D0889715

# Soldiers and Societies in Postcommunist Europe

*One Europe or Several?*

Series Editor: **Helen Wallace**

The 'One Europe or Several?' series examines contemporary processes of political, security, economic, social and cultural change across the European continent, as well as issues of convergence/divergence and prospects for integration and fragmentation. Many of the books in the series are cross-country comparisons; others evaluate the European institutions, in particular the European Union and NATO, in the context of eastern enlargement.

*Titles include*:

**One Europe or Several?**
**Series Standing Order ISBN 0–333–94630–8**
(*outside North America only*)

You can receive future titles in this series as they are published by placing a standing order. Please contact your bookseller or, in case of difficulty, write to us at the address below with your name and address, the title of the series and the ISBN quoted above.

Customer Services Department, Macmillan Distribution Ltd, Houndmills, Basingstoke, Hampshire RG21 6XS, England

# Soldiers and Societies in Postcommunist Europe

## Legitimacy and Change

Edited by

Anthony Forster
*Department of Politics*
*University of Bristol, UK*

Timothy Edmunds
*Department of Politics*
*University of Bristol, UK*

and

Andrew Cottey
*Department of Government*
*University College Cork, Republic of Ireland*

First published 2003 by
PALGRAVE MACMILLAN
Houndmills, Basingstoke, Hampshire RG21 6XS and
175 Fifth Avenue, New York, N. Y. 10010
Companies and representatives throughout the world

PALGRAVE MACMILLAN is the global academic imprint of the Palgrave
Macmillan division of St. Martin's Press, LLC and of Palgrave Macmillan Ltd.
Macmillan® is a registered trademark in the United States, United Kingdom
and other countries. Palgrave is a registered trademark in the European
Union and other countries.

ISBN 0–333–94622–7

This book is printed on paper suitable for recycling and made from fully
managed and sustained forest sources.

A catalogue record for this book is available from the British Library.

Library of Congress Cataloging-in-Publication Data

   Soldiers and societies in postcommunist Europe : legitimacy and
change / edited by
   Anthony Forster, Timothy Edmunds, and Andrew Cottey.
      p. cm.—(One Europe or several?)
   Includes bibliographical references and index.
   ISBN 0–333–94622–7 (cloth)
      1. Civil–military relations—Europe, Eastern. 2. Civil–military
relations—Europe, Central. 3. Sociology, Military—Europe, Eastern.
4. Sociology, Military—Europe, Central. I. Forster, Anthony, 1964–
II. Edmunds, Timothy. III. Cottey, Andrew. IV. Series.

JN96.A38C5867 2003
322′.5′094091717—dc21                              2003051428

10   9   8   7   6   5   4   3   2   1
12   11   10   09   08   07   06   05   04   03

Printed and bound in Great Britain by
Antony Rowe Ltd, Chippenham and Eastbourne

# Contents

# Preface

This book is the product of a research project on 'The Transformation of Civil–Military Relations in Comparative Context', funded by the Economic and Social Research Council's 'One Europe or Several?' research programme (award number L213 25 2009). The project examines the transformation of civil–military relations in the countries of postcommunist central and eastern Europe, exploring emerging patterns of civil–military relations in the region, the policy challenges these raise and the implications for more general understandings of the changing nature of civil–military relations in the contemporary world. Within this context, this book provides a comparative analysis of the development of military–society relations since the collapse of communism. This volume is the third in a series of four volumes to be published in Palgrave's ESRC 'One Europe or Several?' series. The first volume, Cottey, Edmunds, Forster (eds), *Democratic Control of the Military in Postcommunist Europe: Guarding the Guards*, addressed issues of democratic control of armed forces in central and eastern Europe. The second, Forster, Edmunds, Cottey (eds), *The Challenge of Military Reform in Postcommunist Europe* addressed questions of military modernisation and professionalisation in the region. A final volume will explore patterns and trends in civil–military relations in central and eastern Europe.

The chapters in this book were first presented at a conference on 'The Armed Forces and Society in Central and Eastern Europe: Legitimacy and Change', funded by the Directorate for Central and Eastern Europe of the UK Ministry of Defence at Lake Bled in Slovenia in March 2002 in cooperation with the Department of Defence Studies at the University of Ljubljana. The analysis, opinions and conclusions expressed or implied in this paper are those of the editors and authors alone, and do not necessarily represent the views of the UK Ministry of Defence or any other government agency. We wish to express our thanks to the contributors to this volume, to the Directorate for Central and Eastern Europe and to the University of Ljubljana.

ANTHONY FORSTER, TIMOTHY EDMUNDS, ANDREW COTTEY

# Notes on Contributors

**Alex J. Bellamy** is a lecturer at the School of Political Science and International Studies at the University of Queensland.

**Laura Cleary** is a senior lecturer in the Department of Defence Management and Security Analysis at Cranfield University.

**Andrew Cottey** is Jean Monnet Chair in European Political Integration and a lecturer at the Department of Government, University College Cork.

**Pál Dunay** is Director of the International Training Course in Security Policy at the Geneva Centre for Security Policy.

**Timothy Edmunds** is a lecturer in the Department of Politics, University of Bristol.

**Anthony Forster** is Professor of Politics and International Relations and Director of the Governance Research Centre at the Department of Politics, University of Bristol.

**James Gow** is Professor of International Peace and Security at the Department of War Studies, Kings College London.

**Ljubica Jelušic** is Head of Defence Studies and Associate Professor at the Faculty of Social Sciences, University of Ljubljana.

**Andrius Krivas** is Counsellor in the NATO Integration Division of the Ministry of Foreign Affairs of the Republic of Lithuania.

**Paul Latawski** is a senior lecturer at the Royal Military Academy, Sandhurst.

**Marjan Malešic** is Head of the Defence Research Centre and Associate Professor at the Faculty of Social Sciences, University of Ljubljana.

**James Sherr** is a fellow at the Conflict Studies Research Centre, Royal Military Academy, Sandhurst.

**Jan Arveds Trapans** is a senior fellow at the Geneva Centre for Democratic Control of Armed Forces.

**Marybeth Peterson Ulrich** is Associate Professor of Government, Department of National Security and Strategy, at the US Army War College.

**Larry L. Watts** is a security sector reform consultant in the Office of the Romanian Presidency.

**Marie Vlachová** is a senior fellow at the Geneva Centre for Democratic Control of Armed Forces.

**Ivan Zveržanovski** is a research student in the Department of War Studies at King's College London.

# 1

# Armed Forces and Society: a Framework for Analysis

*Timothy Edmunds, Anthony Forster and Andrew Cottey*

Armed forces and societies in central and eastern Europe have undergone dramatic changes since the collapse of communism, with important implications for military–society relations. Communism in the Soviet Union and eastern Europe produced a particular model of military–society relations.[1] For four decades after the Second World War, all the countries of the region had large armed forces based on conscription. As a result, almost all adult males experienced military service. The military also received a relatively large share of state resources – significantly higher in percentage terms than in the West. As a result communist societies and economies were often highly militarised. The physical presence of uniformed personnel throughout society and the symbolic and economic significance of the armed forces within the socio-political system were striking features of communism throughout central and eastern Europe. The main official justification for the armed forces in the communist states was one focused around external threat. This took a variety of different forms including the capitalist West, fascism during the 1930s and 1940s, and the Soviet Union itself for Yugoslavia after 1948 and Romania from the mid-1960s.

Communist armed forces also performed domestic political and social functions. They were one of the institutions used by elites to promote communist values and all conscripts received political education along-side their military training. The armed forces were often viewed as a socially unifying force, helping to break down old barriers between social classes and ethnic groups. In the Soviet Union, for example, the military was one of the key *Soviet* institutions, with the communist leadership using it as mechanism to help break down ethno–national loyalties and encourage the development of a single Soviet identity. Thus, the prevailing model of military–society relations was one in which the

1

majority of people had direct experience of the military, the military was a major presence within society, and the legitimacy of the armed forces rested upon a particular combination of external threats and internal socio-political roles.

The collapse of communism and the end of the Cold War dramatically altered the domestic and international context of military–society relations in central and eastern Europe and fundamentally challenged the domestic rationale for and role of the region's armed forces. The end of the Cold War similarly removed the external justification for the armed forces and the wider militarisation of society. In response to these developments, at the beginning of the 1990s armed forces were significantly reduced in size and defence spending was cut sharply across the region. The number of personnel that were conscripted into the military was reduced and conscription periods cut, while conscientious objection and draft avoidance grew – in some cases quite dramatically. Armed forces were given new missions, including not only national defence under new circumstances, but also contributing to international peacekeeping missions, as well as domestic roles such as providing assistance in response to natural disasters. In the cases of the states emerging from the Soviet Union, Yugoslavia and Czechoslovakia, the change in military–society relations has taken place in the further complicating context of building new states with new armed forces.

The end of communism has also produced wider social changes with significant implications for military–society relations. For example, there has been a decline in deference towards state institutions such as the military and growing attention paid to gay and women's rights, with concomitant demands that both groups be permitted to serve as equals in the military. In combination, these developments have resulted in the demise of the old communist model of military–society relations and an undermining of the traditional bases of legitimacy on which the region's armed forces rested. However, what new patterns of military–society relations are emerging and how far these will provide viable long-term bases of legitimacy for these states' militaries is uncertain and forms the basis for this study.

Military–society relations are further complicated by wider global developments. Many observers argue that a number of global trends – deep long-term changes within societies, important shifts in military technology and warfare and new demands arising from a radically changed international security environment – are dramatically altering military–society relations in the industrialised western democracies and generating new problems in civil–military relations. If this analysis is correct and the drivers of change are indeed global in character, then the countries of central and eastern Europe will also be affected by these wider changes. It is against this twin background of specific regional changes within postcommunist Europe and wider global trends that this book explores emerging patterns of military–society relations in central and eastern Europe. This introductory chapter begins by reviewing the existing debate on military–society relations and laying out a framework for interpreting new patterns of military–society relations in central and eastern Europe. Within this framework, the subsequent chapters assess the development of military–society relations in the various countries of the region. The book's conclusion explores the extent to which identifiable patterns of military–society relations are emerging within central and eastern Europe, the factors which are shaping those patterns, and the wider implications of the changing patterns of military–society relations in the region.

## The existing debate on the military and society

The existing debate on the military and society focuses on two areas. The first of these is concerned with the degree to which the military is linked to the society from which it springs. Is the military a separate or unique institution, with its own imperatives, culture and demands or does it reflect society? If the former, then to what extent can the military remain immune to wider societal change or will it inevitably be shaped by such change? The second focus – which has grown in significance since the end of the Cold War – concerns the extent to which a changing international, technological and societal environment is altering the very nature of societies' relationships with their military institutions.

The first debate – that of whether or not the military has a 'unique' position within society – has long been a subject of the civil–military relations literature. One argument is that the military's 'right to be different' results from the need for combat effectiveness, which necessitates particular 'military' forms of organisation (what has been labelled the 'functional imperative'). Alternatively it is argued that military–society relations are shaped by the need to preserve the domestic sources of legitimacy by remaining close to the society of which it is a part (the so-called 'socio-political' imperative). In turn, the degree to which it is accepted that the military has 'a right to be different' has important policy implications, for example in relation to the extension of civil and human rights legislation into the military environment. In western Europe and North America, these policy implications have been reflected in the ongoing debates about gays or women in the armed forces. Martin Edmonds suggests that the nature of the military's task – where personnel are expected to have 'unlimited liability' and the prospect of being injured or killed is almost a 'definitional' aspect of service – does make it different from other institutions in society such as the police or the civil service. This fact, he argues, necessitates the transfer of individual interests to those of the group, and requires the maintenance of particularly high levels of morale and discipline. As a result, Edmonds suggests that 'armed services fulfil a highly specialized function, the effect of which is to separate them entirely, and geographically to a great extent, from civil society'.[2] However, Edmonds goes on to observe that despite the demands for military uniqueness which arise from this functional imperative, key linkages between the military and society *do* remain. He notes that armed services do tend to reflect the predominant cultural characteristics of their societies. Ultimately, Edmonds argues that the nature of a military's relationship with society is largely dependent on 'society's view of the world', which in turn is influenced by three key variables: first, levels of *technology* and their associated prerequisites – education, industrialisation and the strength of the economy; second the particular *culture* of a society including influences of history, tradition and political ideology; and third, the *socio-economic structure* of society, and particularly the existence, nature and influence of elites.[3]

James Gow takes a different approach, identifying *legitimacy* as the key element in the relationship between the military and society. Gow argues that military legitimacy has both functional and socio-political bases. For Gow, the functional basis of military legitimacy derives from its 'military mission' – which he defines as the protection of the state from external threat. The socio-political bases of military legitimacy are more complex, and stem from the nature of the military's relationship with political authority, its role as a symbol of political unity and national pride (informed by military traditions and past military activities), its contribution to the socio-economic infrastructure of the state, and its role as an instrument of education and socialisation. This military legitimacy is the basis of a 'social contract' between soldiers and the wider socio-political community, and for Gow, 'support [for the military] will be forthcoming if [it] performs effectively, in accordance with its functional and socio-political bases of legitimacy, or if there is some attachment to those bases that overarch poor performance'.[4]

Christopher Dandeker notes that while the armed forces share 'institutional qualities' – such as the need for teamwork, leadership and loyalty to the organisation – with other civilian organisations, their war-fighting role necessitates a level of coercion in military discipline which sets them apart. Thus, he observes that 'the functional imperative of war ensures that the military will always stand apart from civilian society'.[5] Dandeker also addresses the second military and society debate that relates to more fundamental change in the relationship between the military and society. He observes that despite the demands of the military's functional imperative, a series of challenges have emerged to military culture and its 'right to be different' which amount to 'new times' for the military. These include, first, a changed *strategic* context – which in the West entails an end to immediate threats to national security and a more 'globalised' world where challenges to state sovereignty have come both from above, from supranational organisations, and from below, from regionalism and a globalisation of social and cultural relationships. Second, there is a changed *societal* context in which the supporting framework for core military values is increasingly challenged by a more individualistic, egalitarian and litigious society. Finally, and partly as a result of the changed strategic context, there are increasing *cost pressures* which have led to the *civilianisation* of many traditionally military jobs such as logistical support.[6] These themes pick up arguments advanced by Morris Janowitz as early as 1960 that the character of military organisation was changing in response to the organisational demands of evolving weapons technology and developments in the nature of military force. This Janowitz suggested was leading to a different role for the military – the 'constabulary concept' – in which emphasis was shifting from the relatively straightforward task of national defence to a more active contribution to the maintenance of international security.[7]

More recently, Charles Moskos and Frank Wood have suggested that societal pressures are leading western militaries to shift from an 'institutional' structure to a more civilianised 'organisational' one. In turn they argue that this has negative implications for the functional, war-fighting effectiveness of armed forces.[8] Charles Moskos, John Allen Williams and David Segal develop this thesis further with their concept of the 'postmodern military'. They argue that together with changes in the geopolitical environment, societal developments in 'post-industrial' societies have significantly altered the military's traditional position. These societal developments include: first, the weakening of central forms of social organisation, and in particular the nation-state and national markets; second, the decreasing number of authorities in society to which people are willing to defer; and finally a shrinking consensus about what constitutes the public good. These developments have led to a change in the nature of military organisation. Moskos and his colleagues argue that these changes are significant enough to be considered a new, 'postmodern' phase of military organisation and military–society relations. For them, the 'postmodern military' is characterised by an increasing interpenetrability between civilian and military spheres; a diminution of differences within the military itself, particularly between different ranks and services; non-traditional military operations such as peacekeeping; the increasing importance and prevalence of supranational or multinational command structures; and the internationalisation of the military themselves through multinational military operations and structures.[9]

Similar themes are picked up by Martin Shaw, with his twin concepts of the 'post-military' and the 'common risk' society. For Shaw, the Cold War period in much of the industrialised world was characterised by the militarisation of society through the necessity for mass armies and conscriptions. Moreover, in many states, such as France, this militarisation was reinforced by a conception of society which emphasised a 'contract' between the state and its citizens. Thus, in return for their rights, citizens were expected to provide service to the state through conscription. Shaw argues that geopolitical changes coupled with economic growth and a 'revolution of rising expectations' are increasingly undermining this militarisation leading to a 'post-military' society where military service and experience are the exception rather than the norm.[10] More recently, Shaw has refined this theme, arguing that the militarisation along national lines so characteristic of the Cold War period has been replaced by a 'common risk' society, in which perceptions of threat – from problems such as global warming – are perceived to be increasingly transnational. In conjunction with the changes associated with the 'post-military' society, this shift of perception has resulted in the replacement of traditional military symbols and status in national cultures with 'spectator sport militarism', where societal engagement with the military is limited to passive observation through the media.[11]

### Reconsidering the existing debate

Perhaps with the exception of Samuel Huntington, who conceptualised the degree and quality of military uniqueness as essentially fixed once and for all,[12] most military sociologists see armed forces–society relations as fluctuating over time and space as a function of dominant missions, of technological, organisational and doctrinal changes, and of historical legacies and domestic influences. However, most of the models offered are nominalist and leave the study of contextual factors to country case studies or regional syntheses. Applicability to non-western settings has thus been possible, as shown by the short volume Morris Janowitz wrote in the mid-1960s on armed forces in 'new nations',[13] or again by the striking parallel between the writings of Kolkowicz, Odom and Colton[14] – students of Soviet civil–military relations in the 1960s and 1970s – and those of Huntington, C. Wright Mills and Janowitz one or two decades earlier.[15]

However, the current debate on the military and society suffers from two main difficulties. The first is that it does not systematically address the reasons why particular societies have developed particular kinds of armed forces – and why they have the particular relationships with those armed forces that they do. A brief consideration of the diverse nature of western European armed forces illustrates this point. The British armed forces comprise a mixture of professional soldiers and reserves. British society retains a rather functional relationship with its armed forces, and over the past fifty years has shown itself willing both to allow governments to deploy military force and to tolerate casualties in pursuit of national interests. In contrast, the German military retains an intimate link with German society through its *Innere Führung* system. This centralises the socio-political nature of the military's role, with *Innere Führung* functioning as both an agent of socialisation and a mechanism for civilian control over the armed forces. The German military has generally been used in a very different way from that of Britain, and for constitutional and historical reasons the *Bundeswehr* did not engage in direct military action until 1992. Military diversity within Europe is further illustrated by such widely differing militaries and military–society relationships as the Greek, Swedish, Swiss and French. While the existing debate on the relationship between the military and society does go some way towards exploring the generic influences driving this relationship, it does not provide an adequate framework for comparing national differences. Why, for example, when the influences of Cold War or postmodern or post-industrial society apply throughout Europe is there still such diversity? When the diverse evolution of military–society relations in central and eastern Europe is also considered, the limited explanatory power of current perspectives on military–society relations is further highlighted.

The second difficulty with the current debate is a tendency to distinguish too easily between the functional and socio-political imperatives which shape the military–society relationship and to accord the former too much explanatory power. Thus, for example the military's war-fighting imperative is often seen to result from an objective, unproblematic and inevitable mission, the defence of national territory. In practice, however, the prioritisation of different military roles often results as much from socio-political perceptions of threat as from the 'objective' security environment.[16] For example, the Soviet Union's almost universal system of conscription and indeed the Soviet army's relationship with Soviet society resulted from both the need to address external military threats and the need for a far reaching mechanism for politicisation and socialisation. Crucially, the nature of the Soviet military–society relationship developed as a result of the Soviet military's roles – and these roles were *both* functional *and* socio-political. Thus the need for a mass conscript army to address a threat to Soviet national security resulted from an identification of this threat by the Soviet state, and then the socio-political construction of a particular force structure to address it. This particular force structure did not emerge from nowhere, however, but resulted from the historically informed choices of the Soviet state and Soviet society.

Much of the existing literature on the military and society recognises that both military uniqueness and the nature of the functional imperative fluctuate in relation to dominant missions; technological, organisational and doctrinal forms; as well as historical legacies and domestic influences. However, the role of socio-political imperatives in determining the nature and character of military–society relations is all too often underplayed.[17] The point of departure for this study is that when analysing current armed forces–society relations, there is a need for a better understanding of two core issues: first, the reasons why particular societies have prioritised particular imperatives – be they functional or socio-political; and second, the implications of this for the military's relationship with society and its bases for military legitimacy.

## A framework for understanding military–society relations

Military–society relations, and the salience of those relations, vary significantly from country to country. Differing patterns of military–society relations have differing implications, and raise different issues and problems. However, we argue that it is possible to identify five broad roles for the military, each of which has important implications for the character of military–society relations in any particular context. These are: *National Security, Nation Builder, Regime Defence, Domestic Military Assistance* and *Military Diplomacy*. The roles themselves are functional – in that they derive from functions allocated to the military – but socio-political in both their implications and construction. A role affects military–society relations in two ways. First, it influences the nature of civilian or societal perceptions of the armed forces. Second, it influences the way in which the military perceives the society of which it is a part. In common with Gow, we suggest that the legitimacy of the military in relation to society is dependent on societal acceptance of the military's roles and the military's ability to fulfil the demands of these roles effectively.

The military roles we identify are 'ideal' types. In practice of course, most armed forces have a variety of roles and the balance of the five different roles we identify varies from state to state. In some cases one or two role(s) may predominate. In other cases there may be a more complex mix. In addition, military–society relations are not static and in any given case the balance between the different roles we identify is likely to evolve over time. The advantage of the ideal-type models we identify is that they allow us to conceptualise different patterns of military–society relations and explore the factors shaping them in a rigorous manner.

Of the five military roles we identify, National Security and Regime Defence are the most prominent and central roles of armed forces, reflecting the fact that military force is the *ultima ratio* of the external security of the state and the internal survival of any regime. However, as Bernard Boëne notes, this is only true *in the abstract* and should not obscure the fact that in some contexts the functional 'natural' order of priority between the different military roles may change.[18] Nor should this overshadow the fact that the other military roles we identify can profoundly affect military–society relations. It is therefore important to analyse much more holistically the nature and function of the military as an institution.

## Military roles and society

*National Security.* The National Security role corresponds to the 'functional' imperative identified in much of the existing literature on military–society relations. National Security concerns the military's role in defending the state from threats to its security. Traditionally this is conceived in terms of the defence of the territory of the state and perhaps also that of allies against attack by other states. However, the 9/11 terrorist attacks on the United States dramatically highlighted the danger that external attack may also come from non-state actors, and does not necessarily require the existence of formally constituted armed forces. As a consequence, for the United States and many of its allies, the

National Security role now also includes the role of the military as a means of countering international terrorism. As well as responding to direct threats to the physical security of the state and its citizens, armed forces are often also asked to undertake international missions outside the territory of the state – ranging from the interventions of the European imperial powers in past centuries to international peace support operations today. For some, such activities are part of a wider definition of national security which can be threatened by the consequences of instability elsewhere in the world, even when there is no direct physical threat to the state concerned. Others do not consider such operations to be so closely linked to the national security agenda and have even criticised them as detracting from more important security challenges. These divergent views suggest that the boundary between the National Security role and the Military Diplomacy role (discussed below) may be blurred. In addition, the National Security role may also have significant internal dimensions. Terrorism or violent domestic disorder may threaten the integrity or even the survival of the state and the security of its citizens and the military may be called upon to respond to such threats. In practice, what constitutes an internal threat to national security is a deeply political and often contested question. Authoritarian regimes, for instance, often define threats to the survival of the regime as threats to national security. Thus, the distinction between the National Security and Regime Defence roles can also sometimes be blurred.

The National Security role has important implications for military–society relations. It is significant in all armed forces and in most cases has been their foundational purpose. To the extent that the majority of the population accepts what constitutes a threat to national security and the military performs effectively in dealing with those threats, the National Security role is likely to be a source of legitimacy for the military within society as a whole. It may also be a means of mobilising society in support of the military, in relation, for example, to issues such as conscription or defence spending. In so far as the military is seen to be able to address key threats to citizen's security, the National Security role may also generate a sense of connection between a society and its armed forces. This is particularly the case in times of perceived high military threat – as was the case in Europe during the Second World War. Where the National Security role is given substance through conscription, the experience of universal (male) military service may play an important role in generating links between the armed forces and society. However, where societal threat perceptions are low or the military fail to perform the National Security role effectively, the legitimacy of the armed forces in the eyes of society may be undermined. Thus, for example, the Czech military's legitimacy in the National Security role has been undermined both by the end of the Cold War, and by its failure to defend Czechoslovakia from invasion in 1938 and 1968.[19]

*Nation Builder.*   The military has often played the role of Nation Builder. Indeed, as was the case with the Yugoslav People's Army (*Jugoslavenska Narodna Armija* – JNA), in many countries the military is one of the only real *national* institutions, and conscription forms the basis of one of the only truly common national experiences. In these circumstances the military can act as a mechanism to transmit 'national' values to all parts of the population, regardless of background. In fact, in almost all countries – including long-established ones such as the United States or France – the military's fundamentally *national* role of National Security means that it also contributes to this Nation Builder role by acting as a symbolic embodiment of national interests and values. The Nation Builder role is usually associated with conscription because universal (male) military service is the primary means by which the military performs this role. In this sense, the military is often viewed as the 'school of the nation', acting as a key instrument for promoting national values. Thus, in the UK calls to reintroduce conscription have often been premised on the perceived ability of the military institution to inculcate a particular set of social or moral values.[20] In all the communist militaries, conscription provided an opportunity for political and social indoctrination in an all-encompassing institutional environment.

The Nation Builder role inherently links the military to society and gives it a key societal function. From the societal perspective, the military is familiar because most of the population have served in it as conscripts. In turn, the military identifies itself as a fulcrum in the relationship between citizens and the state. Military legitimacy in the Nation Builder role is a product of two factors. The first of these is a societal perception that the military embodies a particular set of common values, and second, the perception that it is uniquely placed to inculcate them into the population. The Nation Builder role may arise from a number of circumstances: a deliberate decision by a civilian political leadership to use the military as a means of promoting national unity or particular national values; the assumption of the role by the military because it – and especially the officer corps – believes it has a special role or duty in maintaining national unity or particular national values; a more spontaneous growth of national consciousness in which the military becomes significant; or a combination of these factors.

*Regime Defence.* The Regime Defence role involves the military supporting or upholding the power of a particular set of political interests – most often a regime, but sometimes those of a particular political party or individual. The Regime Defence role usually relates to authoritarian regimes. Such regimes often depend to a significant degree on physical coercion to maintain their power whereas democratic governments depend primarily on the legitimacy provided by the democratic process. The most extreme model of the military's Regime Defence role is when the military itself assumes power. Under the central and eastern European communist systems, the military was one element of the 'Iron Triangle' alongside the state and the Communist Party, and 'defending communism' was one of the functions of communist armed forces. While communist militaries ultimately failed to protect their regimes from collapse in the late 1980s, this did not preclude the regimes themselves attempting to utilise their armed forces in this way.[21]

However, the Regime Defence role also makes the regime dependent on the military, since the military may withdraw its support or even actively oppose or overthrow it. Authoritarian regimes and rulers thus often have deeply ambiguous relationships with their armed forces, being both dependent and wary of them. They have responded to this problem with a variety of strategies, which include using divide and rule tactics towards different groups within the military, buying the military's support by providing them with privileged socio-economic circumstances, and/or establishing parallel armed services – such as internal security troops or special presidential guards – as counterweights to the regular armed forces. Thus, while the military was one of the institutions of communist rule in central and eastern Europe, communist parties generally sought to maintain strong civilian control over the military and preferred to use separate internal security police forces to maintain domestic order and regime survival.

The Regime Defence role has important implications for military–society relations. Most significantly, the military's primary reference point in the Regime Defence role is not society, or the nation, but the political interests of the regime or ruler to which it is bound. This in turn can lead to a degree of separation of the military from society. From the societal perspective, the military is seen to be linked first to the regime, and only second to the nation or the *populus*. From the military perspective, society poses a threat to the regime *in potentia*, and so is a potential opponent if any fundamental clash of interests between the regime and society as a whole emerges. The Regime Defence role tends by its authoritarian character to work against military legitimacy in society. However, some authoritarian regimes gain legitimacy through exploiting popular or nationalist politics or by providing domestic stability or macroeconomic progress. In these circumstances the military may gain legitimacy by association with the regime's goals or achievements. In other circumstances, the military may retain legitimacy in the eyes of society because it is viewed as (or indeed genuinely is) a reluctant tool or even victim of the authoritarian regime.

*Domestic Military Assistance.* The military can play a variety of roles in relation to the internal governance of the state that are distinct and separate from the Regime Defence role in both authoritarian and democratic regimes. We define this as the Domestic Military Assistance role. Official UK government terminology divides the Domestic Military Assistance role into three subcategories which provide a useful framework for conceptualising this role. The first subcategory is military aid to the civil community (MACC), where support is given to the civil community in dealing with severe socio-economic problems such as natural disasters. For example in the Czech Republic in 1998 the armed forces were used extensively in this role during the widespread flooding which afflicted parts of the country.[22] The second subcategory is the provision of military aid to other government departments (MAGD) to assist the civil authority. For example the military might be used as a parallel or substitute provider of state goods – such as welfare, labour, medical care and so on – where other government departments are not able to do so effectively. Thus, in the Soviet Union, conscript labour was often used on national construction projects or to help bring in the harvest.[23] The third subcategory is maintaining law and order (MLO), where the police or government fear they cannot ensure public safety during political and social unrest such as strikes or demonstrations. For example, in Romania in 1999 the regular military were mobilised, though in the event not used, in response to demonstrations by striking miners.[24] Military legitimacy in the Domestic Military Assistance role stems from two factors. First, it is the indirect product of the authority and legitimacy of the civilian regime which is utilising the armed forces in this way. As noted in our previous discussion of the Regime Defence role, the extent of such legitimacy depends on the nature of the civilian regime itself, the character of the military's relationship with that regime, and the specific threat to law, order and public safety. Second, legitimacy may stem from societal perceptions of the effectiveness of the military in meeting the demands of the Domestic Military Assistance roles.

*Military Diplomacy.* The Military Diplomacy role involves the use of the armed forces by the government as a foreign policy instrument in the outside world, for example, by promoting democracy, supporting other states in developing more effective armed forces, or using military cooperation as a form of confidence-building measure with former or potential enemies. Military Diplomacy is implicitly – if not always explicitly – normative, in that it involves an effort to promote particular values and international cooperation.[25] There is an important distinction to be made between the Military Diplomacy activities of armed forces and the National Security function. Military Diplomacy involves *peacetime cooperative defence activities*, as distinct from the operational use of military force in peacekeeping and humanitarian tasks (which for the most part we include as elements of National Security). Military Diplomacy therefore involves international peacetime cooperation between armed forces, defence ministries and related national security structures and includes four types of activity: first, bilateral and multilateral military cooperation agreements, training and exchange programmes; second, military reform assistance; third, assistance to states in developing defence and broader security sector management structures; and fourth, military confidence-building measures (CBMs) and military support for arms control and defence conversion as part of broader conflict prevention strategies. Despite many areas of commonality, the Military Diplomacy role differs from the National Security role in that the military's bases for legitimacy in this role originate from an appeal to normative values – the preservation of international peace and security or the promotion of democracy and human rights, for example – rather than directly to national security.

We advance these five categories of National Security, Nation Builder, Regime Defence, Domestic Military Assistance and Military Diplomacy as distinctive roles for the armed forces which have different implications for the military's relationship with society and its bases for military legitimacy. However, underpinning this framework of analysis is the understanding that some or all of these different roles coexist. Moreover, there are inevitable and obvious links and cross-overs between certain functions within these categories. When governments deploy armed forces in peacemaking operations (an aspect of our National Security category), a motivation is often to use the armed forces to defend the security interests of the state, but participation in such operations may also be motivated by a desire to use the armed forces to promote particular values and policies – the key feature of the Military Diplomacy role discussed above. Likewise, when the armed forces are used for maintaining law and order in support of the police (an aspect of Domestic Military Assistance), for example during legitimate public demonstrations and strike action, this function can be intimately linked to upholding the political power of a particular set of political interests, often the elected government (the Regime Defence role).

## Factors shaping military roles and military legitimacy

The degree of importance given to different roles, and the emergence of, or transition to, different models of military organisation result from a variety of domestic and international factors and influences. These influences shape the character of the military–society relationship in the various ways outlined above and can be conceptualised as follows: threat perceptions and the geostrategic context; international pressure and aid; technological developments; historical legacies; domestic political context; economic constraints; and societal change. The balance between these factors will help to explain the particular roles which develop for armed forces in particular national contexts and the resulting patterns of military–society relations. Broadly, these can be divided into international and transnational influences and domestic influences.

### International and transnational influences

*Threat perceptions and the geostrategic context.* Informed by the geostrategic context, societal and elite threat perceptions are clearly significant factors influencing the development of military roles. During the Cold War period the strong perception of mutual threat between the Warsaw Pact and NATO resulted in the prioritisation of the National Security role amongst all engaged countries. For both sides in the East–West confrontation, the threat of invasion appeared to be a very real possibility and this justified the development of the military towards National Security functions – resulting in particular military–society relationships. In these circumstances, for example, the West German population was much less concerned about the maintenance of large, conscript-based armed forces and a high defence budget than it is today. Indeed, across Europe the end of the Cold War led to a widespread re-evaluation of the National Security role for the military and the high level of resources it consumed as a result. Thus, changing threat perceptions resulted in the questioning of the military's established role and undermined the existing foundations of its legitimacy in wider society.

*International pressure and aid.*   The influence of other states also plays an important part in shaping military roles in particular national contexts. Soviet dominance in the Warsaw Pact, for example, was perhaps the defining factor in the development of particular roles for the military in much of central and eastern Europe.[26] In a less direct example, the concentration on the development of deployable, NATO compatible forces in the countries of central and eastern Europe owes a great deal to the perceived demands of the NATO accession process. In the Baltic States, for example, there has generally been elite and societal consensus over the importance of NATO accession as a foreign and security policy goal since the mid-1990s. In response to the perceived requirements of NATO accession, the Baltic States have prioritised the development of forces capable of participating in international peace support operations (PSOs), especially alongside NATO forces, as in the Alliance operations in the Balkans. This has had significant implications for military–society relations in these countries, with less priority attached to conscript-based forces as a means of linking the military to society and military legitimacy increasingly based on the armed forces' ability to contribute to international missions.[27]

*Technological developments.*   Technological developments are important because they can alter the ways in which armed forces are organised and function, with significant implications for military–society relations. Thus, one of the main arguments of the civil–military relations literature since the 1960s has been that there has been a shift away from armed forces based on mass mobilisation of ground forces towards more technologically sophisticated forms of warfare. This in turn has required a move away from conscript-based systems of military organisation to smaller, more professional and technically skilled militaries, a move which has had significant implications for military–society relations. As Edward Luttwak has argued more recently, developments in military technology have led to the expectation in the United States that certain sorts of military roles can and should be fulfilled at a distance, with minimal engagement and hence minimal exposure to risk and potential casualties of military personnel.[28] In doing so, Luttwak illustrates that the development of particular technologies can help to re-legitimise certain military roles by making their accomplishment more feasible and less costly in the eyes of society. Many observers now contend that the so called 'revolution in military affairs' (RMA) – the latest phase in the evolution of military technology – will result in or require a wholesale transformation of the armed forces of the United States (and perhaps also its militarily more advanced allies).[29] This in turn may reinforce what is argued to be a growing gap between a small technologically sophisticated professional military and wider society.

## Domestic influences

*Historical legacies.* Historical legacies obviously play an important role in shaping military roles and military–society relations. Particular historical circumstances give rise to particular patterns of military–society relations. These patterns may in turn become deeply rooted as societal and military attitudes are entrenched and internalised. Thus, for example, the British armed forces have a history of overseas deployment and combat in both the colonial and post-colonial periods. This historical legacy has meant that the UK military has found it reasonably easy to develop its Military Diplomacy role in the post-Cold War period.[30] Moreover, the UK's historical experience has meant that military legitimacy in relation to this role is strong at both elite and societal levels. In France, the Nation Builder role for the military has traditionally been underpinned by a historical legacy which emphasises the importance of national military service in a contract between the state and its citizens.[31] In Romania, the use of the military in the Domestic Military Assistance role is controversial because of a strong tradition of the non-involvement of the regular armed forces in domestic politics.[32] The extent and particular bases of military legitimacy in any society are thus strongly influenced by historical experience. Mechanisms for legitimacy that work in one country are not necessarily inherently transferable or equally effective in another. Moreover, as circumstances change, particular historically-inherited patterns of military–society relations and bases of military legitimacy may be challenged. As France moves away from conscription, for example, previous assumptions about the relationship between citizens and the armed forces may be called into question.

*Domestic political context.* The domestic political context has an important influence on the development of military roles, and can help to shape the nature of a particular society's relationship with its military. Different political systems have different mechanisms for civil–military relations, and these in turn have important implications for the extent to which wider society views the military and its particular roles as legitimate. Thus, for example, in a stable democracy, with an established system of democratic control over the armed forces, many aspects of the Regime Defence role are largely unnecessary but also implicitly unacceptable and illegitimate. Some elements of the Domestic Military Assistance role – notably calling in the armed forces to maintain essential public services or using their presence to affect the outcome of strikes – are also problematic. Domestic political elites may also play an important role in shaping military–society relations. For example, the Regime Defence role among the communist militaries of central and eastern Europe developed largely from the ideologies and political strategies of domestic communist political elites. Similarly, the NATO accession debate in central and eastern Europe – with all its accompanying implications for the development of military roles – has occurred largely amongst domestic political elites, with a spillover into societal consideration of the issue especially when referenda on NATO membership take place or there are major divisions between the leading political parties. Political elites are also important in mobilising societal support for particular military roles, and the military's legitimacy in the eyes of society is likely to be fundamentally undermined if support among elites dissipates.

*Economic constraints.*   Economic constraints influence the ability of a state to develop a particular role for its military and the willingness of society to accept the legitimacy of this role. Doubts have recently been expressed in the UK, for example, about the ability of the military to fulfil its Military Diplomacy commitments on current budgets.[33] In a slightly different context, one of the major civil–military implications of the collapse of communism in central and eastern Europe was the damage done to military legitimacy when the (in society's view illegitimate) sizes of communist-era defence budgets were made public. Military legitimacy, therefore, is dependent on a successful marrying of societal priorities in relation to the role of the military with wider societal priorities regarding the economy and state spending.

*Societal change.*   Changes in more general societal values and standards also influence the development and legitimacy of particular military roles and particular modes of military organisation. Indeed, if societal values change then the emphasis which society places on particular military roles is also likely to change. Military sociologists such as Dandeker and Shaw suggest that a more individualistic or 'post-deferential' society has emerged in Europe over the past few decades. In turn, this has led to greater societal resistance to conscription and a decline in the legitimacy of the Nation Builder role for the military. In combination with the change in the geostrategic environment brought about by the end of the Cold War, these societal changes have increased pressure on states across Europe to abandon conscription.[34]

## Conclusion

Through the application of our analytical framework this volume offers new insights into the complex and multifaceted relationship between armed forces and societies in postcommunist central and eastern Europe. It seeks to identify the types of roles armed forces are playing in contemporary central and eastern Europe and resultant patterns of military–society relations, including the extent to which patterns of military–society relations in the region are converging and diverging, and the extent to which they mirror those observable in the established democracies of western Europe and North America. This book also analyses the different factors that shape military roles and military–society relations. In undertaking this task, we explore the relationship between military role and military organisation on the one hand and military legitimacy – that is the legitimacy of the military in the eyes of wider society – on the other. This introductory chapter has laid out a framework for thinking about military–society relations. In particular, it has defined five distinct military roles, which we argue have major implications for military–society relations and the bases of military legitimacy: the National Security role, the Nation Builder role, the Regime Defence role, the Domestic Military Assistance role and the Military Diplomacy role. These roles result from both international and domestic influences. In turn they require particular types of military organisation and create particular challenges for the military's relationship with society and its bases for legitimacy.

The importance of the functional imperative in the National Security, Regime Defence and Domestic Military Assistance roles is noteworthy. There are two reasons for this. First, National Security and Regime Defence and the military aid to the civil power element of the Domestic Military Assistance function (especially maintaining and restoring law and order) relate directly to the core functional purpose of armed forces – the direct application of military force. Second, while the armed forces may have roles other than war fighting, notably the Military Diplomacy and Nation Builder roles, without the ultimate justification provided by the various 'hard' security functions, armed forces would not exist in the first place, and such non-military functions would have to be discharged by other agencies or through other channels. In the case studies that follow it is where what Bernard Boëne calls this 'natural order of priority'[35] is reversed that some of the most challenging questions are posed by the relationship between the armed forces and society in central and eastern Europe.

In terms of the factors shaping military roles and military–society relations, we argue that international influences include the geostrategic context and related societal and elite threat perceptions, international pressure and aid and technological change. Domestic influences include historical legacies, the domestic political context, economic constraints and societal change. The character of military–society relations can thus be influenced in three interrelated ways. First, by a change in the drivers which have influenced the military's development of particular roles. Second, by a societal perception that the military is not effectively fulfilling the roles which are the foundation of its legitimacy. Third, by a change in the nature of military organisation (for example, as a consequence of technological change such as the RMA) that entails a renegotiation of both the military's roles and the bases for its legitimacy. It is to a case-study based analysis of these issues that this volume now turns.

## Notes

1. For an introduction to debates on communist civil–military and military–society relations, see: Z.D. Barany, 'Civil-Military Relations in Communist Systems: Western Models Revisited', *Journal of Political and Military Sociology*, vol.19 (Summer 1991); T.J. Colton, *Commissars, Commanders, and Civilian Authority: the Structure of Soviet Military Politics* (Cambridge MA and London: Harvard University Press, 1979); R. Kolkowicz, *The Soviet Military and the Communist Party* (Princeton NJ: Princeton University Press, 1967); W.E. Odom, 'A Dissenting View of the Group Approach to Soviet Politics', *World Politics*, 28:4 (1976); A. Perlmutter and W. LeoGrande, 'The Party in Uniform: Toward a Theory of Civil–Military Relations in Communist Political Systems', *American Political Science Review*, 76:4 (1982).
2. M. Edmonds, *Armed Services and Society* (Leicester: Leicester University Press, 1988), 43.

3. Edmonds, *Armed Services*, 68–9.
4. J. Gow, *Legitimacy and the Military: the Yugoslav Crisis* (London: Pinter Publishers, 1992), 27–32.
5. C. Dandeker, 'On "The Need to be Different": Recent Trends in Military Culture', in H. Strachan (ed.), *The British Army, Manpower and Society into the Twenty-First Century* (London: Frank Cass, 2000), 174–5.
6. Dandeker, 'On "The Need to be Different"', 175–85. See also: C. Dandeker, 'The Military in Democratic Societies: New Times and New Patterns of Civil–Military Relations', in J. Kuhlmann and J. Callaghan (eds), *Military and Society in 21st Century Europe: a Comparative Analysis* (New Brunswick and London: Transaction Publishers, 2000), 27–31; C. Dandeker, 'A Farewell to Arms? The Military and the Nation State in a Changing World', in J. Burk (ed.), *The Military in New Times: Adapting Armed Forces to a Turbulent World* (Oxford: Westview Press, 1994), 117–39.
7. M. Janowitz, *The Professional Soldier: a Social and Political Portrait* (London: The Free Press of Glencoe Collier-Macmillan Ltd, 1960), 417–42.
8. C.C. Moskos and F.R. Wood, 'Introduction' and C.C. Moskos, 'Institutional and Occupational Trends in Armed Forces', in C.C. Moskos and F.R. Wood, *The Military: More than a Job?* (Exeter: A. Wheaton & Co. Ltd, 1988), 3–26.
9. C.C. Moskos, J.A. Williams and D.R. Segal, 'Armed Forces after the Cold War', in C.C. Moskos, J.A. Williams and D.R. Segal (eds), *The Postmodern Military: Armed Forces after the Cold War* (Oxford: Oxford University Press, 2000), 2.
10. M. Shaw, *Post-Military Society: Militarism, Demilitarization and War at the End of the Twentieth Century* (Cambridge: Polity Press, 1991), 184–90.
11. M. Shaw, 'The Development of "Common-Risk" Society: a Theoretical Overview', in J. Kuhlmann and J. Callaghan (eds), *Military and Society in 21st Century Europe: a Comparative Analysis* (New Brunswick and London: Transaction Publishers, 2000), 24–6.
12. S.P. Huntington, *The Soldier and the State* (Cambridge: Harvard University Press, 1957).
13. M. Janowitz, *The Military in the Political Development of New Nations* (Chicago: University of Chicago Press, 1964).
14. Kolkowicz, *The Soviet Military*; Odom, 'A Dissenting View', 12–26; Colton, *Commanders, Commissars and Civilian Authority*.
15. Huntington, *The Soldier and the State*; C.W. Mills, *The Power Elite* (New York: Oxford University Press, 1956); M. Janowitz, *The Professional Soldier* (Glencoe: Free Press, 1960).
16. Buzan, Wæver and de Wilde call this process 'securitization'. They argue strongly that threats to security do not exist in a vacuum, but are socially and politically constructed – or 'securitized'. B. Buzan, O. Wæver and J. de Wilde, *Security: a New Framework for Analysis* (London: Lynne Riener Publishers Inc., 1998), 23–9.
17. The authors are grateful to Bernard Boëne for highlighting this point.
18. The authors are grateful to Bernard Boëne for highlighting this point.
19. M. Vlachová, 'Democratic Control of Armed Forces in the Czech Republic: a Journey from Social Isolation', in A. Cottey, T. Edmunds and A. Forster (eds), *Democratic Control of the Military in Postcommunist Europe: Guarding the Guards* (Basingstoke: Palgrave Macmillan, 2002).

20. See, for example, J.C.M Baynes, *The Soldier in Modern Society* (London: Eyre Methuen, 1972), 76.
21. Both Erich Honecker in the GDR and Miloš Jakeš in Czechoslovakia attempted to utilise their armed forces to suppress pro-democracy movements in 1989.
22. M. Vlachová, 'Professionalisation of the Army in the Czech Republic', in A. Forster, T. Edmunds and A. Cottey (eds), *The Challenge of Military Reform in Postcommunist Europe: Building Professional Armed Forces* (Basingstoke: Palgrave Macmillan, 2002).
23. See, for example, C. Donnelly, *Red Banner: the Soviet Military System in Peace and War* (Coulsdon: Jane's Information Group Ltd, 1988), 94, 148.
24. See Chapter 8, L.L.Watts, 'Ahead of the Curve: the Military–Society Relationship in Romania'.
25. *The Strategic Defence Review* (London: The Stationery Office, 1998), 4.
26. See, for example, Pál Dunay, 'Building Professional Competence in Hungary's Armed Forces: Slow Motion', and Laura Cleary, 'The New Model Army?: Bulgarian Experiences of Professionalisation', in Forster et al., *The Challenge of Military Reform*.
27. A. Cottey, T. Edmunds and A. Forster, 'Reforming Postcommunist Militaries', in Forster et al., *The Challenge of Military Reform*, 249–52.
28. E.N. Luttwak, 'From Vietnam to Desert Fox: Civil–Military Relations in Modern Democracies', *Survival*, 41:1 (Spring 1999), 108.
29. For an example of this thinking, see United States Department of Defense, *Quadrennial Defense Review Report* (30 September 2001), http://www.defenselink.mil/pubs/qdr2001.pdf.
30. UK armed forces have been heavily involved in numerous overseas deployments which fit the Military Diplomacy role over the past ten years. These include the Gulf War and subsequent action against Iraq (1991–present); Croatia (1992–1995); Bosnia (1992–present); Kosovo (1999–present); East Timor (1999); and Sierra Leone (2000–present).
31. While conscription in France ended in 2001, this development has not been without considerable societal soul-searching in relation to the decline of the military's socialiser role.
32. Watts, 'Ahead of the Curve'.
33. See, for example, C. McInnes, 'Labour's Strategic Defence Review', *International Affairs*, 74:4 (1998), 841.
34. Belgium and the Netherlands abolished conscription in 1992 and 1996 respectively. France, Italy, Portugal and Spain will have followed suit by 2006.
35. The authors are grateful to Bernard Boëne for highlighting this point.

# Part I
# Central Europe

# 2
# The Polish Armed Forces and Society

*Paul Latawski*

Polish society has long held favourable perceptions of the Polish armed forces. The nineteenth century laid the foundations of the high prestige enjoyed by the armed forces in Poland that continues to the present day. This prestige, however, was built around the legitimacy ascribed to the National Security role of the armed forces as the defender of nation and state. Although the armed forces have acted as Nation Builder and in Regime Defence in the last century, these roles were not seen as being fully legitimate from the perspective of Polish society. Indeed, as a consequence of the legacy of Regime Defence in the twentieth century, the Domestic Military Assistance role can be seen as being tainted, certainly with regard to dealing with civil disorder as compared to less controversial activity such as disaster relief. Since 1989 and the demise of communist Poland, the National Security role remains central but has undergone considerable reinterpretation in the light of the new security environment and national policy goals. There has been a gradual shift away from its more traditional guise of territorial defence of the Polish state towards a role that would see the needs of national security met by armed forces more readily employed on power projection operations in the context of NATO or in other forms of military coalition. Poland's membership of NATO is undoubtedly a major external factor in this reorientation of the National Security role. Its long-term legitimacy in terms of Polish society, however, has not been fully tested. A corollary to the new external power projection focus in the National Security role is the armed forces' adoption of a more prominent Military Diplomacy role, and the number of the military's bilateral and multilateral contacts has grown enormously since 1989. Polish initiatives and contributions to the creation of peacekeeping units with neighbouring states is evidence of the effort being invested in this very new role.

This shift toward greater external contributions on the part of the armed forces comes at a time when Polish society, in geopolitical terms, generally feels safe. In addition, the domestic influences on military–society relations in the present and the foreseeable future are likely to be shaped by the shift under way in the armed forces towards the projection of military power. As this change in emphasis is moving the armed forces in the direction of an all-volunteer professional force, better equipped and trained for power projection, this is confronting Polish society with a number of issues, including the willingness of society to fund the expensive changes that are required. Such a decisive move to all-volunteer forces also entails the end of conscription, which would substantially reduce society's contact with the armed forces. On the other hand, from the perspective of Polish society, there is little evidence that many of the social questions that are high on the agenda of long-standing NATO member states have yet emerged in the Polish military–society relationship. In Poland, the only equal opportunities issue that has come to the fore in a very limited way is the place of women in the armed forces. But although the values of Polish society remain traditional, they are nevertheless under increasing pressure as social and economic transformation moves Polish society closer to those of western European and north American states. This chapter takes as its focus the roles of the armed forces and their impact on legitimacy along with domestic and transnational influences on military and society relations in order to explore these issues in further depth.

## Context

### Historical legacies

Poland has a very deeply rooted military tradition that has contributed to the prestige of the armed forces in Polish society. The struggles to regain an independent state from the late eighteenth century to the early twentieth century created strong bonds between society and its soldiers, although these bonds were qualified by a number of factors. The strength of these bonds can be seen in the way that Tadeusz Kościuszko, the military and political leader of the insurrection to thwart the final partition of Poland in 1794, reached out to the peasantry offering social reform in return for their support in defending the Polish state. The subsequent images of Kościuszko, however, wearing peasant garb and rallying peasants wielding scythes on the field of battle brought to life a vision of unshakeable solidarity between society and its soldiers that was far from uncontested. Not all groups in Polish society were enamoured or totally united around the aims of and costs imposed by the great national uprisings between 1795 and 1863.[1] The change in the nature of Polish society from a gentry-dominated to a mass society by the beginning of the twentieth century meant that military–society relations, when the opportunity arose, would have to be fundamentally re-grounded.[2]

One of the paradoxes of the relationship between the Polish armed forces and society is how the consistent prestige enjoyed by the armed forces was maintained despite the fact that not all of the roles that the armed forces adopted in contemporary history met the approval of Polish society. Since the re-establishment of an independent Polish state in 1918, the armed forces of Poland have served a number of roles. In the period of independence between the two world wars, the central role of the armed forces was that of National Security. For a country having regained its independence in circumstances of armed conflict, the victory of the army in the Polish–Soviet war of 1919–21 conferred not only prestige in the eyes of society but also confirmed its central mission of national defence. The army also had a strong Nation (and state) Builder role as an integrative force in education, and in the promotion of patriotism and a common identity.[3]

However, not all of the army's actions won favour in Polish society. Marshall Józef Piłsudski's military coup d'état of May 1926 followed by the arrest and illegal detention at the Brest Litovsk fortress of major political figures and their subsequent ill treatment and trial in the early 1930s did not win universal favour in Polish society.[4] After Piłsudski's death in 1935, a regime dominated by a coterie of colonels clung to power with its legitimacy steadily declining.[5] This culminated in the failure of the army in its National Security role in the form of its catastrophic defeat in September 1939. Despite these blows to its prestige, Polish society demonstrated a remarkable degree of tolerance towards the interwar army that can be explained only by society's support for the army's central role as guardian of the reborn Polish state.[6]

The unprecedented brutality of the Nazi and Soviet occupations of Poland forged strong bonds between Polish society and its soldiers both at home and abroad. The support given to the underground struggle of the Home Army (*Armia Krajowa* – AK) against the occupation that culminated in the ill-fated Warsaw Uprising (August–October 1944) was an important measure of the military's bonds with Polish society. The Polish armed forces in the West, fighting from exile, enjoyed enormous prestige and legitimacy as the heirs of the armed forces of the interwar

Polish state. This can be seen in the strong links between the Polish government-in-exile in London, its armed forces and the Home Army.[7] The air, land and naval contributions of these Polish forces in military operations in north-west Europe was distinguished, but wartime East–West politics precluded their return as the basis of Poland's post-war armed forces.[8] Parallel to the forces in the West was a second exile army that emerged in the Soviet Union from 1943.[9] This communist-led force lacked legitimacy in Polish society. It was highly dependent on the Soviet Union, and its officer corps was made up of a high percentage of non-Polish Soviet officers.[10]

The roles of the post-war Polish People's Army (*Ludowe Wojsko Polskiego* – LWP) were very much tied to the security and ideological demands of the Soviet Union. In military terms, the army was meant to be a reliable instrument of Soviet security policy in the framework of the Warsaw Treaty Organisation. Throughout almost half a century of existence, the LWP was at best a nationally autonomous rather than a truly sovereign national military organisation. The LWP's National Security role was illustrated in an article that appeared in the Polish military publication *Zolnierz Wolnosci* in December 1982: 'It is evident that the foremost and fundamental task of the armed forces, as always in the history of the Polish people's armed forces, is the defence of the country against the foreign enemy in a brotherly alliance with the Soviet Army and other Warsaw Pact armies.'[11]

Conformity and commitment to Soviet ideology underpinned the strong Regime Defence role of the LWP. This had both international and domestic aspects. For example, it was an active participant in the Soviet-led intervention in Czechoslovakia in August 1968 to protect the 'socialist commonwealth' and extinguish the 'revisionist' experiment of Alexander Dubček. However, within Poland the LWP also played a very strong Regime Defence role in defending 'real socialism' during major episodes of domestic upheaval that threatened the supremacy of the communist Polish United Worker's Party (PUWP). In the second half of the 1940s, the LWP operated in a counter-insurgency role against the remnants of the western-orientated AK and on a considerable scale against Ukrainian nationalists in eastern Poland.[12] In quelling major domestic unrest, the LWP played an important role in Poznań in June 1956, Gdańsk in December 1970 and in the imposition of martial law in an attempt to crush the Solidarity movement on 13 December 1981.[13] Interestingly, the LWP's participation in the December 1970 events in Gdańsk gave rise to some 'myths' about the alleged reluctance of the armed forces to employ coercive military power against the civilian population. The use of lethal force by the army during the 1970 disturbances was authorised by the then defence minister, General Wojciech Jaruzelski.[14] Subsequently, a myth grew that he actively opposed the use of force in his dealings with the communist political leadership.[15] Paradoxically, however, the respect for the LWP as a military institution did not substantially diminish despite its record of defending the communist regime.[16] The deployment of about 70,000 troops to implement martial law in December 1981 in a complex domestic operation only underscored the LWP's utility throughout its history in the Regime Defence role.[17]

The LWP also had an overt Nation Builder role albeit within the confines of communist ideology. In the immediate post-war years, for example, the LWP was responsible for de-mining large areas of the country as well as contributing to the rebuilding of essential infrastructure.[18] In ideological terms the LWP functioned as something of a school for socialism with a long-term responsibility for contributing to economic activity that included improvements to infrastructure (railways and bridges), the development of technologies with industrial (and no doubt military) applications and assisting in agricultural harvests.[19] In the communist period, support for the civil community in dealing with such events as floods or other natural disasters was part of the Nation Builder role rather than the Domestic Military Assistance role as it is in many other democratic states. Indeed, military assistance during natural disasters fell under the nation-building rubric just as the domestic use of force was associated with regime defence.[20]

## After communism

Since 1989, the roles of the Polish armed forces have more closely mirrored those of a democratic state. The two postcommunist roles that are well defined in terms of official policy statements are those of National Security and Military Diplomacy. In the Security Strategy of the Republic of Poland adopted on 4 January 2000, the National Security role is explicitly articulated as 'repelling a direct aggression against the territory of Poland' and participation in 'crisis management operations outside Polish territory'. Poland's National Security role thus operates 'both within the national defence system and within the NATO system'.[21] The National Security role moves beyond simple defence of national territory to include power projection operations in the context of the Atlantic Alliance, the United Nations or other international coalitions. Poland's membership of NATO in 1999 obviously created obligations to contribute in some form to power projection operations in support of crisis management. Nevertheless, Polish international activism in contributing to peacekeeping and peace-enforcement operations predates joining NATO and is characteristic of Poland's external policy throughout the 1990s. Deployments to the Balkans alongside NATO, and UN operations further afield, illustrate the postcommunist development of this new role for the armed forces.

The Military Diplomacy role is a new one for the Polish armed forces. Under this heading, the armed forces are expected to undertake 'stability-enhancing and conflict-prevention tasks in peacetime'.[22] Such activity has been particularly evident in the development of bilateral agreements and efforts at regional cooperation. Between 1991 and 1995, for example, twenty-five bilateral military cooperation agreements were concluded between Poland and, principally, other European states. Prior to joining NATO, Poland was a strong participant in the Alliance's Partnership for Peace (PfP) programme and Polish–Danish–German trilateral cooperation eventually led to the formation of a joint corps assigned to NATO.[23] The crowning feature of the Polish armed forces' Military Diplomacy role lies in the creation of bilateral and multilateral joint peacekeeping units with neighbouring states. These are important and historically unprecedented examples of military cooperation and confidence-building projects with Poland's neighbours. The first of these projects was the Lithuanian–Polish Peacekeeping Battalion (LITPOLBAT) launched in February 1995. The Polish–Ukrainian Peacekeeping Battalion (POLUKRBAT) followed in November 1995.[24] A Czech–Polish peacekeeping battalion was mooted in February 1997 but never materialised.[25] This project has been overtaken by the agreement to create a Czech–Polish–Slovak Peacekeeping Brigade signed in September 2001.[26] The scale of development in the area of joint peacekeeping units is a measure of the growing importance of the Military Diplomacy role for the Polish armed forces.

At the same time, two roles previously performed by the Polish armed forces have now disappeared – those of Regime Defence and Nation Builder. The former role was abandoned because of its incompatibility with a democratic state and the second because of its irrelevance in terms of the absence of an ideological driver or perceived need for nation or state integration. But, despite what is undoubtedly the welcome demise of these roles, it does not follow that the Polish armed forces have no further domestic role. As in any democratic state, the Domestic Military Assistance role for the armed forces embraces a range of activities from military assistance to the civil community to deal with things such as natural disasters, to maintaining law and order when the police are overwhelmed by public disturbance. In 1997, for example, the Polish armed forces deployed nearly 50,000 troops in flood relief operations when the Odra river broke its banks and inundated large areas of western Poland including major urban centres such as Wrocław. However, the military's response was not without its critics. For example, one report on Polish Radio 1 alleged that troops had used tear-gas to drive farmers away from flood dykes they were attempting to repair near Wrocław.[27] What is clear is that the armed forces, rightly or wrongly, were tarred with the brush of the Polish public's critical assessment of the way the government handed the emergency.[28] When floods again threatened two years later, the military had clearly assimilated the practical lessons of their previous relief and rescue operations.[29]

While provision exists for the internal employment of the armed forces, given the recent history of the armed forces' involvement in Regime Defence, such a domestic role would be greeted with some suspicion and unease in Polish society.[30] In practice, therefore, the armed forces have not been called on to assist the police in a civil disturbance. In addition, although the Polish president under Article 126 of the 1997 Constitution has the responsibility for safeguarding the 'security of the state' – which must include its internal dimension – the decision-making arrangements for this are complex and involve both the premier and government.[31] Given the historical sensitivity associated with the employment of the armed forces in the context of a domestic disturbance, it is not surprising that this aspect of a Domestic Military Assistance role receives very little official discussion. Instead, the National Defence Strategy of the Republic of Poland of May 2000 merely makes a rather oblique reference to such a role in a paragraph labelled civil–military cooperation: 'The armed forces are being prepared to co-operate with domestic non-military bodies to carry out a variety of tasks on the territory of Poland.'[32]

## Domestic, international and transnational influences on the armed forces and society

Polish society has had a long-standing love affair with its armed forces. Rooted in the historical experiences of the nation in the nineteenth and twentieth centuries, the popularity of the military is woven into the fabric of national consciousness.[33] In broad terms, this support for the armed forces remains firm today, although contemporary society's approval cannot be viewed as uncritical. This can be illustrated by a series of opinion polls assessing public views of the armed forces. In December 1998, the Public Opinion Research Centre (CBOS) opinion poll asked a random sample of just over 1000 Poles how they rated an extensive list of institutions, including the armed forces. In the survey, the armed forces were ranked in seventh place behind Polish radio, the fire brigade, public television, the National Bank of Poland, the Roman Catholic Church and the Presidency. Fifty-six per cent of respondents thought that the armed forces worked well and 18 per cent that they functioned poorly.[34] An opinion poll by the Social Research Laboratory (PBS) that sought a positive or negative opinion of institutions in June 1999 also ranked the armed forces in seventh place but with only 41 per cent of respondents having a positive opinion and 59 per cent taking a negative view.[35] As if to contradict the sliding level of positive opinion of the armed forces as an institution, a CBOS opinion poll in March 1998 asked respondents to rank institutions by their popularity. The armed forces scored highly, occupying third place with 71 per cent. Only Polish radio and television were more popular.[36] Similarly, polling evidence on the Polish public's trust of the armed forces as an institution has been consistently very high for a long period of time. For example, in February 1998 and April 2002 the armed forces occupied first place among institutions with 71 and 79 per cent of respondents.[37] What this opinion polling evidence tells us about attitudes in Polish society is that as an institution, the armed forces are generally held in high esteem, though with important provisos.

The values of Polish society condition its relations with the armed forces, though in ways that are generally not consistent with the 'postmodern' agenda found in the societies of long-standing NATO member states.[38] Indeed, Polish society may be characterised as being in a contradictory position, where traditional values still run strongly in the mainstream but are increasingly challenged by processes of major economic and social change driven by the postcommunist transformation.[39] Although Poland is counted among the more successful examples of economic transformation, the cost to society has been impoverishment and increasing economic stratification.[40] This contradictory picture is best illustrated by contrasting the fact that Poland since the end of communism has seen the expansion of the number of Roman Catholic archdioceses and dioceses – suggesting the strength and enduring qualities of traditional values – at the same time as a growth in opportunities for women in business and the professions.[41] Although the latter development cannot be seen as more than the first tentative step towards a postmodern society, it does suggest that major social change is under way in parts of Polish society. This mixture of tradition and change can be readily seen in military–society relations.

In 1991 and 1993 respectively, the field ordinariates (Bishoprics) for the Roman Catholic Church and the Polish Autocephalous Orthodox Church were created in the Polish armed forces. These represented an effort to strengthen the armed forces' links to the dominant values of Polish society. In 1995, a military chaplaincy was established for Protestants in military service.[42] By contrast, during the communist period, the Christian churches faced serious obstacles to their work in the armed forces. Given the denominational composition of Poland, the Catholic ordinariate dwarfs the representation of the other Christian churches making it a dominant influence.[43] Nevertheless, in terms of relations with Poland's tiny national minorities the creation of the Autocephalous Orthodox ordinariate represents an important effort to cater to the needs of the small Belorussian and Ukrainian minorities in Poland. Traditionally in central Europe, religious affiliation is an important indicator of national identity. Church activity in the armed forces, however, has provoked some criticism. There are officers who think that the priest in uniform has replaced the political officer as a guide of ideological orthodoxy.[44] The discontent that has surfaced over alleged clericalisation, however, is not overwhelmingly present even among officers groomed under the pervasive influence of Marxist–Leninist ideology prior to 1989. The revitalisation of the influence of Christian churches on armed forces personnel serves an important role. It helps to reconnect the Polish military to the mainstream values of Polish society.

Where the armed forces are facing very modest pressure for change is in the acceptance of women into military service. Women are clearly one group with extremely low levels of representation in the armed forces. Apart from the impact of traditional values in Polish society, there exist major barriers to increasing the number of women in the armed forces in the military itself. In a January 1992 interview, the then defence minister, Rear Admiral Piotr Kołodziejczyk, demonstrated the resistance in the armed forces to increasing the participation of women:

> To my mind, there is no room for a woman, a lovely and fragile being, on the brutal and cruel field of battle. Still, I perceive a niche for women in the armed forces. At present we have some 60 lady officers, chiefly in the medical service, but ladies could also serve in signal troops or monitoring services ... I still cannot imagine that a 20-year-old girl in whom the maternal instinct might arise at the

most unexpected moment could sign a contract for five years of
regular military service.[45]

The Polish armed forces only began to accept women into the armed
forces as volunteer professional soldiers at the end of 1988. Even then,
the only area in which women could serve was in the medical services.[46]
In addition, the total numbers of women serving represented a minus-
cule proportion of the armed forces. With a strength in excess of
200,000 in 1995 there were nevertheless only around 100 women in military service. By December 1997, this total had increased to 143 women
(139 officers and four warrant officers). These women serve only in medical services, with many of them highly qualified doctors.[47] In contrast,
the British armed forces contained 17,040 women of all ranks in 2002
and approximately 70 per cent of all military trades were open to
them.[48] Moreover, while reductions in the personnel strength in the
Polish armed forces have continued, the proportion of women has
increased in numbers to a degree which can only be described as negli-
gible. In January 2001, only 277 women served in the Polish armed
forces representing about 0.1 per cent of the total serving personnel.[49] In
comparison with other NATO members this was less than the Czech
Republic (3.7 per cent) and Hungary (9.6 per cent) and very far from the
United States' 14 per cent.[50] By the end of 2001, numbers of women in
military service had risen to 288 with 230 in training.[51]

The most significant increase in numbers of women serving and their
opportunities was prompted by changes introduced in 1999. The
number of corps (or specialist areas) that women could join in the
armed forces was expanded with the list now including signals, the air
force, administration, electronic engineering, logistics and medicine.[52]
Moreover, the increase in numbers of women in training after 1999
can be explained by the fact that women could now enter officer training establishments and schools for warrant officers and NCOs.[53] The
opening of military schools to women has led to a debate on physical
fitness requirements for women because there is no uniform set of criteria for admission.[54] Yet, while there is some progress, it has not been
supported by major policy changes. Indeed, the official policy on
women in the armed forces can be described as cautious to the point of
regression:

> The increase in the number of women was not spectacular but the
> situation of the reduction in the Armed Forces is generally not
> conducive to recruiting women to the military service … Currently

there are no programmes of maintaining the recruitment of women due to the deep restructuring changes in the Armed Forces of the Republic of Poland.[55]

For the time being, women thus represent a tiny element in the personnel structure of the Polish armed forces. Some pressure for change may come from the direction of NATO's Committee on Women in NATO Forces, but this external influence is not likely to be very significant.[56] Polish society, however, is changing rapidly and the traditional roles of women are coming under pressure. Although the legal framework has expanded opportunities for women, radical changes are likely to be a long-term proposition.[57] Over time it is inconceivable that the armed forces of Poland will be immune from the wider changes in society that are expanding the role of women. At present, however, the armed forces are not prepared either in attitude or in practical terms to meet the challenges of having larger numbers of women in the military.[58]

The impact of the large-scale manpower reductions on military–society relations, particularly among the volunteer non-conscript element of the armed forces, is not well understood. Despite the sizeable numbers of officers and warrant officers discharged since 1989, not much study has been made of their reintegration into society. The armed forces have developed a resettlement programme that has seen thousands of officers participate during the period between 1996 and 2000. However, the results seem somewhat meagre in terms of the numbers who actually gain employment through this programme.[59] The considerable turbulence in the officer corps caused by successive years of downsizing nevertheless seems not to have adversely affected either the perception of the officer corps in wider Polish society or in the officer corps itself regarding the prestige of the military profession. These remain generally high. Opinion polling evidence shows that in a hierarchy of prestige among professions, being an army officer stands in fifth position. Only doctors, managing directors of major firms, university professors and diplomats are held to be more prestigious.[60] Since 1988, evidence indicates that the prestige of the officer corps in the eyes of society has increased.[61]

The external influences on military–society relations in Poland come particularly from the broad integration process into western institutions, but above all from the economic and social change prompted by Poland's efforts to join the European Union (EU). Many of these changes in the economic and social spheres are generalised in their impact on the attitudes of Polish society. In the longer term they may lead to increasing convergence with the postmodern values of western European states. In the short to medium term, however, it is the economic and social costs of transformation and preparation for EU membership that have the most immediate impact. Indeed, it is likely that the competing economic and social desires in Polish society will make defence a lesser priority. For Poland, like many of its regional partners, 'in the absence of any direct external military threat, the internal crisis [of transformation] of each country is, by far, the dominant source of anxiety'.[62] Since joining NATO, preoccupation with economic and social transformation issues is complemented by the fact that Poles also believe that their country is now well protected from external threat by virtue of NATO's collective security guarantees.[63] Indeed, although NATO may bring a feeling of security to Polish society, it also presents challenges to the military–society relationship.

## Conclusions

Relations between the armed forces and society in Poland are governed by three interrelated factors: first, the requirements of NATO membership; second, the move towards all-volunteer armed forces and the growing unpopularity of conscription in Polish society; and third, economic constraints on defence spending. It is clear that Polish membership of NATO brings with it a shift within the national security role towards power projection in keeping with the Alliance's new emphasis on 'crisis management' operations. In broad terms this means that Polish society is being confronted with deployments to conflicts outside national borders that carry a number of risks – not least the possibility of Polish casualties. Opinion polling suggests that members of the Polish armed forces are willing to serve abroad.[64] However, the support of Polish society cannot be taken for granted so easily. When the Polish public was asked what kind of cooperation with NATO was most acceptable in an August 2001 opinion poll, the largest number, 80 per cent, supported the category of Polish missions in regions of conflict.[65] Yet as regards the Polish public's reaction to sending troops to join coalition operations in Afghanistan in October 2001, 65 per cent were opposed to sending troops.[66] By January 2002, opposition had lessened considerably but views were evenly split with 43 per cent in favour and against.[67] This suggests that support for Polish participation in operations abroad, whether in the context of NATO or not, will be given only on a case-by-case basis.

The new missions for the Polish armed forces underscored by NATO membership have contributed to the emerging prospect that Poland will eventually have all-volunteer armed forces. Indeed, the Polish Defence Minister, Jerzy Szmajdzinski has confirmed that although it would not be a rapid process, military reform was certainly increasing, with rapid reaction forces receiving priority.[68] The ultimate consequence of any move towards all-volunteer forces would be an end to conscription in Polish society. Males in Polish society have been subject to conscription since 1918. If one discounts the period of occupation between 1939–44, then conscription has been a feature of military–society relations for 80 years. In Poland, approximately 300,000 young men a year become eligible for conscription. In the first half of the 1990s, between 100,000 and 120,000 were conscripted out of the available pool.[69] In 1997, some 40 per cent of the pool was conscripted; by 2001 this had dropped to little more than 22 per cent.[70] Although conscription is impacting on fewer individuals, should it disappear entirely, it would sever a long-established link between the armed forces and society. It is a link, however, that Polish society seems all too willing to break, though the consequences for military–society relations have not been fully debated.[71]

In the next decade, the most important challenge in Polish military–society relations is the issue of defence expenditure. Defence Minister Szmajdzinski recently stated that 'the greatest problem of the Polish military is its chronic underfunding'.[72] The significant changes to the employment of the armed forces entailed by NATO, military reform and the end of conscription require the application of substantial resources. Indeed, some analysis argues that even deeper manpower cuts might be necessary to create all-volunteer professional armed forces and adequately fund modernisation within the likely resource base.[73] With the competing resource demands of a difficult economic and social transition, Polish society is less willing to make defence a priority budget item. As is often the case on key issues at the centre of military–society relations, democratic societies find it easier to will the ends rather than the means of achieving them.

## Notes

1. S. Kieniewicz et al., *Trzy Powstania Narodowe* (Warsaw: Książka i Wiedza, 1994).
2. I. Ihnatowicz et al., *Społeczeństwo Polskie od X do XX wieku* (Warsaw: Książka i Wiedza, 1996), 551–6.

3. J. Odziemkowski, *Armia i Społeczeństwo II Rzeczypospolitej* (Warsaw: Wydawnictwo Bellona, 1996).
4. J. Rothschild, *Piłsudski's Coup d'état* (New York: Columbia University Press, 1966), 353–6.
5. A. Polonsky, *Politics in Independent Poland 1921–1939: the Crisis in Constitutional Government* (Oxford: Clarendon Press, 1972), 391–447.
6. Odziemkowski, *Armia i Społeczeństwo II Rzeczypospolitej*, 199.
7. K. Sword with N. Davies and J. Ciechanowski, *The Formation of the Polish Community in Great Britain 1939–50* (London: School of Slavonic and East European Studies, 1989), 111–18.
8. A. Liebich, *Na obcej ziemi: Polskie Siły Zbrojne 1939–1945* (London: 1947).
9. C. Grzelak, H. Stanczyk and S. Zwolinski, *Bez mozliwosci wyboru: Wojsko Polskie na froncie wschodnim 1943–1945* (Warszawa: Wydawnictwo Bellona, 1993).
10. P. Latawski, 'Building the Organs of State Power: Soviet "Cadres" and the Polish People's Army, 1945–49', in R.B. Pynsent (ed.), *The Phoney Peace: Power and Culture in Central Europe 1945–49* (London: School of Slavonic and East European Studies, 2000), 337–45.
11. Quoted in *Zolnierz Wolnosci*, 11–12 December 1982.
12. E. Misiło, 'Polska polityka narodowościowa wobec Ukraińców 1944–1947', in W. Wrzesiński, *Polska – Polacy – Mniejszości Narodowe* (Wrocław: Ossolineum, 1992), 400.
13. P. Latawski, 'The Polish Military and Politics', in J. Bielasiak and M.D. Simon (eds), *Polish Politics: Edge of the Abyss* (New York: Praeger, 1984), 268–92; A.A. Michta, *Red Eagle: the Army in Polish Politics, 1944–1988* (Stanford: Hoover Institution Press, 1990), 131–47; E.J. Nalepa, 'Udział Wojska Polskiego w wydarzeniach Poznańskich 1956 r.', *Wojskowy Przegląd Historyczny*, 36:3–4 (1991), 256–74, and his *Wojsko Polskie w Grudniu 1970* (Warszawa: Wydawnictwo Bellona, 1990).
14. Michta, *Red Eagle*, 68.
15. L. Fajfer, 'The Polish Military and the Crisis of 1970', *Communist and Post-Communist Studies*, 26:2 (1993), 213–14.
16. Latawski, 'The Polish Military and Politics', 277.
17. E.J. Nalepa, 'Przybliżanie prawdy', *Prawo i Życie*, 4–11 January 1992.
18. Gen. J. Bordziłowski, 'Wojna skończona, walki trwają', *Wojskowy Przegląd Historyczny*, 18:3 (1973), 557.
19. Gen. M. Obiedziński, 'Ludowe Wojsko Polskie w pokojowej służbie narodu', *Wojskowy Przegląd Historyczny*, 18:3 (1973), 38–71.
20. Ibid.
21. *Strategia bezpieczeństwa Rzeczpospolitej Polskiej*, 4 January 2000, Polish Ministry of Foreign Affairs website at: http://www.msz.gov.pl/polzagr/strategiabezprp.html.
22. Ibid.
23. H.I. Łatkowski, 'Siły Zbrojne – współpraca i współzależności regionale', in J. Fiszer (ed.), *Państwa narodowe w euroatlantyckich strukturach* (Poznań: 1996), 75–88.
24. POLUKRBAT has been sent out to Kosovo as part of KFOR and it remains unique insofar it is the only such joint peacekeeping formation to deploy as a unit among the many joint peacekeeping projects that have materialised in the region.

25. P. Latawski, 'Bilateral and Multilateral Peacekeeping Units in Central and Eastern Europe', in D.S. Gordon and F.H. Toase (eds), *Aspects of Peacekeeping* (London: Frank Cass, 2001), 67–70.
26. 'Poparcie dla brygady', *Polska Zbrojna*, 10 March 2002.
27. Text of report by Polish radio, 22 July 1997, BBC Mon EU1 EuroPol oemb/mmr, BBC Monitoring 1997.
28. CBOS Opinion Poll, 29 and 30 July 1997, in report by Polish News Agency PAP, 11 August 1997, BBC Mon EU1 EuroPol oemb, BBC Monitoring 1997.
29. W., 'Mądry Polak po…wodzie', *Polska Zbrojna*, 8 August 1997, 20–21 and 'Woda nie śpi', *Polska Zbrojna*, 16 April 1999, 17–18.
30. M. Kowalewski, 'The Polish Model of Military Assistance to the Civil Authorities in Democracies', in NATO Defence College (ed.), *Military Assistance to the Civil Authorities in Democracies: Case Studies and Perspectives* (Frankfurt am Main: Peter Lang, 1997), 101.
31. See Chapter V, Article 126, *Konstytucja Rzeczpospolitej Polskiej*, April 1997.
32. *Strategia obronności Rzeczypospolitej Polskiej*, Polish Ministry of National Defence website at: http://www.wp.mil.pl/bezpieczenstwo/1_1_2.html.
33. J.J. Wiatr, 'The Public Image of the Polish Military: Past and Present', in C.M. Kelleher (ed.), *Political-Military Systems: Comparative Perspectives* (Beverly Hills: Sage Publications, 1974), 199–201.
34. Opinion poll by CBOS, *Gazeta Wyborcza*, 29 December 1998.
35. Opinion poll by PBS, *Rzeczypospolita*, 29 June 1999.
36. Opinion poll by CBOS, *Gazeta Wyborcza*, 10 March 1998.
37. Opinion polls by OBOP, in: Polish News Agency PAP, 16 February 1998 and 'Polacy ufają mundurowi', *Polska Zbrojna*, 28 April 2002.
38. C.C. Moskos, J.A. Williams and D.R. Segal (eds), *The Postmodern Military: Armed Forces after the Cold War* (New York: Oxford University Press, 2000).
39. M. Ziółkowski, 'The Pragmatic Shift in Polish Social Consciousness: with or against the Tide of Rising Post-Materialism?', in E. Wnuk-Lipiński (ed.), *After Communism: a Multidisciplinary Approach to Radical Social Change* (Warsaw: ISP-PAN, 1995), 170.
40. J. Danecki, 'Social Costs of System Transformation in Poland', in S. Ringen and C. Wallace (eds), *Societies in Transition: East-Central Europe Today: Prague Papers on Social Responses to Transformation Vol. I* (Prague: CEU Press, April 1993), 47–60.
41. J. Kofman and W. Roszkowski, *Transformacja i postkomunizm* (Warszawa: ISP-PAN, 1999), 101 and 125.
42. *Wojsko Polskie: Informator '95* (Warszawa: Bellona, 1995), 139–142.
43. Interview with Brig. Gen. S.L. Glodz, Field Bishop of the Polish Army, in 'The Church should Fill a Great Role in the Army', *Przeglad Katolicki*, 1–8 March 1992 in JPRS-EER-92-050.
44. M. Ciecerski, 'Pluton śpiewa!', *Polityka*, 1 May 1993.
45. Interview with Rear Admiral P. Kołodziejczyk, *Wprost*, 12 January 1992 in JPRS-EER-92-015, 7 February 1992.
46. A. Dębska and M. Kloczkowski, 'Kobieta w wojsku, wyzwanie dla wojska i socjologii', in Jan Maciejewski (ed.), *Socjologiczne aspekty bezpieczeństwa narodowego* (Wrocław: Wydawnictwo Uniwersytetu Wrocławskiego, 2001), 79–80.
47. E. Mazurkow, 'Podwójne powołanie', *Polska Zbrojna*, 8 March 1995 and report of Polish news agency PAP, 26 December 1997.

48. *UK Defence Statistics 2002*, Government Statistical Service, 55; and N. Vinson, 'A Fairer Front-Line? The Role of Women in the Combat Arms', *RUSI Newsbrief*, November 1997, 81–3.
49. *National Report – Military Service of Women in Poland – 2001*, Polish Ministry of National Defence website at: http://www.wp.mil.pl/_en_about/e_6_n.htm.
50. A. Dąbrowska, 'Od makijażu do kamuflażu', *Polska Zbrojna*, 9 December 2001, 14.
51. A. Dąbrowska, 'Od makijażu do kamuflażu', 14
52. Dębska and Kloczkowski, 'Kobieta w wojsku', 86.
53. *National Report – Military Service of Women in Poland – 2001*; see also E. Szewerniak-Milewska and R. Kowal, 'Emancypacja przy karabinie', *Polska Zbrojna*, 1 January 1999.
54. Poland, Committee on Women in NATO Forces, 26 March 2002, NATO website at: http://www.nato.int/ims/2001/win/poland.htm; and A. Wojtyś, 'Taryfa ulgowa', *Polska Zbrojna*, 17 February 2002, 20.
55. *National Report – Military Service of Women in Poland – 2001*.
56. Committee on Women in NATO Forces, International Military Staff, NATO website at: http://www.nato.int/ims/2001/win/poland.htm.
57. Dębska and Kloczkowski, 'Kobieta w wojsku', 82–4.
58. Report of Polish news agency PAP, 23 November 1998.
59. *Obrona Narodowa 2001* (Warsaw: MON BPI, December 2001), 162.
60. S. Jarmoszko, *Oficerowie Wojsko Polskiego przełomu wieków: Zarys socjologii empirycznej zawodu oficera* (Warsaw: Adam Marszałek, 2002), 86.
61. Jarmoszko, *Oficerowie Wojsko Polskiego*, 89.
62. M. Boguszakova, I. Gabal, E. Hann, P. Starzynski and E. Taracova, 'Public Attitudes in Four Central European Countries', in R. Smoke (ed.), *Perceptions of Security: Public Opinion and Expert Assessments in Europe's New Democracies* (Manchester: Manchester University Press, 1996), 34.
63. Opinion poll by SMG/KRC, *Zycie Warszawy*, 27–28 March 1999.
64. A series of opinion polls by the Military Sociology Research Organisation indicated that about 80 per cent of professional soldiers supported deployments outside Poland, *Polska Zbrojna*, 26 August 2001, 8.
65. Opinion poll by WBBS, *Polska Zbrojna*, 21 October 2001, 8.
66. Opinion poll in *Rzeczpospolita*, 27–28 October 2001.
67. Opinion poll by CBOS, *Polska Zbrojna*, 10 February 2002, 8.
68. Article by Polish Defence Minister, J. Szmajdzinski, *Polska Zbrojna*, 25 April 2002.
69. W. Modzelewski, *Pacyfizm w Polsce* (Warsaw: PAN-ISP, 1996), 42.
70. T. Mitek, 'Zaproszenie w kamasze', *Polska Zbrojna*, 3 March 2002.
71. P. Latawski, 'Professionalisation of the Polish Armed Forces: No Room for Amateurs and Undereducated Soldiers' in A. Forster, T. Edmunds and A. Cottey (eds), *The Challenge of Military Reform in Postcommunist Europe: Building Professional Armed Forces* (Basingstoke: Palgrave Macmillan, 2002).
72. Article by Polish Defence Minister, J. Szmajdzinski, *Polska Zbrojna*, 25 April 2002.
73. R. and J. Telep, *Kierunek Armia Zawodowa?* (Warsaw: Bellona, 2002), 122–33.

# 3
# The Integration of the Czech Armed Forces into Society

*Marie Vlachová*

The last decade of change in the Czech Republic has introduced a market economy, a pluralistic political system, and democratic values of liberalism, freedom and individualism. In this context, Czech society identified quick integration with Europe and its security system as a political priority. Both politicians and the public recognised that reform of the Czech Republic's own internal and external security systems would be a precondition of this integration process, and so began to pay significant – if selective – attention to it. Internal security issues – and in particular the establishment of democratic oversight of the intelligence services and the reform of the police – were given priority. In contrast, military issues were de-prioritised. Czech society was convinced early on of the armed forces' loyalty to the new government and of the reality of democratic civilian control. Once these issues were addressed, society's attention turned to more vital economic, social and political problems. As a result, the reform of the Czech armed forces became the almost exclusive concern of the politicians in the Ministry of Defence, and senior military officers. It was only after NATO accession and the Kosovo crisis that Czech society began to pay more attention to specifically military issues. This process was intensified by the events of 11 September 2001. Thus, military–society relations in the Czech Republic over the past decade have been characterised by the armed forces' slow emergence from their social isolation of the communist period. This chapter analyses the reasons for the relative success of this endeavour, looking at the historical context of Czech military– society relations, the development of new roles for the armed forces, international and domestic influences on this relationship and future challenges it is likely to face.

## Historical context

In recent history, military–society relations in the Czech Republic have oscillated between two extreme positions, with society either taking an indifferent attitude towards the military or celebrating it as a defender of national sovereignty. Thus, on the one hand, the anti-militarist literary figure of the 'good soldier Sweik' was lauded as an embodiment of the Czech's position on the military, while on the other the whole nation supported the army in its ill-fated mobilisation against Nazi invasion in 1939. Indeed, the army's role in protecting state sovereignty was strongly promoted by President Tomas Masaryk in the pre-war period, and formed the basis of the Czech legions' successes during the First World War. This ambivalence in societal attitudes was also demonstrated in the actual performance of the Czechoslovak military during the Second World War. Its capitulation to Nazi invasion severely undermined its standing in society and encouraged a widespread anti-militarism among Czechs. At the same time, the fact that the army had been ordered not to fight by the civilian government of the time, and the successes of Czechoslovak soldiers who fought for other countries on both the western and eastern fronts both contributed to the military's legitimacy in society.

During the communist period, the military's legitimacy was dependent on that of the regime and was acceptable so long as the communist regime was supported. Up until the 1960s, when socialism was strong in Czechoslovakia, the majority of people considered the military to be an inevitable attribute of communist state power. This is not to say that it was wholeheartedly supported – those opponents of the socialist regime exposed to so-called 're-education' during their conscript service had different opinions – but the bases for the legitimacy of the armed forces in society were firm.[1] The character of Czechoslovak military–society relations improved during the short period of the 'Prague Spring' of 1968, when many military officers actively supported the reform process. However, this brief increase in military legitimacy was cut short by the Warsaw Pact invasion, and the Czechoslovak army's failure to put up any serious resistance to it. The aftermath of 1968 saw a strengthening of communist control in Czechoslovakia and communist civilian control over the military. This was accompanied by an extremely high defence budget, overstaffing in the military, and close linkages between the armed forces and armaments manufacturers. In this context, the Czechoslovak armed forces became isolated, and society approached military issues with neglect and indifference. Moreover, the attractiveness of the military profession was further devalued by its requirement for compulsory membership of the Communist Party.

The social isolation of the Czechoslovak military became increasingly evident after the regime change of 1989. Media revelations about the enormous size of communist Czechoslovakia's defence budget and evidence of communist plans to use the military for internal repression during the 'Velvet Revolution' helped to contribute to the general mood of mistrust. However, given that the army was not, in practice, used in this way and that postcommunist civilian control of the armed forces was quickly established, Czechoslovak society quickly lost interest in defence and military matters. Indeed, in the first years after 1989, almost all important decisions relating to the armed forces were made by a narrow circle made up of the Prime Minister and his ministers of defence, foreign affairs and the interior.[2] For its part, the media concentrated mainly on negative phenomena such as a lack of transparency in military procurement, bullying of conscripts and the army's decline in combat readiness. Constant changes in the senior positions in the Ministry of Defence also added to the steady political marginalisation of military matters. This situation only began to change with the launch of the NATO accession process which helped to highlight the importance of defence reform issues in the Czech Republic's wider process of European integration.

## Current roles

The security strategy of the Czech Republic identifies the defence of state sovereignty and territorial integrity, the defence of the democratic regime, and the freedom of citizens as the country's primary vital interests. It also recognises natural disasters, terrorism, international organised crime, and migration resulting from regional instability as threats to these interests. In addition it states that as a member of NATO the Czech Republic in formulating its defence tasks takes into account the collective security interests of NATO members.[3] In the main reform document, the Concept of Professionalisation and Mobilisation of the Czech Armed Forces, the country's defence strategy is outlined as the prevention of military conflict on Czech territory. In this respect, the Concept states the importance of an operational military, capable of participation in Alliance operations outside Czech territory, whose quality will discourage potential enemies from attacking the country. This is identified as the first pillar of defence of the Czech Republic. Furthermore, the country must be able to defend its own airspace with its own national air force and as part of the NATO Integrated Extended Air Defence System (the second pillar of defence). Finally, the Concept identifies the third pillar of defence as being the country's ability to host Alliance forces on its territory at times of crisis.[4]

The National Security, Nation Builder, Domestic Military Assistance and Military Diplomacy roles outlined in Chapter 1 thus all appear in the concepts and practice of the Czech armed forces to some extent. The National Security role is expressed through the Czech Republic's balance between providing for its own national defence, and its ability to fulfil its NATO obligations. However, an awareness of the difficulties that a small state like the Czech Republic will have in providing for both territorial and collective defence has led the country down the path of quite radical military reform. This is likely to be a long and demanding process for the Czech armed forces and the success of the process will depend on the capability of senior military officers in predicting future NATO requirements and adapting them to national circumstances. It will also require the support of politicians and their ability to persuade the public that solutions suggested by the Ministry of Defence are realistic and necessary.

The Domestic Military Assistance role is included in the Constitutional Act on the Security of the Czech Republic, which obliges the armed forces to temporarily fulfil tasks such as the guarding of borders and providing internal order and security if the police are unable to do so.[5] For example, during the World Bank and International Monetary Fund's Prague Summit in 2000, military units were on standby to intervene if the anti-globalisation riots escalated out of control. In addition, the Czech armed forces have traditionally played a strong role in aiding the civil authorities during times of natural disaster and catastrophe such as the widespread flooding of 1998 and 2002, and this role is specifically included in Czech defence and military legislation. The Military Diplomacy role, however, is a new one for the Czech Republic, having emerged in the wake of the country's accession to NATO. In particular, promoting solutions that are reasonable from the point of view of national interests and helpful in shaping the future form of the Alliance has become a vital part of the Czech armed forces' capabilities. Moreover, with EU accession becoming an increasingly realistic prospect within the next five years, the Czech military will have an important role to play in negotiating the country's contribution to the European Defence Policy and EU rapid reaction corps.

From 1989, the roles of the Czech armed forces have undergone a substantial change. The specifically national defence agenda has gained an importance very different to its standing at the time of the Warsaw Pact, and a new dimension has been added by the introduction of new roles related to the Czech Republic's membership of NATO. These international activities are an important element in the increase in the prestige of the Czech Republic internationally, and the armed forces themselves at home. The military – via NATO – is seen as a guarantor of national security, democracy and the future pro-western development of the Czech state. Today, the armed forces are seen as the Czech Republic's leading envoy to the western democracies and their institutions. Given the poor state of military–society relations at the beginning of the 1990s – characterised by distrust and disinterest – the speed and direction of this change is really quite remarkable.

## International factors influencing military–society relations

Immediately after the Velvet Revolution Czech foreign policy was dominated by a regional cooperation oriented mostly to the CSCE/OSCE and so-called Visegrad group (Poland, Czechoslovakia and Hungary). Soon afterwards, however, the new centre-right government re-prioritised its foreign policy towards potential NATO and EU membership. With the exception of the Communist Party, this refocusing was evident in the programmes of all the parliamentary political parties. Throughout this period, the transformation of the country's armed forces was allowed to drift in the shadow of political and society prioritisation of other areas of political and economic reform. Many politicians were aware that neither the military nor the country more widely were technically prepared for NATO membership. However, they correctly assessed that the first round of NATO enlargement would be driven by political rather than technical criteria and lobbied hard on this basis – supported by the successes of Czech troops in peace support operations (PSOs) in the Balkans.

The NATO accession process succeeded in engaging the Czech public in defence and security issues in a way that had not happened before. However, after accession itself, and the end of the Kosovo crisis directly after, this exceptional wave of popular interest fell away. This was mirrored at a political level, and responsibility for fulfilment of Alliance requirements was once again left mainly to defence ministers, officials and senior military figures in the Ministry of Defence. This situation changed again towards the end of 2000, when NATO criticism of the military's inability to meet its membership obligations aroused fierce debates in the media. This combination of criticism from outside and growing dissatisfaction within the army itself has led to a new round of radical reforms for the Czech armed forces which have focused on the introduction of an all-volunteer force with high levels of mobility, flexibility and professionalism and strong role specialisation in areas such as chemical and biological weapons detection.[6] In the aftermath of 11 September 2001, the Czech Republic was vocal in declaring its willingness to fulfil the new demands of the Alliance and to combat the threat of terrorism – tasks which have fitted well with the priorities identified in the military reform process.[7]

## The main domestic influences on military–society relations

### Economic resources and military reform

One of the basic factors influencing the quality of military–society relations is the willingness of society to invest in the development of the armed forces. The system of defence planning and budgeting used during the communist period has changed substantially since 1989. The military budget suffered huge cuts, was opened to much wider political and public scrutiny, and new western standards of defence planning and budgeting were introduced. The year on year decline of the defence budget has stabilised since NATO accession, when the Czech government pledged to gradually increase its defence expenditure to 2.2 per cent of GDP in line with NATO standards. However, while governmental resolutions guarantee the gradual increase of the defence budget at least up to 2004, these levels of spending are dependent on the achievement of high predicted levels of economic growth.[8]

The ability to spend funds allocated to the armed forces in a rational manner is central to the maintenance of a positive public image for the Czech military. However, the shift to more transparent and efficient standards of defence planning and budgeting has been a demanding process. Until 2001, when the radical reform of the armed forces was launched, priorities for military modernisation were not specified in a sufficiently coherent way to act as a guide for long-term defence planning. Indeed, in the early 1990s, when the reform process first started, many experts actually left the armed forces for jobs in the private sector which appeared to offer more attractive prospects, particularly for those with skills in economics.

Prior to 2001, the Czech government's approach to defence planning was essentially limited to completing the NATO Defence Planning

Questionnaire and defining the force goals. The planning process ran concurrently at the Ministry of Defence and within the General Staff, but without substantial coordination from government ministers or senior officials, and defence planning and budgeting was slow to permeate the Ministry of Defence. Moreover, the social climate in the early 1990s, in which market forces were presumed to be omnipotent, meant that the costs of the long-term transformation of the armed forces were underestimated.[9] As a consequence the Planning, Programming and Budgeting System (PPBS) introduced in the ministry in 1997 collapsed. The absence of a robust long-term and sustainable plan for modernisation also led to some ad hoc decisions that drew away funds that were badly needed for training. In turn, this meant that the combat readiness of the military – with the exception of some elite brigades – has decreased.[10]

Since 2001, a new and more systematic approach to planning has been tied tightly to existing resource constraints, and as a result, future defence budgets and plans now have to take account of economic realities. In addition, the responsibilities and powers of each separate element involved in the process are precisely defined. Planning is now based on strategic documents and NATO requirements and runs in six-year cycles with approved budgets offering stable points of reference.[11] Moreover, a more modest variant of the military reform package has been prepared in case of lower economic growth than expected.

## Public opinion on the military and its reform

Public perceptions of defence, the military and military profession are an important indicator of the changing image of the Czech armed forces. In 1990 only one-third of the Czech population trusted the military, compared to two-thirds at the end of 2001. The same 2001 poll identified the Minister of Defence and the Chief of General Staff – together with the President – as the most credible representatives of the state, and the armed forces and police as the most trustworthy state institutions.[12] This dramatic increase in the prestige of the armed forces in the Czech Republic is partly a reflection of changing public perceptions of security since 11 September 2001. However, it is also representative of a more long-term and persistent trend in the country – as suggested by opinion polls taken over time.[13] In addition, the Czech public's evaluation of the professional qualities of its soldiers has been growing steadily more positive.[14] In general, Czech society is supportive of a radical reform of the armed forces and the introduction of all-volunteer forces, with this support understandably being higher among the young male population.[15]

Czech society perceives its military's primary function to be the National Security role, in particular the defence of national territory from outside aggression. However, it also ascribes great importance to the armed forces' non-military functions.[16] The Czech armed forces' participation in NATO expeditionary obligations is considered less vital, but, nevertheless, opinion polls show growing support for them as well. Until 11 September 2001 threat perceptions among the Czech public were very low, with only a quarter of citizens in 2001 believing that military aggression against the Czech Republic was a future possibility. Since 11 September 2001, public threat perceptions have changed greatly, and previous feelings of living in a secure region – which had been intensified after NATO accession – disappeared.[17] In general, public trust of the country's security institutions has increased significantly, along with popular support for NATO, the EU and the United States. However, the most striking illustration of this change in attitude is the strong support now given to the Czech Republic's participation in anti-terrorist activities.[18] Thus, for example, most Czechs support the development of special military units that are capable of contributing to the International Security Force in Afghanistan. Moreover, they see a future all-volunteer structure for the armed forces as a more effective guarantor of their security, and increasingly understand that the provision of effective security arrangements is likely to be costly. In general, the Czech public has therefore become more aware of the connection between international and domestic policy, and are more informed about questions concerning the future missions and structures of the Czech armed forces.[19]

Public opinion towards NATO has traditionally been somewhat lukewarm in the Czech Republic, though this too has begun to change recently. In 1996, barely half the population supported the country's NATO membership, though this had risen to 70 per cent in 2001. After two years' experience of membership, most people see the main security benefit for the Czech Republic as being the way membership has contributed to the professional qualities of the armed forces and to the international prestige of the country.[20] In addition, after 11 September 2001, much of Czech society sees membership of the Alliance as the country's best chance of combating international terrorism – although it also remains sensitive to the potential additional risks this may entail. Further NATO enlargement is also strongly supported.[21]

## The strategic community as a bridge between the military and society

Political culture in the Czech Republic still lags behind that of the West. Democratic politics in the country faces challenges including a lack of transparency in political life, a lack of accountability amongst decision makers, and corruption. These problems also characterise the defence field, as evidenced by a number of recent scandals in relation to procurement and military reform.[22] Civil society in the Czech Republic is strong, and based on a rich tradition. This dates back to the end of the nineteenth century, when the institutions of civil society acted as substitutes for the Czech nation-state in Austria-Hungary. Nevertheless, the communist regime tried to suppress this tradition, and although it did not succeed entirely, the development of civil society in the post-communist period has not been easy. Today, there are numerous civil society organisations in the country, though most are underdeveloped and dispersed, unable to coordinate their activities with state institutions and, as a consequence, restricted in their ability to influence Czech defence policy.[23]

The Czech strategic community – that part of civil society that is concerned with defence and security issues – consists mainly of independent experts, non-governmental organisations (NGOs) and specialist journalists. In general, it is still too small and fragmented to be able to have any visible influence on state security and defence policy, though it has made some limited progress in this area in recent years. In 1999, for example, the first Czech NGO devoted specifically to defence issues – the Club for Security, Defence and the Protection of the Society and State (BOOSS) – was established with support from the Ministry of Defence. Since its foundation, it has organised meetings and workshops on topical issues of defence reform, and prepared a concept for the overall system of management of the Czech security sector. Similarly, during the Bosnian conflict, Czech humanitarian NGOs had significant contact with Czech peacekeeping units, which provided them with protection and material help. Similarly, public expressions of support for the Czech peacekeepers from independent civilian NGOs contributed significantly to the positive image change the Czech armed forces experienced from the mid-1990s.[24] The Czech strategic community, although limited in number, represents an important source of independent opinion and analysis on defence and security issues in the country, and parliamentarians have increasingly begun to use it as an alternative source of expertise. Moreover, the Ministry of Defence has begun to invite elements of the strategic community to ministerial public events, discussions, workshops and briefings.

## Future challenges in linking the Czech armed forces and society

The reforms of the Czech armed forces will bring fresh challenges to military–society relations. The main goal of the reform is to create small, sustainable and responsive forces with balanced air–ground and specialisation capabilities that are able to meet peacetime and contingency requirements as well as respond to natural disasters.[25] The number of headquarters, bases and garrisons will be reduced, and the military education system will also be downsized in order to adapt it to the needs of an all-volunteer force. In addition, a completely new system of mobilisation will be established. An important aim of the reform is 'to achieve a situation where the armed forces are perceived as an indispensable, useful and efficient segment of society'.[26] In practice, over the coming years, the most important areas affecting the character of military–society relations in the Czech Republic will probably be those connected with the management of human resources, the marketing of the military reform to the public, and the role of those politicians responsible for defence and security issues.

Public opinion polling shows that the willingness of young Czechs to serve in the all-volunteer forces is around 17 per cent – which, given the military's future needs is not all that impressive.[27] In practice, the Ministry of Defence will have to make use of every area of the labour market if it is to achieve its aims for the size and quality of the all-volunteer force. This will mean creating an effective system of human resource management and marketing in the armed forces, being able to detect target groups at a regional level, and establishing a comprehensive, merit-based career structure. Because of demographic pressures, it is likely that the Czech armed forces will try to recruit soldiers on a long-term – even career-long – basis. As a consequence, the creation of good working and living conditions for military personnel is seen as an important goal to enable effective recruitment of young men and women.

The armed forces will also have to pay more attention to nontraditional target groups in the young population, such as women and the Romany community. Today, 2000 women serve in the Czech military, making up 10 per cent of the professional corps, mainly at NCO level, working in logistical, technical and administrative posts.

Almost 200 women have served in foreign monitoring and peacekeeping missions, and on average these numbers have been slowly but steadily rising since 1992. The Ministry of Defence has taken some small steps towards meeting NATO standards in this area, and has established a working group to look at the issue of equality in the armed forces. In the all-volunteer force, the percentage of women serving in the military is planned to rise from the present 10 per cent to 20 per cent, and it is likely that in the future women will be given greater opportunities to achieve higher ranks. However, Czech society remains conservative and traditional as regards the role of women in the labour market more widely, and therefore the reaction of the Czech public to such an increase in their numbers in the armed forces is uncertain. Recruitment from the Romany population poses even greater problems, both because of a history of discrimination against them in Czech society, and also because poor health and education levels mean that in the past few recruits have been selected for the armed forces.

There are certainly risks inherent in the reform process of the Czech military, resulting from the relatively short time it which it must be accomplished, limited financial resources, and its radical nature. The reform is an integral concept in which all steps are connected. Thus, a change in the military's force structure also requires the creation of a new system of human resource management. In turn, this will not be effective without a new system of performance evaluation. Feedback from military personnel, the public and elected politicians as to their concerns and attitudes towards the reform will also play a crucial role in its success. In order to accomplish this in a positive way, the armed forces will themselves have to keep the process of reform transparent, using the media and the strategic community as channels of communication to society. In particular, the defensive and passive relationship that the Ministry of Defence has developed with the media over the past decade will also need to change. The ministry will need to be more active in highlighting the benefits of reform and the progress made – and it will need the confidence to be honest where difficulties and problems arise.

The strategic community will also need to play a more mature role in military–society relations. While there is general public agreement with the reform goals, debate on individual issues has been weak and inconsistent. The current debate is dominated by the media's tendency to concentrate only on particular issues, such as the deadline for the abolition of conscription or the purchase of supersonic aircraft for the Czech air force. This will need to change in order to address the wider implications of the reforms. Thus, for example, the reform will heavily influence infrastructure and job opportunities in some regions. As a result, the Ministry of Defence will have to find some creative solutions to help mitigate the local impact of closing garrisons, bases, storehouses and military schools. Moreover, since the impact of the reform will be felt most keenly at a local level, fierce lobbying by local authorities will be inevitable and will have a particular impact on parliamentarians who are dependent on local electoral opinion. In the long run, an active, careful and sensitive approach by ministers and officials to the impact of the reforms at a local level is a prerequisite of their success, and an important element of sustaining good relations between the military and society.

Marketing the reform to military personnel is of equal importance and modern management methods will have to be employed if ongoing support for the change is to be sustained among military personnel. This will require not only new channels of information, but also the creation of fora that will allow opponents and sceptics within the armed forces to present their ideas, and give the authors of the reform the opportunity to explain their policies. Moreover, because the reform is a long-term process, its success will be dependent on the ability of the Ministry of Defence to ensure that the rationale for the necessary investment of 2.2 per cent of GDP in the defence budget over the next ten years is clearly understood by politicians and the public.

## Conclusion

Over the past decade, the Czech armed forces' relationship with society can best be described as a journey out of social isolation. The armed forces have struggled hard to overcome the negative legacies of the communist period, during which they lost their last vestiges of being defenders of the national interest in the eyes of society. Since the collapse of communism, the armed forces' reintegration with society has been successful in the sense that they are no longer perceived as a threat to democracy or as a marginal and ineffective institution with an unclear mission and substandard personnel. The present armed forces have become embedded in society through new bases for legitimacy. These stem in particular from the professional successes of Czech soldiers in NATO peacekeeping operations and in providing assistance to the civil community during the severe flooding of 1998 and 2002. New reforms aim to establish a volunteer force by 2007, and the military increasingly comprises a transparent institution with a rational and realistic vision of its future role and structure. Amongst the general population, the military today is genuinely considered to be an envoy of the Czech Republic in its return to the democratic world, and as an effective guarantor of national security and sovereignty.

Perhaps the most significant factor that has influenced these developments has been the Czech Republic's 1999 invitation to join NATO. The armed forces have benefited from membership in many ways, not least through the defence advice and assistance offered by other NATO members. NATO pressure on the Czech government over the speed of the country's defence reforms has had a positive impact on the armed forces themselves, by making the government increasingly cognisant of the need for quicker and more radical defence transformation. The need to find a balance between the demands of national and collective defence has also compelled the military to abandon some of its more unrealistic modernisation plans, and to begin to structure its forces in a way that is compatible with the financial and human resources the Czech Republic has available. Domestically, a political system based around the strong partisan interests of political parties has hampered the engagement of civil society in defence matters, though recently this situation has begun to change offering some basis for optimism.

Over the next decade, military–society relations in the Czech Republic will face a number of challenges. In the wake of the abolition of conscription, the military will have to guard in particular against renewed societal isolation. It will have a strong motivation to preserve the societal links it has built up over the past decade, but it will also have to create new ones. Above all, recruitment needs will require the military to be sensitive to societal opinions, views and attitudes. A high priority will have to be given to a more systematic analysis of the labour market and identification of key target groups for enlistment, while military career structures will need to be strengthened and developed to improve the armed forces' professional attractiveness. In addition, the Czech armed forces will have to develop new public relations strategies and relationships with the country's strategic community. This should lead to greater transparency in military–society relations and allow more effective monitoring of the armed forces' development. The next ten years offers great challenges and opportunities for military–society relations in the Czech Republic. If the armed forces and politicians can seize these opportunities, the Czech military's decade-long journey out of social isolation looks set to continue.

## Notes

1. The hero of one of the most celebrated Czech novels, 'Tank Battalion' by Josef Škvorecký, published in 1969, expresses his disapproval of the communist regime through his experience of conscript service.
2. See Marie Vlachová, 'Democratic Control of Armed Forces in the Czech Republic: a Journey from Social Isolation', in Andrew Cottey, Timothy Edmunds and Anthony Forster (eds), *Democratic Control of the Military in Postcommunist Europe: Guarding the Guards* (Basingstoke: Palgrave Macmillan, 2001).
3. *Security Strategy of the Czech Republic* (Ministry of Foreign Affairs: Prague, 2001).
4. *Koncepce výstavby profesionální armády České republiky a mobilizace ozbrojených sil České republiky* (The Concept of Professionalisation and Mobilization of the Czech Armed Forces) (Ministry of Defence: Prague, 2002), 6.
5. *Act on Armed Forces of the Czech Republic* 219/1999.
6. See Marie Vlachová, 'Professionalisation of the Army in the Czech Republic', in Anthony Forster, Timothy Edmunds and Andrew Cottey (eds), *The Challenge of Military Reform in Postcommunist Europe: Building Professional Armed Forces* (Basingstoke: Palgrave Macmillan, 2002).
7. Former Prime Minister Miloš Zeman, speech on Czech television, *The Czech Press Agency*, 3 October 2001.
8. In 1996 the Czech Republic spent 4.4 per cent of its GDP on defence. This had dropped to 1.5 per cent in 1997. The recovery began in 1998 when defence spending rose to 2.8 per cent. For 2002 this figure was expected to rise to 4 per cent, and for 2003 at least 3 per cent should be achieved.
9. Vladimír Karaffa, 'Peripetie procesu obranného plánování' (Turnabouts in the process of defence planning), *Vojenské rozhledy*, No. 4 (2000), 35–42.
10. *Analýza požadovaných schopností, cílové struktury a složení ozbrojených sil České republiky* (Analysis of Required Capabilities, Target Structure and Composition of the Armed Forces of the Czech Republic) (Ministerstvo obrany ČR: Praha, 2001), 10.
11. *Koncepce výstavby*, 10.
12. In 1996 only about 40 per cent of Czechs trusted their armed forces, while in 2001 two-thirds of the population expressed their belief that the military was a trustworthy institution. See Jiří Hendrych, *Armáda a společnost České republiky, kontinuální výzkum 1996–2001* (The military and the society – a continual survey) (Ministry of Defence: Prague, 2002), 12.
13. Jiří Hendrych, *Armáda a společnost*, 27–30.
14. In spite of the fact that Czechs are very cautious in positive evaluation of their armed forces, there is a visible trend of prevailing positive opinions concerning the qualities of Czech professionals. In December 2001, 44 per cent of people were sure that the military was well trained, 40 per cent thought the soldiers would be able to sustain any combat successfully, 60 per cent of Czechs appreciated their expertise as professionals and 50 per cent had the same opinion about their physical fitness. More than half of Czechs were persuaded that professional soldiers are fully integrated into democratic society. See Jiří Hendrych, *Armáda a společnost*, 9–11.

15. The radical reform of the armed forces has been supported by more than 80 per cent of Czechs and approximately the same number of people are sure that the reform will be successful. See Jiří Hendrych, *Armáda a společnost*, 16.

16. Such as rescue operations and help to the civilian population in case of natural disasters, economic help and some policing roles (in the fights against drug trafficking, illegal immigration and so on).

17. Jiří Šandera, *Mění se postoje k NATO v důsledku boje proti terorismu?* (Are the public attitudes to NATO changing under the impact of the fight against terrorism?), press conference of STEM (12 December 2001) STEM website, at: http://www.stem.cz/index.php?id=209&tisk=1&url=source_clanky/209/index.php.

18. In November 2001, 60 per cent of the population thought that the Czech Republic should participate actively in the anti-terrorist fight, even if meant extra defence spending. The deployment of Czech combat and special units in Afghanistan was supported by 74 per cent of the population. See Ivan Gabal and Lenka Helšusová, *Pohled české veřejnosti na protiteroristickou kampaň, bezpečnost a politiku ČR* (The Czech public view of anti-terrorist campaign, security and policy of the Czech Republic), *Mezinárodní politika*, 4/2002.

19. There is unanimous support for civil defence courses to return to the school curriculum.

20. See Ivan Gabal, Lenka Hlešusova and Thomas Szayna, *The Impact of NATO Membership in the Czech Republic: Changing Views of Security, Military, and Defense*, www.gac.cz/documents/CzechPaper.doc.

21. Ivan Gabal and Lenka Helšusová, *Pohled české veřejnosti*, 35–6.

22. The purchase of non-functional parachutes from a private company founded by former soldiers was the first of a series of acquisition blunders and deceits that were made public and widely reported in the media. In 1999, 10 ministerial officials were accused of deception in purchases for the Ministry of Defence. In 2000, public attention was attracted by reports about several purchases of defective spare parts for MI-24 attack helicopters.

23. Martin Potůček (ed.), *Průvodce krajinou priorit pro Českou republiku* (A guidebook of the landscape of Czech priorities) (Praha: Gutenberg, 2002), 346–7.

24. Marie Vlachová and Štefan Sarvaš, 'Czech Soldiers in Peacekeeping Operations in Former Yugoslavia', in J. Callaghan, M. Schoenborn and J. Kuhlmann, *Warriors in Peacekeeping: Points of Tension in Complex Cultural Encounters* (Garmisch-Partenkirchen: The Marshall C. George European Center for Security Studies), 2003.

25. The present force size of 50,000 military personnel and 20,000 civilians will be reduced to 34–36,000 military personnel and 10,000 civilians, with a total wartime strength 1.8 times higher than the peacetime one.

26. *Koncepce výstavby*, 25.

27. Zdeněk Dvořák and Ladislav Halberštát, *Možnosti personálního marketingu při profesionalizaci AČR* (The possibilities of human resources marketing to recruit personnel for all-volunteer forces) (Prague: Ministry of Defence, 2001).

# 4
# Armed Forces and Society in Slovakia

*Marybeth Peterson Ulrich*

> The Slovak Armed Forces have the primary responsibility for
> the Defence of the country against all military threats, for
> potentially contributing to the full range of alliance missions,
> and for providing support to other national agencies against all
> non-military threats to the state.[1]

This excerpt from Slovakia's Military Strategy clearly states the principal
roles that have been ascribed to the Army of the Slovak Republic (ASR).[2]
However, consensus among Slovak political elites regarding its military's
roles is only a recent development. Prior to 2001 Slovakia lacked a full complement of national security policies stating the threats and challenges of
the contemporary security environment and the role of the armed forces in
meeting them. The sequential approval of a Security Strategy (March 2001),
Defence Strategy (May 2001), Military Strategy (October 2001) and Long
Term Plan for the Armed Forces' Development (July 2002) has marked an
era of consensus building among Slovak political elites concerning the purpose of the ASR in the life of the new Slovak state.

The result has been a shift away from conceptualising the armed
forces as primarily devoted to the unilateral protection of the territorial
integrity of the state towards the development of armed forces suitable
for collective defence. In addition threat assessment has expanded to
include regional stability and the global terrorist threat. This chapter
will explore the evolution of the ASR's roles throughout the postcommunist era, focusing on the implications of these developments for
Slovak society and its relationship with the Slovak armed forces. The
argument advanced in this chapter is that significant progress has
occurred at the elite level, but that gaining societal acceptance for these
decisions is only beginning.

National Security is the ASR's primary role. The legislation outlining the tasks of the Slovak armed forces lists guaranteeing the defence of the Slovak Republic against the external armed attack of a foreign power as the first task.[3] Should such a conflict occur, defence planners assume that Slovakia will not have to fight such an enemy alone. A common theme across Slovak national security documents is that the probability of a major armed conflict that threatens the state's sovereignty is low. Slovak security documents point to the possibility of regional conflict as more likely. Here the embedded assumption is that regional threats to security will be addressed collectively within the framework of international organisations. Restructuring and reform of the ASR therefore focuses on creating capabilities to contribute to cooperative regional security operations, with internal security a role shared between the armed forces, police, and state and local organs.[4]

In sum, the ASR's National Security role has evolved as the elite consensus on threats to Slovak security has developed. Regional armed conflict, terrorism, illegal transfer of weapons, international organized crime, and unfavourable refugee flows, are threats whose likelihood is identified as moderate to high in the Military Strategy. Fulfilling the National Security function thus entails adapting capabilities in order to contribute to the collective management of regional and global security challenges.

The ASR's Nation Builder role was prominent in the early years of independence, but is receding as Slovakia begins to implement its plan to reform its armed forces and eliminate conscription by 2006. In the creation of national institutions the armed forces have, in the past, played an important symbolic role embodying the concept of Slovak national identity. This role has diminished as the concept of an independent state has become well established in Slovak society.[5] However, as Slovakia has progressed in its transition, Slovaks who support an end to conscript service now outnumber those opposed to it.

Young men and their parents are placing a higher priority on pursuing educational and work opportunities than benefiting from attending the 'school of the nation' via conscripted service. While 20 years ago Slovak society would have looked down upon young men who avoided military service, such a stigma is no longer the norm.[6] In this respect the Nation Builder role has gradually ceded influence to the National Security role with its demands for professional soldiers to undertake a range of missions in the post-Cold War era. Consequently, the ASR faces the prospect of losing the military–society link that conscription ensured while simultaneously taking on the increasingly difficult challenge of recruiting volunteers to fill the ranks of the professional military.

Of the roles outlined in this volume, that of Regime Defence appears least relevant to contemporary Slovak military–society relations today. The ASR's ability to garner a 70 per cent approval rating among the public and its status as the country's most trusted institution can be credited to the public's perception that since independence the ASR has generally steered clear of political manipulation.[7] Although some elements of the military were politicised in the Meciar era between 1993 and 1998, their actions were not transparent to the public and the ASR was able to project an image of political neutrality. Until the end of 1999, the Ministry of Defence (MOD) was located in Bratislava while the General Staff resided at Trencin, 100 kilometres away.[8] During this time, the General Staff retained its independence as an autonomous entity above politics. To the extent that politicisation occurred it was largely confined to a group of former political officers who were influential within the MOD.[9] However, such elements lost their influence in the post-Meciar Dzurinda government and presently the ASR enjoys an apolitical reputation. There is no evidence of inappropriate support to particular political parties or individual politicians.

The recent recasting of the ASR's roles and missions includes the retention of significant Domestic Military Assistance roles. In addition to the mandate to defend the Slovak Republic from external attack and to fulfil the state's commitments to its international obligations, legislation passed in July 2002 assigns to the Slovak armed forces the tasks of contributing to the maintenance of public order, protection of the borders, search and rescue functions and disaster relief. The ASR is also authorised to be used for the protection and defence of facilities as directed by the government, anti-terrorist operations, and for the 'solution of extraordinary events'.[10] While the ASR's legal basis includes some capacity to respond to crises of public order, no police or gendarmerie role is part of the ASR's non-emergency functions. Conscripts were, until 2001, used to man the ranks of the railroad troops, but were subsequently replaced with paid labourers. Interestingly, Slovakia's three military hospitals remain part of the state health-care system, continuing the practice of making military doctors and the military health infrastructure available to the population at large.[11]

The Slovak armed forces have a robust Military Diplomacy role. The ASR has entered into bilateral agreements with almost all NATO countries, all neighbouring countries (Poland, Austria, Hungary, Czech Republic and Ukraine) and other 'countries of interest'. In 2001, 1700 activities took place as a result of bilateral cooperation. These events included educational and training exchanges, exercises, and a wide variety of cooperative defence activities such as the formation of joint multinational units and training initiatives.[12] In 2002, 473 activities were planned that were specifically related to achieving designated partner goals within Slovakia's Individual Partner Programme (IPP) conducted with the objective of gaining NATO membership.[13] Military reform assistance has also been extensive. The United States has provided the most extensive financial backing for reform providing US$20 million in Warsaw Initiative funds.[14] Most of these funds have been spent on equipment, training and education related to bolstering Slovakia's application for NATO membership. Much of the bilateral cooperation is also focused on supporting partner goals.

As this volume's editors note in Chapter 1, the distinct roles outlined above at times coexist and are interlinked. The defence cooperation inherent in the Military Diplomacy role has been an important factor in the formation of Slovak political elites' normative values regarding Slovakia's responsibility to participate in regional conflict prevention efforts and cooperative approaches towards the preservation and promotion of international peace. It is important to note, too, that in its status as a NATO aspirant, Slovakia has been eager to take on peacekeeping roles and to contribute to the US's global war on terrorism to demonstrate its commitment to the western democratic values that underlie these military operations. Thus, when explaining to the Slovak press the significance of sending an engineering platoon of 40 soldiers to Afghanistan to assist US forces in the reconstruction of an airport, Defence Minister Jozef Stank, remarked that such an action brings Slovakia closer to NATO through participation in the anti-terrorist coalition.[15]

Slovak society, however, has only a limited understanding of non-Article 5 issues. 'People understand war, but not things short of war.'[16] The exception is the participation of the ASR in peacekeeping missions. These activities have received a great deal of publicity and many Slovaks have met or know one of the more than 700 soldiers who have been deployed to serve in peacekeeping missions abroad.[17] However, the reorientation of the ASR's roles and missions since 1993 has mostly been an elite-driven affair. At present, the ASR is in a critical period of attempting comprehensive reform that will shape both its functional and socio-political bases of legitimacy within society. At stake is societal acceptance and support for a more normatively-based military role rooted in compatibility with NATO forces and the capacity to contribute to transnational threats as well as national defence. Such a shift in national security strategy is effecting change in the ASR's relationship with society as the emphasis on conscription-based forces shifts towards all-volunteer forces.

## The National Security context

The Slovak armed forces and society have a unique relationship among postcommunist states. While the legacy of communist rule is held in common across the former Eastern bloc, Slovakia shares with the newly independent states of the former Soviet Union the challenge of building a new state. The ASR has a mixed legacy comprised of both the positive reputation earned as a result of its war-fighting record in the service of the independent Slovak state in the Second World War and its reputation for passivity, shared with the Czechs in the Czechoslovak armed forces. While the Czechs in the Czechoslovak armed forces had no choice but to serve abroad with either the British or the Russian allies when the Germans established the protectorate of Moravia and Bohemia in 1939, the Slovaks retained their role as the military force of the independent puppet Slovak government.

In this era, the Slovak armed forces were actively engaged in the terri-torial defence of Slovakia – fighting against Hungary which invaded its eastern province and with the Germans against the Russians on the east-ern front. Professional soldiers also played a critical role in organising the revolt against the Nazis in the Slovak National Uprising in August 1944. However, this record must be balanced against the paucity of more recent military heroism and in particular the inability of the Czechoslovak military to stand up to the foreign occupations of 1938 and 1968, complicity in the Soviet coup in 1948, and its offer to defend the failing communist regime in 1989.[18] Present day societal legitimacy is a composite of the mixed historical legacy of the Slovak military as a tool to defend the country and the so-called 'Munich Complex' resulting from the periods when the military was not used to defend the state.[19]

November 1989 ushered in sweeping socio-political change as Czechoslovak society and the Czechoslovak army adjusted to the intro-duction of a democratic political system. Democratic institutions were created as communist era features were dismantled and the shift in the political system from communism to democracy caused marked changes in societal norms and values regarding the military. In the communist era, since the Party controlled all levers of socialisation – the workplace, the schools, the media, and to some extent the home – militarism and respect for the military institution were deliberately fostered until they became hallmarks of political culture in the Soviet bloc.[20] The political socialisation task in the satellite countries, however, was two-dimensional in that emphasis was placed on both socialist patriotism, or nationalism, and socialist internationalism, or obedience to Moscow.[21]

In the Eastern bloc the compatibility of military and societal values was high. Conscription in particular served the secondary function of socialising conscripts in order to transmit a common set of values across society.[22] Satellite states faced the additional burden of dealing with the legitimacy problem of imposed communist regimes, which led to a greater gap between the values of the societies at large and the military institutions that allegedly defended them. The disconnection of the militaries from the communist political regimes has been an opportunity for the divisions between postcommunist societies and their armed forces to heal.[23]

The new Slovak political elite placed a high priority on the immediate disengagement of the Communist Party from its prominent position in society and as a pillar linking the military to society and the state. The postcommunist Slovak constitution and laws were consequently written to ensure that armed forces would not retain the influence they had in the communist era. The legacy of this distrust between society and the armed forces is the rigid legal framework that restricts the autonomy and decision-making capacity of the national security apparatus. For example, the Slovak legal framework prohibits actions from occurring that are not explicitly authorised in law. Paradoxically, this is a tremendous obstacle to the Slovak military's current reform effort, because every proposed change to policy requires the passage of legislation permitting the desired action to take place. The problem is rooted in the lack of trust and confidence that the first Slovak postcommunist parliaments had in the still communist-dominated armed forces.

Slovakia's difficult adjustment in the first years following the fall of communism took on an entirely new form when political entrepreneurs in the Czech and Slovak national councils manoeuvred towards partition of the two regions into separate states.[24] At this point a fundamentally new relationship was born between an independent Slovakia and the Army of the Slovak Republic. The ASR has enjoyed a relatively smooth relationship with Slovak society; however, observers report that this positive public perception is not based on substantive information on national security matters. In many respects, the ASR is still a closed institution and one legacy of the communist era security culture is a reluctance to reach out to society to build the necessary bridges to share the responsibility for national security with society.[25] This general resistance to sharing information is a limitation that plagues the Slovak national bureaucracy across the board. Minister of Defence Stank noted that much of the progress made in the post-Meciar government has not been shared with either citizens or members of the armed forces not directly involved in drafting the reforms.[26]

## Domestic, international and transnational influences on the armed forces and society

Domestic political factors have had a profound effect on the evolution of Slovak security policy and the interface between the Slovak armed forces and society. In particular, Slovakia's endurance of the Meciar regime delayed the development of democratic institutions across Slovak society and within the national security infrastructure. Under Meciar, little in practice was accomplished on defence reform.[27] As a result, competency and military capability were sacrificed. The Slovak military was not a leading democratising institution, but the Meciar era did not inflict lasting damage on society–army relations because the public was largely unaware of the politicisation that occurred. Society and the media were generally satisfied with their perceptions of the armed forces and there was neither sufficient interest in nor access to the closed world of the armed forces to alter these views.[28]

Corruption, bankrupt economic policies, untransformed communist bureaucratic structures and repeated violations of democratic norms ultimately led to Slovakia's pointed exclusion from the first wave of NATO enlargement in 1997. These factors helped to galvanise a broad-based coalition against Meciar's party that unseated him in 1998. Prime Minister Dzurinda's government of leftist social democrats, a Green party, and right-leaning Christian democrats shared a common foreign policy agenda of integrating Slovakia into European economic and security structures.[29]

Although Slovakia has been in pursuit of NATO membership since it submitted its Partnership for Peace Framework Document in early 1994,[30] this source of external pressure did not reach a critical mass in Slovak intergovernmental circles until the Dzurinda government was well under way. The Dzurinda government gradually came to realise that significant measures would have to be taken to make progress towards its goal of becoming integrated into Europe. A negative external defence assessment[31] in 2000 was the impetus for the government's order to conduct a comprehensive defence review in order to improve on the capability deficiencies noted in the report and to reinvigorate Slovakia's campaign for NATO membership. American and British Defence assessments released in the spring of 2000 were key influences on the decision of the government to launch Slovak Republic Force 2010, a major reform effort aimed at structuring and implementing plans for total military reform.[32]

The assessments coincided with critical feedback in the dialogue between NATO and Slovakia in the Member Action Plan (MAP) process that Slovakia was not doing enough to remain a viable candidate for NATO membership.[33] Senior Defence Ministry civilians brought in by Minister Stank to facilitate change in the armed forces believed that prior to their arrival the 'ministry was doing what it wanted and that the Army was incapable of changing itself'.[34] The new leadership, committed to accomplishing the government's foreign policy goals, realised that the improvements that NATO was seeking were not possible without a comprehensive reform of the entire national security system. State Secretary Kacer recognised that 'process is directly linked to capabilities' and that 'all capabilities must have set procedures and planned resources'.[35] He credited the external pressure of the MAP process for producing an epiphany of sorts within the strategic community comprising a recognition that addressing these fundamental concepts would lead to both internal efficiency and accountability. These elements were necessary to gain capability and boost societal legitimacy through increased accountability of defence expenditure.[36]

The evolution of Slovak national security strategy and practice described above largely took place at the political elite level. Actually accomplishing the strategic concept required the national security leadership to engage society in order to articulate a compelling strategic vision and communicate to society both the progress made and its expected role in supporting national security. Since 2001 much progress has been made in elite participation and in acceptance of an increasingly coherent approach to national security.

The reform plan, Slovak Republic Force 2010, offered several critical links with society.[37] First, the plan embodied Slovakia's hopes for NATO membership. As a blueprint it outlined how the ASR would transform itself into a small, but capable force interoperable with NATO and appropriately structured, trained and equipped to meet the national security needs of the state while contributing to the Alliance. Scrapping the conscription model and securing budgetary support for a scaled-down, more capable force depends on developing and sustaining societal support.

Beyond a credible plan for reform, however, the Slovaks are also under pressure to demonstrate that the public supports NATO membership. As a result, the Ministry of Defence has initiated several programmes to educate the public on national security affairs. In the run-up to the Prague Summit in November 2002, the focus was on building support for NATO membership through a joint Ministry of Foreign Affairs (MFA) and Ministry of Defence information campaign.[38] A specific initiative, the Campaign for Increasing Information about NATO Membership, targeted schoolteachers at all levels, in the hope that armed with information about the Alliance, educators would promote a pro-NATO image to their students.

Some have criticised the effort for emphasising benefits over obligations in order to influence opinion polls. Thus, for example, M. Durina, the head of the Publishing and Information Agency of the Slovak MOD has noted that: 'the MFA is trying to demilitarise NATO, but NATO is not EU number two. It's not just a political question. [We want] people to remain interested [in security affairs] permanently, not temporarily.'[39] One danger is that political elites have chosen to downplay the threat assessments that are the basis of the Slovak security strategy they endorse. In particular, acceptance of NATO membership is being promoted on the basis that it will enhance social security as well as the 'hard' security that the state is seeking. There is therefore some evidence that the Slovak government may be making similar mistakes to those of the Czech government as they prepared their electorate for NATO membership in 1999–2000. Czech national security elites failed to fully prepare their society for the obligations of NATO membership, especially participation in and support for non-Article 5 contingencies.[40] Consequently, when the Operation Allied Force bombings began within days of Czech accession to NATO, both political and societal support quickly evaporated.

Slovaks are mistrustful of elite-led efforts to shape attitudes and others have reacted negatively to the information campaign, viewing the effort as political indoctrination.[41] The impact on army–society relations has not been distrust so much as scepticism towards directive attempts to influence political attitudes rooted in the experience of living under communism. The Slovak government has struggled with sustaining public support for NATO membership. After several years of hovering at or below the 50 per cent mark, in the summer preceding the November 2002 Prague Summit public support for NATO membership reached its peak of 60 per cent.[42] Experts credit much of the gains in the polls to the endorsement that Meciar's party, Movement for a Democratic Slovakia (HZDS) had given for NATO accession. The main remaining wild-card in military–society relations is the possibility of a referendum on NATO membership. Post-Prague, popular support for membership has dipped back to the 50 per cent mark and activists are working to get the necessary number of signatures to force a referendum. Prime Minister Dzurinda, Defence Minister Simko and Foreign Minister E. Kukan are undertaking a coordinated campaign to educate the public on the political and economic benefits of NATO membership.[43] It seems that the proper management of military–society relations post-Prague continues to pose a key challenge for the Slovak political elites.

This effort to shape public attitudes positively towards NATO membership, while simultaneously constructing the bridges to society necessary to build a professional military, does highlight a fundamental problem in Slovak army–society relations – a gap in the perceived threats to security between the political elites and society at large. While Slovak security elites are retooling the ASR to contribute to regional cooperative security operations and to respond to global transnational threats, such as terrorism, the Slovak public does not count regional or global security threats as among their primary concerns.[44] Slovaks' sense of insecurity derives primarily from their perceived lack of social security stemming from a struggling economy.

Members of the Slovak national security community repeatedly emphasise that there is a pressing need for political elites to take responsibility for accurately shaping public attitudes towards the nature of the threat environment. With the exception of international organised crime, there is a serious difference between the strategic vision and assumptions laid out in Slovak strategic documents and what most Slovaks actually feel. Particularly lacking is a collective or cooperative security mindset. Although Slovaks are aware that terrorists, rogue states, weapons of mass destruction and general instability are all components of the international environment, the general perception is that these are not direct threats to Slovakia.[45]

Moreover, while much attention has been focused on gaining support for NATO membership, army–society relations have not yet reached the point where the public can participate in a general national security dialogue within which citizens will understand the connection between security issues and their day-to-day lives.[46] Although the ASR has consistently been ranked as the most trustworthy institution in Slovakia,[47] experts contend that the 'public knows nothing about the Army or security policy'.[48] Trust is high, but interest in the military or national security affairs is low. Consequently, public debate of security issues has been practically non-existent.[49]

A factor contributing to the political elites' struggle to effectively shape public opinion is Slovakia's immature national security community.[50] A national security community consists of civilian professionals with national security responsibilities throughout the government – such as in the Ministry of Foreign Affairs, Ministry of Defence and Ministry of Finance – legislators serving on national security committees and the intelligence service, who must coordinate their efforts with military professionals. The national security community extends to society at large with the inclusion of academics, journalists and non-governmental organisations (NGOs) that specialise in national security affairs.

Slovakia's security community is underdeveloped in several key areas. First, civilians with national security responsibilities lack the expertise necessary to perform their jobs effectively. Furthermore, military officers rather than civilian civil servants continue to hold many jobs in the Ministry of Defence, raising issues of accountability. These officers argue that they cannot be replaced because civilians with their level of expertise simply do not exist.[51] Second, many military officers serving at the strategic policymaking level lack the necessary education and knowledge of politics and international relations to offer effective strategic advice to civilian policymakers. Finally, the government lacks partners across civil society to inform the public on security issues, foster the debate necessary for civil accountability of the armed forces and security policy, and to motivate citizens to participate directly in national security affairs through either military or government service.[52]

## The current and future major challenges of linking armed forces to society

There are a variety of interrelated and complex factors that pose a challenge to sustaining effective military and society relations in Slovakia. First, the Defence Ministry and General Staff are just beginning to develop national security planning processes that will effectively set priorities, coordinate resources to focus on the achievement of the stated objectives and ensure that the means allocated to defence are optimised. As Slovak society becomes more aware of its security interests and national security programmes it will need both evidence and reassurance that scarce public resources are being well spent. There is therefore likely to be a continuing challenge to ensure that the political and military leadership remains engaged, interested and competent in promoting security as a public policy to the electorate.

The possibility of the return to power of either Meciar or the HZDS in the September 2002 national elections threatened the continued progress in military–society relations. The last polls prior to the election showed HZDS holding the strongest relative position at 18.7 per cent vis-à-vis Prime Minister Dzurinda's party, the SDKU (the Slovak Democratic and Christian Union), with a showing of 8.5 per cent. Support for the ruling coalition was slipping due to the public's dissatisfaction with record high unemployment and the perception of corruption. Other centre-right parties – SMK (the Hungarians), KDH (Christian Democrats) and ANO (New Citizens Alliance) – were polling at 10.2, 7.2 and 7.8 per cent respectively. Meanwhile, a third force was rising on the Slovak political scene rivalling HZDS in opposition. Robert Fico's SMER party, which some observers had labelled 'Meciar-lite', was gaining ground, polling at 15.2 per cent with its mixed platform of populism and criticism of the Dzurinda government.

Fearing an outcome with either HZDS or SMER coming out on top, key external actors including US Ambassdor to NATO, Nicholas Burns, and US Ambassador to Slovakia, Ronald Weiser, issued clear statements that an HZDS victory 'would be a fundamental obstacle to Slovakia's entry to NATO'.[53] The return of a government less committed to realising the goals of integration, and a second NATO rejection could cause reform to stumble badly, seriously affecting the ability of the ASR to recruit a professional army and leading to the resignations of the young officers committed to reform.[54]

Observers credit the strong and clear message from the West as a key factor in shaping the perception of the electorate that the return of HZDS or even the victory of a SMER-led coalition would be a rejection of the Dzurinda government's generally pro-reform course. Ultimately Dzurinda pulled off a surprising victory. His SDKU almost doubled its pre-election polling numbers with a showing of 15.2 per cent on election day. HZDS and SMER pulled in 33 per cent of the vote combined, but the contribution of the centre-right parties' votes pushed the SDKU-KDH-ANO-SMK combination over the top enabling Dzurinda to form a coalition, with their combined 78 seats resulting in a narrow parliamentary majority without including either HZDS or SMER in the governing coalition. The major governing posts – Prime Minister, Foreign Minister and Finance Minister – did not change hands. Ivan Simko (SDKU) moved from the Interior to the Defence Ministry but has thus far made a strong effort to sustain public and internal support for continued reform.[55] In addition, Chief of the General Staff, Lt. General M. Cerovsky was reappointed to another four-year term in December 2002.[56]

### Current and future major challenges of linking armed forces to society in relation to recruitment and retention

Western-trained Slovak officers instrumental in the planning for Slovak Republic Force 2010 contend that 'understanding NATO values is a big problem for Slovak officers'.[57] Many of the Russian-trained officers are good military experts but have difficulty adapting to the underlying philosophy of the defence transformation effort.[58] As democratisation and integration into European institutions deepens, commensurate adaptation of the armed forces into a western-oriented professional force will be essential to keep Slovak society and the ASR linked. Retaining officers convinced that they have a bright future in a transformed ASR capable of providing an adequate quality of life, professional advancement opportunities, valuable training experiences, and a mission valued by the Slovak people is a key factor to the successful implementation of defence reform.

Similarly, the goal of moving to an all-volunteer force depends on a successful recruitment campaign to fill the ranks of the non-commissioned and commissioned officer corps. In an effort to attract junior officers, the ASR has introduced a one-year course of military training, prior to commissioning, that results in a master's degree. To meet its goals, the Slovak Ministry of Defence has already funded a number of marketing campaigns for recruitment to its newly envisioned NCO corps. In 2001 the goal of recruiting 1600 contract soldiers to fill the professional non-commissioned officer ranks was met, but observers suggest that this was principally the attraction of serving in peace-keeping missions.[59] Clearly, sustaining recruitment goals to fill positions across the ASR in an increasingly competitive labour market will be more difficult in the years ahead.

Some steps have already been taken. In July 2002, the Slovak parliament passed a law that raises non-commissioned officers' salaries by 48 per cent and provides for an enlistment bonus.[60] Additional quality of life initiatives are being considered, but such investments are being balanced with other investments needed in defence infrastructure and modernisation. Another deterrent to military service is the perceived and practical experience of life in the ASR. Conscripts dissatisfied with military service appear not to be keen to volunteer for a long-term career. Presently, there is a provision in effect that requires all volunteer soldiers to come from the conscript ranks.[61] Ultimately, the successful introduction of all-volunteer armed forces will depend on the development of military–society relations that can directly communicate to potential recruits and society at large improved conditions in the armed forces and attractive career prospects through a variety of jobs and missions.

## Current and future major challenges of linking armed forces to society in relation to legitimising armed forces

The legitimacy of the armed forces in Slovak society is dependent on social acceptance of the ASR's roles and its ability to fulfil the demands of its roles effectively.[62] Slovak Republic Force 2010 is indicative of the security elites' shift in recent years towards the National Security and Military Diplomacy roles. The key challenges of legitimising this transformation are closing the 'threat gap' between society and political elites and sustaining long-term commitment to the reform process. However, it is important to note that the role preference of Slovak elites at this point in time is more of a goal than a reality and much will depend on successful implementation. The ASR therefore confronts the dual tasks of gaining societal support for its reform plan and actually delivering on it.

Serious questions remain concerning the ASR's ability to implement the comprehensive organisational changes that the professionalisation path is dictating. Will the new four-party coalition keep the reform process on track? Will the external pressure inherent in an imminent NATO invitation evaporate once membership is in hand? Will political elites take the steps necessary to shape public attitudes in order to close the 'threat gap'? Will the economic picture allow the investment of resources necessary to adopt the ASR's new roles? Societal legitimacy largely depends on the extent to which the Slovak people are included in a defence dialogue and in society's subsequent willingness to participate in and support the armed forces' activities. Slovakia's long campaign to earn international support for its NATO bid has been successful. However, much work remains to convince the Slovak public that pursuing security within the NATO framework is the way to go.

## Current and future major challenges of linking armed forces to society in relation to the deployment of military force

There are two main issues related to the deployment of military force and linking the ASR to Slovak society. The first concerns projections regarding the ASR's capacity to actually deploy force. The second concerns the degree to which Slovak society will support such operations. At present Slovakia has a limited capacity to deploy its forces, and only a few elite units have made regular contributions to regional security operations, primarily through the Partnership for Peace programme.[63]

The goal is to transform the ASR so that existing units will have the necessary capacities to deploy. As the new security strategy takes effect and operations reflect a coherent and increasingly predictable pattern of deploying forces, sustained support from Slovak society will depend on its acceptance of the ASR's new roles and its willingness to fund them. Comprehensive military reform will require the participation of citizens seeking military careers, sustained public support for defence spending, and societal commitment to the security strategy towards which personnel and economic resources will need to be directed.[64]

### Current and future major challenges of linking armed forces to society in relation to securing appropriate public expenditure for the armed forces

In conjunction with its approval of the long-term plan for ASR reform in July 2002, the Slovak parliament itself committed to a defence spending level of 2 per cent of GDP, beginning in 2003.[65] The increase from the 1.89 per cent level is attributed to recommendations from NATO officials that the 2 per cent level is the minimum expected for all NATO candidates.[66] A stable figure is a critical component for long-term defence planning. In parliament, the media, and society at large there is no real opposition to these levels. A 'guns versus butter' campaign led by a few leftist parliamentarians in recent years met with only marginal support and anyway such initiatives contrary to the will of the political elite in Slovak society are rare.[67]

Defence Minister Stank contended that approval of the long-term plan and the commitment to fund it was a critical step towards ensuring that reforms continued after the September 2002 elections.[68] The specific amount of funds available for defence from year to year will depend on the economic growth rate. A prosperous society will be able to contribute more towards the fulfilment of Slovak security goals.

However, many postcommunist states have proved that greater defence spending does not necessarily equate to greater defence capabilities. Additional resources pumped into unreformed defence structures may not gain any additional defence capacities and until 2001 this was also true in Slovakia. In 2000 only 2.3 per cent of the budget was spent on procurement, which proved inadequate in making significant progress in its military reform programme, but 2001 marked a break with past budgets, allocating 10.8 per cent towards MAP partner goals and modernisation of elite units for deployments abroad. Extremely ambitious investment objectives of 25 per cent are laid out in Slovak Republic Force 2010.[69] Such a radical redistribution of defence resources will require accomplishing objectives that have proved elusive since independence: personnel levels will have to be reduced and absorbed into society; a systematic reordering of priorities throughout the defence planning system will also be required – in a system which to date has proved itself incapable of rationally allocating resources.

The human factors associated with implementing such massive change should not be underestimated. Legislation passed in July 2002 provides funds to support officers who are made redundant. Effective communication of the changes that take place is a critical strategic goal in itself, to attract recruits, legitimise the new defence model, and to convince society that its scarce resources are being spent wisely. With no substantial additional resources on the horizon, military reform will be expensive and incremental. As a senior western officer serving as an adviser to General Cerovsky observed, the Slovaks 'will have to live with the outputs of a transforming system'.[70] The challenge will be to deliver some tangible results right away while simultaneously living with the reality of a slowly changing system.

## Conclusions

A number of key factors have emerged as Slovak military–society relations have evolved since 1989 – the gap that separates Slovak society and its political elites over the perceived threat, the conservative cultural legacy and the influence of the NATO accession process over Slovak national security affairs. In turn, these factors are interrelated in that the 'threat gap' stems from the adoption of an alliance-based cooperative approach to security influenced by western liberal democratic values. Making headway in the NATO accession process has required the gradual shedding of a myriad of communist-era legacies, from force structures to bureaucracies. These developments, meanwhile, rely upon the acceptance of a culturally conservative society that prefers maintenance of the status quo to radical change. Other significant factors include the clear communication of political elites' activities and progress in the defence reform plan, and building up a base of experts to nurture the development of a national security community capable of fostering interest in security affairs in the general public.

Slovak national security policy in the postcommunist era has thus been the result of the decisions of political elites and not the product of popular participation in politics.[71] The elites have crafted National Security and Military Diplomacy roles for the ASR, with underlying threat assumptions that depart significantly from the threat perceptions held by society at large. Societal participation, however, will be required to effect real change and achieve the national security objectives. Legitimacy for these changes will manifest itself in two main areas – social and financial support for and participation in a professional army. Sustaining the legitimacy of the armed forces depends on societal acceptance of the threat perceptions and alliance-centred strategy that defence planners currently envisage. The roles and missions outlined in the ASR's new set of security documents have yet to be internalised and accepted by society.

To achieve its goals, the ASR and the national security elites will need to embrace the challenge of establishing robust civil–military relations to educate and inform the electorate about the changed strategic environment, national security affairs and the government's vision of the role the electorate will need to play. The realisation of the ASR's roles will require the sustained availability of scarce national resources and the commitment of individual Slovaks to support and staff the effort. At present, there is no significant debate over sustaining the current level of defence spending. The danger is that a resource-strapped Slovak state, having achieved NATO membership, and confronted with the demands of economic development and the costs of EU membership, will find it increasingly difficult to sustain public support for military reform.

Much work remains to be done to build ties between the ASR and Slovak society – indeed, a transformation of attitudes has yet to occur uniformly within the ASR itself. Reformers conduct their work with some fear that robust bipartisan support for military reform is a chimera. Although the ASR now recognises to some degree the need to build ties with society, Slovak society has been a more reluctant partner. Over the next decade, the consolidation of societal support represents a major challenge in the quest to develop professional and legitimate armed forces in Slovakia.

## Notes

1. *Military Strategy of the Slovak Republic* (Bratislava: Ministry of Defence, December 2001), 15.

2. The Army of the Slovak Republic is an all-inclusive term encompassing the land and air forces of the Slovak Republic.
3. 'The Armed Forces of the Slovak Republic' (Bratislava: Ministry of Defence, 2002), http://www.mod.gov.sk/english/rezort/armada.asp.
4. *Security Strategy of the Slovak Republic* (Bratislava: Ministry of Defence, 25 October 2001), 10.
5. A. Hrnko, Acting Head of NATO Section, Slovak Republic Ministry of Defence, interview by author, Bratislava, July 2002.
6. Hrnko interview.
7. Bratislava TA3 Television, 'Slovak Young Men Show Increased Interest in Army Career', 6 May 2002; *FBIS*, EUP20020506000197 (6 May 2002).
8. M.P. Ulrich, 'Developing Mature National Security Systems in Post-communist States: the Cases of the Czech Republic and Slovakia', *Armed Forces and Society*, 23:3 (2002), 414.
9. M. Korba, Slovak defence expert and scholar, interview by author, Bratislava, July 2002.
10. NR SR Act 321/2002, http://www.mod.gov.sk/english/rezort/armada/ armada.asp.
11. J. Pivarci, State Secretary, Slovak Republic Ministry of Defence, interview by author, Bratislava, July 2002.
12. Examples of this cooperation include such activities as the establishment of a Polish–Slovak–Czech peacekeeping brigade command centre, creation of a Slovak–Dutch joint helicopter unit, and Hungarian–Ukrainian–Romanian–Slovak multinational catastrophe prevention unit.
13. Hrnko interview.
14. Hrnko interview.
15. Bratislava Narodna Obroda, 'Defence Minister Believes Afghan Mission Brings Slovakia Closer to NATO', 11 June 2002, 7; *FBIS*, EUP20020612000269 (11 June 2002).
16. Interview with senior civilian official, Slovak Republic Ministry of Defence, by author, Bratislava, July 2002.
17. M. Bergeson, Major, USA, Chief, US Office of Defense Cooperation, interview by author, Bratislava, July 2002.
18. C.S. Leff, *The Czech and Slovak Republics* (Boulder, CO: Westview Press, 1997), 232–5; M.P. Ulrich, *Democratizing Communist Militaries: the Cases of the Czech and Russian Armed Forces* (Ann Arbor, MI: University of Michigan Press, 1999), 102–4.
19. Hrnko interview.
20. Ulrich, *Democratizing Communist Militaries*, 21.
21. Ulrich, *Democratizing Communist Militaries*, 22.
22. Ulrich, *Democratizing Communist Militaries*, 40.
23. Ulrich, *Democratizing Communist Militaries*, 40.
24. C. Krupnick and C. Atkinson, 'Slovakia and Security at the Center of Europe', in *Almost NATO: Partners and Players in Central and East European Security* (New York: Rowman and Littlefield, 2002), 2.
25. Korba interview.
26. Frantisek Jasek, 'Support for NATO Entry Went Up Again: the Army Reform is Waiting for Parliament's Definitive Decision', *Bratislava Novy Den*, 7 May 2002, 8; *FBIS*, EUP2002058000481 (7 May 2002).

27. R. Kacer, State Secretary, Ministry of Defence of the Slovak Republic, interview by author, Bratislava, July 2001.
28. Korba interview.
29. M. Ulrich, 'Professionalisation of the Armed Forces in Slovakia', in A. Forster, T. Edmunds and A. Cottey (eds), *The Challenge of Military Reform in Central and Eastern Europe: Building Professional Armed Forces* (Basingstoke: Palgrave Macmillan, 2002), 13.
30. 'Signatures of Partnership for Peace Framework Document', 23 April 2002, http://www.nato.int/pfp/sig.cntr.htm.
31. *Defence Assessment of the Slovak Republic* (Washington, DC: Department of Defence, 2000).
32. Interviews with Slovak defence officials, by author, Bratislava, July 2001 and July 2002.
33. Interview with senior civilian defence official, Slovak Ministry of Defence, by author, Bratislava, July 2001.
34. Kacer interview.
35. Kacer interview.
36. Kacer interview.
37. The plan is available at the Slovak Ministry of Defence website: http://www.mod.gov.sk/english/index.asp.
38. I. Samson, Analyst, Slovak Foreign Policy Association, interview by author, Bratislava, July 2001.
39. M. Durina, Head Publishing and Information Agency, Slovak Ministry of Defence, interview by author, Bratislava, July 2001.
40. Ulrich, 'Developing Mature National Security Systems', 410–12.
41. Samson interview; *Organising National Defences for NATO Membership: the Unexamined Dimension of Aspirants' Readiness for Entry* (Groningen, Netherlands: Centre for European Security Studies, 2001), 83.
42. The Defence Ministry reported in May 2002 that a poll that it commissioned confirmed that 61 per cent of the population supported Slovakia's entry into NATO. Bratislava TA3 Television, 'Slovak Young Men Show Increased Interest in Army Career'.
43. BBC Monitoring International Reports, 'Slovak Premier Announces Campaign to Raise Support for NATO Entry', 26 January 2003.
44. Korba interview.
45. Korba interview.
46. Durina interview.
47. According to 64.8 per cent of respondents polled in January 2000 by Markant. *Bratislava TASR*, 'Slovak Armed Forces "Most Trustworthy Institution"', *FBIS*, EUP20000214000381 (14 February 2000).
48. Samson interview.
49. Pavol Vitko, Spokesman and Head of Media and Public Affairs Division, Ministry of Defence of the Slovak Republic, interview by author, Bratislava, July 2001.
50. See Ulrich, 'Developing Mature National Security Systems in Postcommunist States: the Cases of the Czech Republic and Slovakia'.
51. Ulrich, 'Developing Mature National Security Systems in Postcommunist States: the Cases of the Czech Republic and Slovakia', 419.

52. M. Korba, *Civil–Military Relations in Slovakia from the Perspective of NATO Integration* (Bratislava: Slovak Foreign Policy Association, 2001).

53. Czech News Agency, 'Slovakia Not to Join NATO with Meciar and HZDS – USA', 20 June 2002.

54. Interview with western observer of Slovak military affairs, by author, Bratislava, July 2002.

55. BBC Monitoring International Reports, 'Slovakian Defence Minister Says Ministry Was Reformed "Far More Than Others" ', 29 December 2002.

56. *Sme, Bratislava*, 'Slovak Army Chief of Staff to Remain in Post', 6 December 2002.

57. J. Viktorin, Colonel, Department of Integration and Foreign Affairs, Slovak Republic Ministry of Defence, interview by author, Bratislava, July 2001.

58. Viktorin interview.

59. Interview with western observer of Slovak military affairs, by author, Bratislava, July 2002.

60. *Bratislava Pravda*, 'Parliament Raised Professional Soldiers' Salaries', 3 July 2002, 2; *FBIS*, EUP20020704000440 (4 July 2002).

61. Interview with western observer of Slovak military affairs, by author, Bratislava, July 2002.

62. See Chapter 1.

63. Slovak troops are assigned to fifteen separate deployments around the globe ranging from service in the former Yugoslavia to UN peace support operations in the Middle East.

64. J. Kazocins, Brigadier, British Military Adviser to Slovak General Staff and P. Svec, Colonel, Slovak General Staff, interviews by author, Bratislava, July 2001.

65. *Bratislava Pravda*, 'Parliament Confirms Slovak Army Professionalisation', 12 July 2002, 2; *FBIS*, EUP20020714000009 (14 July 2002).

66. B. Hocevar, Major, US Army International Political–Military Affairs Officer, interview by author, Headquarters US European Command, Stuttgart, June 2002.

67. Korba interview.

68. *Bratislava Pravda*, 'Parliament Confirms Slovak Army Professionalisation'.

69. *Organising National Defences for NATO Membership: the Unexamined Dimension of Aspirants' Readiness for Entry*, 89–90.

70. Kazocins interview.

71. *Organising National Defences for NATO Membership: the Unexamined Dimension of Aspirants' Readiness for Entry*, 82–3.

# 5
# The Armed Forces in Hungarian Society: Finding a Role?

*Pál Dunay*

The armed forces of Hungary have always faced difficulties in their relationship with society. Historically, the country has no glorious war-fighting tradition. It lost every war between 1487 and 1991, and failed to defend itself against Soviet invasion in 1956. These negative legacies were further aggravated by successive Hungarian regimes, all of which publicly criticised both their predecessors and the performance of the armed forces. Thus, for example, Hungary fought alongside the German fascists right up until the end of the Second World War. For the newly incumbent post-war communists it was easy to depict their forerunners as 'the last satellite' of fascism. In 1956 the armed forces were dissolved. They did not provide any organised support for the Hungarian uprising, which was subsequently suppressed with the support of Soviet arms. For those who sympathised with the revolution the armed forces' inaction demonstrated their irrelevance.

In some ways, this lasting legacy of doubtful political reliability on the part of the Hungarian armed forces has, ironically, actually contributed to their professionalism. The military had little political bargaining power and its leadership were not represented in the Party Politburo.[1] The armed forces carried out their responsibilities as determined by the political leadership and the demands of the Warsaw Treaty Organisation (WTO), and were not overt actors in the Hungarian communist system. As a result, during the negotiated system change of 1989, they were not directly criticised. Moreover, Hungary, which had been effectively occupied for many decades, had no real national institutions, and these had to be 'created' after the system change of 1989. Since the armed forces did not present any challenge to this process of transformation, for some considerable time defence issues were not treated as a political priority. Indeed, throughout the 13 years since the fall of communism, the entire defence issue appears to have fallen into the category of 'important, but not urgent'. As Ferenc Molnár bluntly put it: 'The new political elite was not interested in the armed forces.'[2] In this environment, expertise in defence and security issues developed very slowly, and the whole issue of national defence only began to attract interest when NATO accession became a real possibility.

In the period since 1989, the Hungarian armed forces have clearly played the classical, narrowly defined role of the military of a liberal democracy. They provide for the defence of the state against a potential external enemy and they contribute to international cooperation through peace support operations and as part of Hungary's commitment to NATO – the National Security and Military Diplomacy roles. The armed forces are also employed in case of natural and human disasters – the Domestic Military Assistance role. According to a current publication of the Hungarian Ministry of Defence the following functions are attributed to Hungarian armed forces:

> the defence of the territorial integrity inside NATO. The aversion of catastrophes and the elimination of their consequences follow the basic function. The defence of NATO territory, the aversion of catastrophes abroad and participation in blue helmet (UN) operations are mentioned as the third most important task.[3]

Thus Hungary has a well-established National Security and Domestic Military Assistance role for its armed forces, with an emphasis on the defence of the national territory. As regards the Military Diplomacy role, Hungary – as a new NATO member – has begun to play an active role in providing support to other countries seeking NATO membership and is working to fulfil its requirements under the Membership Action Plan (MAP). Given their questionable contribution to Hungary's 1100-year history, the armed forces play no role in consolidating national identity. The same is true of the Regime Defence role.[4]

The relationship between the Hungarian armed forces and Hungarian society currently faces a variety of pressures, and these are overwhelmingly of domestic origin. In particular, the most important challenge for this relationship is closely connected with a shift to all-volunteer armed forces. This process will sharpen the contradiction between those who propose to complement the volunteer core with some residual national guard type territorial defence force and those who deem this unnecessary. However, there is wide-ranging political and societal consensus about the desirability of professionalisation, and so even this issue is unlikely to directly challenge the legitimacy of the armed forces. Moreover, there are a complex set of pressures exerted upon the government relating to the funding of the armed forces. Domestically, these pressures come from different directions. In general, most Hungarians appeared willing to support an increase in defence spending as long as it did not take place at the expense of other important projects, activities and portfolios. However, despite the extra legitimacy provided by the armed forces' international commitments, occasionally helping to protect the financial resources of the defence portfolio, in general defence has usually lost out in any budgetary struggles.

During the last decade Hungarian defence has followed the same development pattern as many other central and eastern European countries. Professional incompetence prevailed both within the senior echelons of the military and among civilians dealing with defence matters both within the Ministry of Defence and in parliament. Reform plans followed each other so rapidly that it was impossible to introduce sound military planning. In particular, the weakness of the military resulted in the widespread civilian intervention in many traditional areas of military autonomy. Indeed, even decisions on military-technical matters were often taken out of the hands of senior military officers. In the light of this situation, it was fortunate that defence reform and military competence were not placed under too much public scrutiny. In the second half of the 1990s the situation changed. First, after a long period of inactivity and neglect, the Horn government realised that NATO enlargement might occur earlier than initially predicted, and this triggered increased government activity, particularly after Hungary's formal invitation to negotiate NATO membership. Following autumn 1999 when the deep-rooted problems of defence became more salient, the first long-term defence reform was agreed upon and its implementation started.[5] However, this happened in a period of further declining public interest in defence reform; though, by contrast, significant attention has been paid to the Hungarian military's future shift to an all-volunteer force, given the wide popular desire for this reform to take place. This selective public interest in Hungarian defence issues has therefore become an important and rather stubborn obstacle to the development of a mature relationship between the Hungarian armed forces and civil society.

## Context

Perhaps the most peculiar feature of the history of Hungarian society is that it is difficult to find an era that can be regarded as a positive point of reference. The history of Hungary is full of occupations, military defeats and loss of territory. Tartars, Turks, Austrians and Soviets invaded and often occupied the country. But Hungary was not always an innocent victim of aggression. She occupied territories as well, and also participated in several wars of aggression. The last era that historians assess positively is the 1867 to 1914 period of the Austro-Hungarian monarchy. It was certainly an undemocratic experience, and not a particularly glorious time for other nationalities within the empire, but it was nevertheless an era of prosperity and military success for Hungary. What followed were two lost world wars, a limited illiberal democracy, alignment with fascism, and decades of Soviet occupation. It is therefore difficult to refer to a period in national history when Hungary had both prestigious and successful armed forces and an acceptable political regime.

Moreover, the Hungarian armed forces had little prestige during the communist period between 1948 and 1989. The military's sporadic appeals to Communist Party leaders did not improve this, in part because the political elite pointed to the responsibility of the military to improve its reputation in society and in part because the Communist Party leadership could not address the root cause of the problem. What is noticeable, however, is that the armed forces' prestige increased at those times when they were most demanding of the political leadership.[6] It is for this reason, among others, that the system change of 1989 was accompanied by a sudden increase in the military's standing.

As historical experience illustrates, the standing of the Hungarian armed forces in society can change quite rapidly. The system change of 1989, the increase of transparency in defence matters, and the adoption of the basic principles of security and defence, occurred in parallel with a growing sense of insecurity, as a result of wars in the Balkans. In this context, 38 per cent of the population of Hungary viewed the armed forces more positively in 1996 than at the beginning of the decade.[7] At the same time, the population was critical in its assessment of their performance, the state of their equipment and their overall level of preparedness.[8]

In analysing the key factors influencing societal opinion of the Hungarian armed forces, three are worthy of note. First, from 1945 Hungary did not fight a war and hence such experience did not play a role in shaping military–society relations. Second was the increase and decrease of tension in neighbouring states and the fear of a violent conflict emerging, especially as a consequence of the Balkan wars. Finally, the ability of Hungary to contribute to military operations in concert with better prepared armed forces from other states, especially during the Kosovo operation of 1999, was also a factor.

Until the late 1980s the Hungarian armed forces did not participate in any Peace Support Operations (PSOs) with the exception of truce monitoring in Vietnam in the mid-1970s. Since 1990, the Hungarian government has continued to be selective in relation to its PSO commitments. Traditionally, the government has refrained from participation in PSOs when the possibility of casualties might be disproportionate to the results of the operation, for example, the UN operation in Somalia and operation Alba in Albania. The Hungarian government has also declined PSO opportunities when the deployment has taken place in neighbouring states, or in a territory where due to historical reasons the Hungarians might be regarded as enemies – such as the former Yugoslavia.[9] However, more recently, the influence of this factor has waned and the two operations where the Hungarian contribution has been largest – SFOR in Bosnia and KFOR in Kosovo – both fall into the second category. In all, around 2000 Hungarian soldiers have been involved in PSOs, and the impact of these deployments on the armed forces has been significant in terms of developing their technical and interoperability capabilities. They have also had a slightly less direct impact on military–society relations. Through such missions, much has been done to promote the idea that Hungarian armed forces can operate alongside those of other nations with larger and more advanced militaries. In addition, the use of Hungarian facilities by other NATO members during the Bosnia and Kosovo interventions visibly demonstrated that Hungary can play a valuable role in contributing to international peace and security. Both these factors have contributed to the rising prestige of the armed forces in Hungarian society.

Moreover, in recent years, natural disasters, and especially major flooding in 1999 and 2000, have required the extensive involvement of the Hungarian armed forces. However, it is difficult to assess the impact of this widely publicised Domestic Military Assistance role on military–society relations since both these events were followed or preceded by other significant defence-related developments. Thus, the first of the two floods occurred just prior to Hungary joining NATO and an intensive public relations campaign leading up to the referendum on membership, and the Kosovo operation followed. Whatever the specific contribution, from 1998 public opinion significantly improved from this point.

In sum, the Hungarian armed forces could not draw on long traditions or the past achievements of a national institution to help reconnect the military to Hungarian society. It has to build up its reputation gradually on the basis of new roles and achievements. As a consequence, the results are modest and fragile and it remains prone to sudden and unexpected changes in levels of public support, both in terms of recruitment and specific military operations.

## Factors influencing the relationship of the armed forces and society

After the system change the first two democratically elected governments of the country – the moderate conservative Antall and the socialist-liberal Horn administrations – shared the assessment that national defence was not a priority issue for government policy. Among other factors, this reflected the fact that the post of defence minister was generally offered to politicians as compensation for not being appointed to more attractive ministerial positions. During the first government, the establishment of functioning democratic institutions and privatisation were the priorities. Circumstances dictated that the Horn government had to shore up Hungary's difficult economic situation, and conditions were simply not conducive to the prioritisation of defence, but poor ministerial appointments to posts in the Hungarian Ministry of Defence have continued during the Orbán government. However, three important differences set the Orbán government apart from its predecessors. First, during the NATO accession talks government ministers made commitments that had to be fulfilled. Second, by the time the Orbán government came to office in 1998 the economy was in a relatively strong condition, and high economic growth provided additional resources to the defence sector. Third, the Orbán government advanced a concept of socio-political development that would allow the armed forces to establish a clear role in the service of a strong state.[10]

Despite the steadily improving relationships between the armed forces and the government and the armed forces and the Hungarian electorate, in recent years, the maintenance of mandatory military service has been the main divisive issue. The liberal Alliance of Free Democrats (AFD) is committed to the immediate abolition of conscription;[11] the Socialist Party has the same objective but over a slightly longer timescale;[12] while the conservatives not only want to defer a decision on the issue, but also want to establish a national guard which would include some mandatory military service. Despite the popularity of a decision to end conscription, throughout the period of the Orbán government from 1998–2002, it continued to resist such a move.

The Prime Minister set out his position in a speech to senior Ministry of Defence officials and officers.

> I would like to give preference to those also in other areas of state service, who fulfilled their military duty... We are not speaking here exclusively about the need for military officers to have respect and recognition. This can be achieved only if conscripts also conclude that it is an honour to serve in the armed forces. It is honourable to serve as contract soldier and it is an honour to serve as conscript... One has more confidence in those colleagues in the state administration who took the military oath... Therefore it is our objective that all young people who are suitable physically, even to the smallest extent would serve and would be committed to the common future of our country.[13]

Despite this view, mandatory military service remains deeply unpopular in Hungarian society and the overwhelming weight of public opinion is in favour of its abolition.

The victory of the Socialist Party and the AFD at the April 2002 parliamentary elections has brought the prospect of ending compulsory military service closer. The government is determined to abolish conscription by 1 January 2006, within the period of its current term of office and a few months ahead of the next elections. As a consequence, the current government is likely to live up to its promise with little objection from the conservative opposition. Indeed, opposing such a decision would make the conservative parties highly unpopular, particularly among young people who tend to vote for the largest conservative party, FIDESZ. In a recent opinion poll which asked when Hungary should have fully all-volunteer armed forces, 40 per cent support abolition in less than five years, 18 per cent within five to 10 years, and 4 per cent within 10 to 15 years. Twenty-three per cent of those polled were of the view that Hungary should not introduce all-volunteer armed forces at all.[14] It is also worth noting that if the conservative opposition parties in parliament refuse to support the necessary constitutional changes, the government could simply decide not to call up conscripts after 1 January 2006 without the approval of the legislature. Thus, the momentum towards all-volunteer armed forces appears irresistible and once implemented it will be both politically and technically difficult to reverse.

Beyond the political pronouncements on conscription, the approach of military professionals themselves is also important. Szigeti suggests that armed forces based on conscription have to be able to carry out war-fighting tasks with their peacetime personnel; reserves must be capable of being mobilised rapidly and have to be regularly retrained.[15] Moreover, conscript-based armed forces are only useful in those countries which prepare for large-scale manoeuvres (seizing and holding territory) or which may face large-scale aggression.[16] Neither set of conditions make the maintenance of conscription necessary in Hungary. Training time has been reduced to a minimum, reservists are almost never called up to serve or to be retrained, and the new army structure is unable to cope with these organisational legacies. Moreover, since 1999, the need to reinforce the armed forces in the unlikely case of an emerging violent conflict is now guaranteed by reinforcement from other Alliance members. Socialist politicians addressing the matter emphasise that the eventual (and unlikely) emergence of a threat facing Hungary is both predictable and can only occur in the long term. In such a case it should prove possible to agree upon any necessary political and military measures, which might induce the provisional reintroduction of conscription should this prove necessary.

If there is no military rationale for keeping conscription, is there a case for maintaining it in order to preserve the link between the armed forces and society? This argument would hold if the switch to an all-volunteer force threatened a rapid and significant decline in societal support for the armed forces. In practice, public attention towards and support for the Hungarian armed forces is likely to decline a little if the military becomes all-volunteer. However, it is also clear that much of the electorate opposes conscription, and in itself this is already an important issue in souring current Hungarian military–society relations. As Table 5.1 illustrates, the level of public confidence in the armed forces has declined irrespective of the question of military service. In addition, societal assessments about the role of the military change rapidly, especially with changes in popular threat perceptions.

The bare fact of the matter is that conscription has very little support in Hungarian society. Draft avoidance is widespread. For example, in 1998, 50 per cent of the eligible population in Budapest avoided military service.[17] In order to combat this problem, the armed forces introduced a more thorough system of medical certification in 2001 which succeeded in reducing the proportion of those unfit for military service by 3 per cent in comparison to the previous year's draft.[18] In addition, compulsory service time was reduced to six months from 1 January 2002, which may reduce the social cost of maintaining the conscript system, but is likely to severely damage the effectiveness of conscript

*Table 5.1*   The change of public confidence in institutions (Median Public Opinion and Marketing Co. Ltd)

|  | Sep 1991 | Jan 1992 | Oct 1993 | Jul 1994 | Apr 1996 | Nov 1998 | Oct 1999 | Sep 2000 |
|---|---|---|---|---|---|---|---|---|
| President of the Republic | 79 | – | 61 | 80 | 70 | 72 | 74 | 68 |
| Constitutional court | 68 | – | 50 | 65 | 65 | 71 | 67 | 67 |
| Courts | 73 | 53 | 49 | 59 | 50 | 54 | 53 | 53 |
| Armed forces | 66 | 52 | 53 | 62 | 55 | 55 | 51 | 42 |
| Churches | 61 | 56 | – | – | 45 | 43 | 47 | 42 |
| Police | 64 | – | 51 | 59 | 54 | 61 | 41 | 45 |
| Local government | 61 | 53 | 47 | 56 | 52 | 54 | 56 | 54 |
| Government | 57 | 43 | 29 | 63 | 42 | 50 | 42 | 42 |
| Parliament | 57 | 33 | 30 | 58 | 38 | 48 | 42 | 43 |
| Trade unions | 39 | – | 33 | 39 | 30 | 31 | 27 | 28 |
| Parties | 37 | – | 26 | 43 | 31 | 38 | 36 | 35 |

*Note*: Averages on a scale of 100. 1 = no confidence at all, 100 = full confidence.

*Source*: J. Eszényi, 'A honvédség iránti lakossági bizalom tíz éve' (Ten years of public confidence towards the home defence forces), *Új Honvédségi Szemle*, 5 (2001), 29.

soldiers' military training. However, given that there is a consensus in Hungarian society over the eventual abolition of conscription, these measures can only be considered temporary and of cosmetic importance.

The conservative opposition's alternative to the continuation of compulsory conscription is to establish a national guard type organisation. Their idea is that this will ensure that – whatever the shape of the regular armed forces in future – every Hungarian will go through some military training in order to help maintain the armed forces' connection with society. As part of the plan, every eligible male would be required to undergo three months basic training, which would be territorially organised. After the completion of basic training further participation would be voluntary. The national guard would also be responsible for retraining those who had previously served in the armed forces, and would train specific units for disaster and catastrophe management. Given the attitude of most young Hungarians to military service, however, it is unlikely that this idea will acquire widespread popular or military support – particularly as the new organisation would be a direct competitor to the regular armed forces in the allocation of the defence budget. In addition, the investment-heavy phase of Hungary's defence

*Table 5.2* More money should be allocated to the Hungarian home defence forces (per cent)

|  | Agree | Disagree | Don't know/ no answer |
|---|---|---|---|
| January 1990 | 20 | 68 | 12 |
| February 1991 | 35 | 47 | 18 |
| December 1992 | 60 | 28 | 12 |
| April 1996 | 65 | 23 | 12 |
| June 1997 | 76 | 19 | 5 |
| April 1998 | 71 | 19 | 10 |
| October 1998 | 70 | 19 | 11 |
| November 1999 | 74 | 17 | 9 |

*Source*: J. Szabó, 'Magyarország és hadserege a modernizáció útján' (Hungary and its armed forces on the road to modernisation), in F. Gazdag (ed.), *Biztonságpolitika* (Budapest: SVKH, 2001), 288.

reforms still lies in the future, and it may run the risk of undermining these reforms by diverting the already limited funds available.

Changing public opinion about the armed forces is also reflected in the economic constraints society imposes on the defence sector. In the early 1990s, Hungarian society was sceptical about defence costs, though as Table 5.2 illustrates, this view changed gradually throughout the 1990s. This change occurred for four main reasons: first, in response to the close proximity of Yugoslav wars; second because of the approach of NATO accession; third, because of a general improvement in the economic situation; and finally because of dawning recognition that even the development of small high quality armed forces has cost implications.

Public opinion responses suggest that individuals assess defence spending differently when questioned about it in the abstract rather than in the context of budgetary competition with other state activities or portfolios. Table 5.3 shows that in comparison to other portfolios, defence still lags behind health-care as a public spending priority, but as a spending requirement, it has come close to the importance placed on public education and internal security.

When Hungary acceded to NATO in 1999, the government made a commitment to increase its defence spending to 1.81 per cent of GDP. However, neither NATO nor the Hungarian government identified capability improvement projects, and as a consequence, the defence budget increased with little improvement to the performance of the Hungarian armed forces. Moreover, since the increase in defence spending co-incided with a period of high economic growth, its implementation did

*Table 5.3*   Imagine that you can distribute 100 billion forints (US$400 million) from the tax revenues of the state. Decide how much you would allocate to different areas so that the whole amount would be spent (average of answers)

| Sector | Allocation (billion forints) |
| --- | --- |
| Health-care | 20.3 |
| Public education | 11.78 |
| Internal security | 11.76 |
| National defence | 11.23 |
| Prevention of catastrophes | 10.18 |
| Labour affairs | 9.11 |
| Protection of the environment | 8.23 |
| Public transport | 7.11 |
| Culture | 6.21 |
| Sport | 4.38 |
| Total | 100 |

*Note*: The opinion poll was conducted in November 1999.

*Source*: J. Eszényi, 'A védelem forintjai: Tények, adatok, vélelmek a honvédelmi költségvetésröl' (The forints of defence: facts, data and assumptions about the defence budget), *Új Honvédségi Szemle*, 1 (2001), 31.

not place any particular strain on military–society relations, or on societal spending priorities, though this may well change if economic growth slows in future, and the competition for scarce state resources becomes more acute.[19]

Public perceptions of the incomes of military personnel are also important. At the beginning of the 1990s, the general public assumption was that the military were overpaid. This had changed by 1993, when most people expressed the opinion that the armed forces were not paid adequately for the job they did.[20] The government and the Ministry of Defence have made efforts to close this income gap between the public sector and the wider economy. The first phase of the current defence reform – implemented between 2000 and 2003 – includes the objective of improving living and working conditions for service personnel, and this includes a significant increase in salaries. However, even after the implementation of these changes, it is likely that military salaries will still not be sufficiently competitive to attract qualified men and women, especially with the registered unemployment rate in Hungary as low as 5.3 per cent, a labour market that makes it increasingly difficult for the armed forces to recruit sufficient qualified personnel.

International assignments have also influenced the income structure of some elements of the armed forces. The average income of Hungarian officers and NCOs is approximately one-eighth of the NATO average whereas it equals the NATO average on international assignment.[21] This situation has already had a negative impact on personnel issues in the armed forces. Interesting assignments are in high demand and income differentials have meant that some positions that require low-level qualifications are filled by more senior NCOs and officers than is strictly necessary.[22] Indeed, in the case of officers and a part of the NCO corps the chance to go on international assignment may well contribute to continued service in the armed forces. On the other hand, in the case of contract soldiers – many of whom intend to stay in the armed forces for only a short while anyway – the income earned on international assignment does not contribute to extending their service in the military, and may even have the opposite effect. Thus, after a completed 'tour', many contract soldiers use the extra income as a spring-board from which to leave.

In terms of threat perceptions, Hungary has passed through a very difficult decade. New neighbours have emerged and old ones disappeared. This had a particular impact as Hungary was the only country that bordered each of the three former multinational federations that disintegrated in the early 1990s: Czechoslovakia, the Soviet Union and Yugoslavia. Indeed, it has been regularly emphasised by successive Hungarian governments that the primary regional problem is the instability accompanying transformation. However, more recently, the concept of Hungary as belonging to a 'zone of instability' has been eroded. This has occurred for four reasons. First, the major shocks of the 1990s – emanating from the emergence of new states out of the Soviet Union and Czechoslovakia – have passed. Second, the decline in living standards which accompanied the 1989 system change did not result in large-scale political destabilisation in the region. Third, Hungarian politicians and civil servants have become increasingly circumspect when referring to their country's threat perceptions in order not to deter western investment and undermine the country's European integration efforts. Finally, Hungary's accession to NATO has had a significant impact on threat perceptions.

Consecutive governments have placed an emphasis on the symbolic importance, rather than the security relevance of this development: 'by NATO membership Hungary has ultimately gained place in the community of Western democracies'.[23] The Hungarian political mainstream is of the view that the accession of the country to NATO has reduced societal threat perceptions to a nearly non-measurable level; that in security terms, the transition era for Hungary has come to an end; and that the country is now primarily a provider rather than a consumer of security. That alliances do not only contribute to the security of their members but also 'distribute' the threat perceptions of others – and thus actually generate additional threats – is not acknowledged by the Hungarian elite. Indeed, the only time when indirect reference was made to the 'dangers' involved in NATO membership occurred during the Kosovo conflict when opposition MPs of the Socialist Party raised the issue whether Hungary – the only NATO neighbour of Serbia – would face mission creep. The landslide domestic political changes in the autumn of 2000 in Yugoslavia meant that six months later the Prime Minister was able to conclude:

> We can see that in this moment the region is stable in military-security sense, I can say more stable than a year ago ... The reason is that matters south of us on the territory of Yugoslavia are in better shape than they were a year ago. With this I do not say that every danger has come to an end as the democratic transformation has not been completed, yet. In spite of all this, I feel that the region is stable today, and one of the pledges of this stability is Hungary.[24]

However, it is important to note that threat perceptions among the political elite do not necessarily coincide with those of the general public. In Hungary, as Tables 5.4 and 5.5 illustrate, fear of armed conflict is low, and popular threat perceptions are noticeably orientated more towards the social problems of transition such as unemployment and crime. Indeed, this was the case even when Yugoslav aircraft violated

*Table 5.4*  In your opinion is it likely that Hungary will become involved in an armed conflict in the near future? (Per cent)

|  | Very probable | Little probability | Not probable | Don't know |
|---|---|---|---|---|
| December 1992 | 9 | 47 | 38 | 6 |
| April 1996 | 4 | 27 | 62 | 7 |
| June 1997 | 2 | 19 | 74 | 2 |
| April 1998 | 1 | 20 | 73 | 6 |
| October 1998 | 9 | 24 | 66 | 1 |
| November 1999 | 4 | 31 | 61 | 4 |

*Source*: J. Szabó, 'Magyarország és hadserege a modernizáció útján' (Hungary and its armed forces on the road to modernisation), in F. Gazdag (ed.), *Biztonságpolitika* (Budapest: SVKH, 2001), 287.

*Table 5.5*   Which areas would you spend
more at the expense of increasing taxes?
(Per cent)

| | |
|---|---|
| Health-care | 70.5 |
| Family subsidies | 54.2 |
| Pensions | 44.6 |
| Public education | 37.3 |
| Protection of the environment | 15.2 |
| Police | 15.1 |
| Unemployment benefits | 12.0 |
| Culture, arts | 7.0 |
| National defence | 3.6 |

*Note*: Opinion poll conducted in spring 1995.

*Source*: J. Eszényi, 'A védelem forintjai: Tények,
adatok, vélelmek a honvédelmi költségvetésröl'
(The forints of defence: facts, data and assumptions about the defence budget), *Új Honvédségi
Szemle*, 1 (2001), 30.

*Table 5.6*   According to your opinion does any
country endanger the peace and security of
Hungary? (Per cent)

| | 1988 | 1989 | 1992 | 1995 | 1999 |
|---|---|---|---|---|---|
| Yes | 23 | 56 | 67 | 46 | 33 |

*Source*: F. Molnár, 'A közvélemény alakulása a biztonságról és a haderök szerepéröl a Cseh Köztársaságban,
Lengyelországban és Magyarországon' (The evolution
of public opinion about security and the role of armed
forces), *Új Honvédségi Szemle*, 8 (2000), 9.

Hungarian airspace in 1991 and dropped bombs on Yugoslav territory
close to the Hungarian border.

Moreover, Hungary – in contrast to Poland and the Czech Republic –
has never perceived any threat from Germany and only exceptionally
from Russia. While instability caused by the conflict in Yugoslavia has
certainly been a concern in the past, the collapse of the Milošević regime
in 2000 has significantly diminished these fears. In addition, as Table 5.6
illustrates, with Hungary's accession to NATO, the possibility of it
being militarily threatened by another state has appeared even more
remote.

Eighteen per cent of the population is of the view that NATO 'fully
guarantees the security of the country', 37 per cent says that NATO

'to a large extent provides for the security of the country' and according to another 28 per cent the NATO security guarantee exists to 'medium extent'.[25] Taken together, 83 per cent of the population is of the view that the Atlantic Alliance provides enhanced security of Hungary. In sum, Hungary is a country that is increasingly confident in its national security. In this environment, and despite the recent increase in defence expenditure, in the medium term defence is likely to continue to be seen as an area of public policy where the central budget can economise.

Hungary has faced international pressures and expectations over a wide range of issues. From a western perspective, perhaps the most important issue is that Hungary should be a source of stability rather than instability in the region. In this respect, Hungary's conservative governments have been warned against using excessively harsh rhetoric towards those countries with Hungarian ethnic minorities. In terms of NATO integration, the Hungarian government has been slow to fulfil its defence commitments, achieving 76 per cent of them in 1999, 50 per cent in 2000, and only 26 per cent in 2001.[26] This has resulted in criticism of the government's performance in NATO by other member state governments and particularly by the US. Despite this, Hungary has been relatively skilful in resisting pressure in this area, using four different means to reflect its efforts in the best light possible. First, in common with both the Czech Republic and Poland, the country has shown itself to be an extremely loyal member of NATO and has not been disruptive over potentially difficult policies. This was illustrated most clearly during the Kosovo operation when NATO decisions were taken as smoothly with 19 members as they would have been with 16. Loyalty was also reflected in Hungary's contribution to the two major NATO-led peace operations – SFOR and KFOR. Second, Hungary contributed to the tasks of the Alliance through its location. NATO has been able to use Hungarian airspace, airfields and other military facilities whenever it has been necessary – and especially in relation to the former Yugoslavia. Third, Hungary has actively participated in intelligence cooperation. Finally, Hungary has compensated for its weak performance in some areas, by offering promises to do better in future – though in practice these have seldom been delivered on.

## Current and future challenges of linking armed forces to society

Current and future challenges of linking the armed forces and society in Hungary fall into four main areas: recruitment and retention, legitimacy, deployment of forces and public expenditure.

As regards recruitment and retention, the Hungarian armed forces reduced the size of its armed forces to a peacetime strength of 45,000, which for the moment is being maintained by the inclusion of approximately 20,000 conscripts. However, conscripts present an increasing liability given the popular objection to the draft. Fast economic growth and decreasing levels of unemployment also make it increasingly difficult to attract qualified personnel. This situation is aggravated by the relatively late introduction of a predictable career path, which throughout the 1990s contributed to a mass exodus from the officer corps. Similarly, the armed forces continue to experience difficulties in retaining the necessary number of contract soldiers. As conscription is widely rejected by society and heavily disliked by the draftees there is no reason to think that its abolition would significantly increase the distance between the armed forces and society. It is a widely-shared view that a smaller, fully professional armed force could actually contribute better to the defence of the country.

The Hungarian armed forces struggled fairly successfully with the legitimacy deficit they faced at the beginning of the 1990s. This resulted from a variety of different factors including the increased threat perception provided by the Yugoslav wars, and the increasing engagement of the Hungarian military in international activities with states that have more developed forces. Military legitimacy in Hungary still remains fragile, however, and the legitimacy gained through international peace operations may not be sufficient to compensate in a lasting 'threat-free' environment. If the gap between the expectation of the population towards defence as primarily identified with the defence of national territory and the perception of a 'threat-free' environment continues, then Hungary may well be left with a defence sector that is not salient to the government, the political establishment or the population at large. This situation would certainly create a major problem between the domestic landscape and Hungary's commitments as a NATO member.

Hungarian society does not reject the international deployment of its armed forces for international peace operations abroad. At the same time, however, the population is of the view that international engagements are not the primary function of the armed forces. It is likely that the change to accepting this function is gradual and may provide legitimacy in the long run only. Hungarian peacekeepers have not yet suffered major casualties in any of these operations, and it remains open to question how far this would be tolerated by the population if it occurred in future.

Due to Hungary's international commitments and the genuine needs of the armed forces after a decade of deprivation the public is largely supportive of providing adequate or at least partly adequate financing for the defence sector. There is little doubt though that this is the armed forces' future weak spot. If economic growth slows, and there is increasing competition for state resources as a result, it is likely that public support for defence spending will erode in favour of areas such as education, health-care or the social services.

## Conclusions

The Hungarian armed forces' standing in society has improved significantly since the system change of 1989. In part, this results from the fact that the collapse of communism transformed the military into more of a national institution than they had been under communism. However, Hungary has no rich military tradition and society is neither fully engaged or particularly interested in defence matters. This tradition continues in 2003 and means that support for the armed forces in Hungarian society is always likely to be volatile. Despite this, the legitimacy of the armed forces is guaranteed for the time being and may even increase if they can continue to contribute successfully to international operations and visibly to perform useful functions during natural disasters. The commitment to introduce an all-volunteer army and the consensus in society around this issue will most probably not 'detach' the Hungarian armed forces from society. In any case, the shortness of the current six-month compulsory military service period is of questionable military value, and its abolition will almost certainly be viewed with relief not only in the country at large, but also among political and military elites. A start has also been made in adequately financing Hungary's armed forces in line with the country's NATO commitments, and the government has made major efforts to increase defence appropriations in the state budget in recent years. Nonetheless, it remains open to question whether the will to finance the defence sector will remain once the current period of economic growth comes to an end.

Long-term predictions have little practical value in relation to the Hungarian military, as the experiences of the last decade have illustrated. If external conditions remain unchanged, Hungary can expect to operate in a benign international environment where military force is used primarily for conflict management and peace operations. Moreover, as the integrated space of Europe expands there is reason to hope that a zone of democratic peace will prevail. This does not mean that the Hungarian armed forces are not going to face challenges in the years to come. Externally these may include the weakening cohesion of

NATO as a defence alliance. In this case, national defence efforts may gain increasing support and new relevance. While it is unrealistic to expect that the current benign atmosphere will prevail between the Russian Federation and the West, at least in the short term there is no reason to assume that any change will have direct military consequences for Hungary. Domestically, the most important challenge will therefore be to complete the personnel reductions of the current defence reform and then to focus on developing the armed forces in a way that will enable them to contribute professionally to multinational and alliance-based power projection operations. A critical factor in this process will also clearly be the development of a more robust relationship between the Hungarian armed forces and Hungarian society.

## Notes

1. 'Professionalism' in this respect should be regarded a relative category for two reasons. The strategic level of military activity remained in the hands of the Soviet general staff and military decision making in the Warsaw Treaty was highly centralised.
2. F. Molnár, 'A közvélemény alakulása a biztonságról és a haderők szerepéről a Cseh Köztársaságban, Lengyelországban és Magyarországon' (The evolution of public opinion about security and the role of armed forces in the Czech Republic, Poland and Hungary), *Új Honvédségi Szemle*, 8 (2000), 9.
3. *A honvédelem négy éve 1998–2002* (Four years of homeland defence 1998–2002) (Budapest: Zrínyi, 2002) 227.
4. There has been only one crisis since 1989 – during the so-called taxi drivers' blockade of 1990 – where the employment of the armed forces or law enforcement agencies could have been considered. Even then, however, it was never a serious possibility.
5. For details of the defence reform plan and its prospects see P. Dunay, 'Building Professional Competence in Hungary's Armed Forces: Slow Motion', in A. Forster, T. Edmunds and A. Cottey, *The Challenge of Military Reform in Postcommunist Europe: Building Professional Armed Forces* (Basingstoke: Palgrave Macmillan, 2002).
6. See J. Szabó, 'Hadsereg és civil ellenőrzés' (The armed forces and civil control), *Társadalmi Szemle*, 4 (1995), 72.
7. See J. Szabó, 'Magyarország és hadserege a modernizáció útján' (Hungary and its armed forces on the road to modernisation), in F. Gazdag (ed.), *Biztonságpolitika* (Budapest: SVKH, 2001), 286.
8. J. Szabó, 'A civil társadalom viszonya a magyar fegyveres erőkhöz' (The attitude of the civil society to the armed forces), *Valóság*, 5 (1997), 96.
9. For more details and data see R. Silek, 'Hungary and Peacekeeping', *International Peacekeeping*, 3–4 (1998), 82.
10. In one of his speeches Prime Minister Orbán emphasised the importance of law and order, the elimination of corruption and the importance of a strong state. See V. Orbán, *Miniszterelnök előadása* (Address of Prime Minister Viktor

Orbán, at the meeting of Hungarian ambassadors in July 1998), 6–7 (unpublished manuscript). More recently *A miniszterelnök a Belügyminisztérium vezetői értekezletén* (The Prime Minister at the Meeting of the Leadership of the Ministry of Interior), Hungarian Government website, 7 February 2001 at http://www.meh.hu/Kormany/Kormanyfo/2001/02/010207.htm.

11. Hungarian News Agency website, at http://hírek.mti.hu/belfold, 12 March 2002.

12. T.J.K., 'A szocialista miniszterjelölt a honvédség átalakításáról' (The socialist candidate for the post of minister of defence about the reform of the Home Defence Forces), *Népszabadság*, 8 March 2002; T.J.K., 'Mikortól legyen profi hadsereg?' (Since when should there be professional armed forces?), *Népszabadság*, 18 August 2001.

13. 'A miniszterelnök a feladatszabó értekezleten' (the Prime Minister at the Task Assigning Conference of the Hungarian Armed Forces), 1 March 2001, p. 4. Hungarian Ministry of Defence website, at: http://www.honvedelem.hu/cikk.php?cikk=717.

14. 'A honvédelem', 226.

15. L. Szigeti, 'A hadkötelezettség alapján fenntartott haderő előnyei, hátrányai' (The advantages and disadvantages of armed forces maintained on the basis of compulsory military service), *Új Honvédségi Szemle*, 9 (2000), 28.

16. L. Szigeti, 'A tömeghadsereg utáni haderő hadkiegészítési kérdései' (The replenishment questions of the post-mass army era), *Új Honvédségi Szemle*, 1 (2000), 22.

17. L. Hülvely, 'Javaslat a személyi kiegészítési rendszer átalakítására 1. rész' (Proposal for the change of the system of personnel substitution, part I), *Új Honvédségi Szemle*, 5 (2001), 6.

18. L. Király, 'Több lett a katonaságra alkalmas fiatal' (More young people are fit for military service), *Népszabadság*, 6 March 2002.

19. L.J. Kiss, 'Die Kostenfrage der ungarischen NATO-Mitgliedschaft', in A. Pradetto and F.M. Alamir (eds), *Die Debatte über die Kosten der NATO-Osterweiterung* (Baden-Baden: Nomos Verlagsgesellschaft, 1998), 172–8.

20. J. Eszényi, 'A katonai pálya presztizsének alakulása' (The evolution of the prestige of military profession), *Új Honvédségi Szemle*, 3 (2002), 6–16.

21. L. Hülvely, 'Javaslat a személyi kiegészítési rendszer átalakítására 2. rész' (Proposal for the change of system of personnel substitution, part II), *Új Honvédségi Szemle*, 6 (2001), 34.

22. See J. Padányi, 'Értékrendi változások a nemzetközi missziókban szolgáló katonáknál' (Changes of values among soldiers on international assignments), *Új Honvédségi Szemle*, 2 (2001), 31.

23. *Az új évezred küszöbén: Kormányprogram a polgári Magyarországért* (On the eve of the new millennium: government programme for civic Hungary) (Budapest, n.p. 1998), 63.

24. 'A miniszterelnök', 2.

25. *A honvédelem*, 227.

26. M. Bak, 'Nem minden vezető maradhat a helyén a honvédelmi tárcánál – Négyszemközt Juhász Ferenccel' (Not every leader can stay in his function in the defence portfolio – face to face with Ferenc Juhász), *Népszabadság*, 28 May 2002.

# Part II
# The Baltic States

# 6
# Armed Forces and Society in Latvia: a Decade of Development

*Jan Arveds Trapans*

In 2000, Latvian Defence Minister Ģirts Valdis Kristovskis issued a 'Report of the Defence Minister to the Parliament on State Defence Policy and the Development of Armed Forces in the Year 2000'. This was a detailed report, with 107 pages and seven chapters, starting with 'The International Security Environment and the Objectives of Latvia's Security and Defence Policy' and concluding with 'The National Armed Forces and Society'. The report was disseminated to the public, and an abbreviated version made available in English through the Defence Ministry's website. The report was known as the Defence Ministry's White Book, and a second report followed in 2001.[1]

These White Books were delivered with a perceptible air of accomplishment. They report on defence and security related endeavours, present summary budgets, indicate for what particular defence needs money is to be spent in short, medium and long-term periods, and present priorities in equipment and weapon acquisitions. In addition, they describe collaboration among the three Baltic States, have chapters on Latvian participation in international peacekeeping missions notably IFOR (Bosnia), SFOR (Bosnia) and KFOR (Kosovo), and have much to say about preparations for NATO membership. In form and content, they are not much different from similar documents issued by western defence ministries.

The second White Book, that of 2001, has a chapter entitled 'Looking to the Future'. Below the title of this chapter there is a photograph showing the Monument of Liberty at the very centre of Riga, the symbol of independence, built during the 1930s, never destroyed but neglected under Soviet rule, and recently restored to its former grandeur. People are placing flowers at the base of the monument; they are commemorating independence regained. A sentry wearing a high-collared, dark-green tunic, the parade uniform of the armed forces worn by the Latvian army before 1940 – the parade dress representing the past, his youth representing the future – looks forward with confidence. A little light-haired girl, clutching a pink toy pig and a small purse, attentively, even sombrely, observes the young sentry. She symbolises society.[2]

This is the image of the armed forces that the defence establishment desires to promote. How closely it depicts the true state of affairs in the armed forces and in society's views of their nature and role is the focus of this chapter. To understand fully the decade of development of the armed forces and society in Latvia, the chapter analyses developments since 1991, the point of departure, when Latvia regained its independence.

## Departure

When the Soviet Army withdrew from Latvia, all 'that was left behind consisted of 26 sunken submarines and ships leaking acid, oil and phosphorous. On this foundation Latvia began building its armed forces.'[3] Western observers said of Latvia: 'It is worth recalling that, at the beginning, neither [a Defence] Ministry nor national Armed Forces existed; that the military infrastructure was in ruins; that equipment and logistical support were almost non-existent; that public support for the professional military was low; that training and experience ... had been gained in a very different Soviet system.'[4] Parliament was inexperienced, the armed forces were in shambles, and there was no Defence Ministry.

The armed forces thus only emerged from the turbulent events of 1990 and 1991 as the Baltic States wrested themselves away from the collapsing Soviet empire. Units were created ad hoc to respond to immediate needs. In 1991 Latvia's parliament established volunteer border guards to show that it had some control over the borders, as a sovereign state should. There was also a special armed unit to defend the parliament. Later, a self-defence force, the National Guard or *Zemessardze* arose spontaneously. The government summoned Latvian officers who had served in the Soviet Army to establish armed forces. The Defence Ministry was established in November 1991. It was staffed with inexperienced civilians who had to manage disjointed formations, activated by competing state and quasi-state authorities or appearing as volunteer self-defence forces.

Considerable effort was required to place these various formations under clear lines of civilian control and to clarify the confused defence situation, organisationally and legally. However, there was a major difficulty, which took some time to resolve. Latvia was creating a small regular conscript force, commanded by professional officers from the former Soviet Army. It also had the *Zemessardze*, the volunteer force with commanders who saw themselves as the leaders of a 'nation in arms', but who had limited military experience. There was therefore distrust between the small professional and large volunteer forces. On the one side there was the condescension of professionals towards amateurs. On the other, there was a suspicion of the former Soviet Army officers. Both the professional and volunteer forces had their supporters and detractors.

Exacerbating this situation was the fact that Latvia's society is not ethnically homogenous. Some 59 per cent of the country's inhabitants are Latvians, 29 per cent are Russians, and 12 per cent belong to other nationalities, principally Belarus, Ukrainians, Poles and Lithuanians. To divide the entire population into 'Latvians' and 'Russians' as sometimes is done in western publications is misleading. Nor are the ethnic Russians a grey mass. Some have come to Latvia recently, others have roots reaching back for centuries; there are Russian workers, teachers, professionals and the intelligentsia. Each group has closer or looser ties to society and different views towards Latvia as a state and its nascent armed forces.

## Context

### The influence of the past

In terms of the influence of the past, armed forces have histories that give society an image of their nature and purpose. The Latvian view of the nature of armed forces contains different and often conflicting images. One of the most important influences is the fact that most Latvians despised the Soviet Army. It was seen as an occupying army, *okupanti*, which had seized a small independent country in 1940 and made possible mass deportations and executions during the Stalin years. Moreover, its many large military training areas despoiled the Latvian countryside and environment. At the political level, it was the Soviet Army that kept the Communist Party in power and provided it with privileges that were denied to most Latvians.

A second influence on military–society relations in Latvia is the past military record of the Latvian Army. During the War of Independence Latvia's armed forces had fought on two fronts, against the Red Army and German forces, and defeated both. Moreover, Latvian regiments and divisions served with distinction in the Imperial Russian Army during the First World War and in the German Army in the Second World War, developing a reputation as elite combat units. The Latvian historical memory of their soldiers – perhaps oversimplified but not without justification – is one of discipline and valour recognised by friends and foes.

However, the reflection of the past did not match the reality of the armed forces in the immediate period following independence. Former Soviet Army officers initially commanded Latvian's small, conscript armed forces and although their loyalty to an independent sovereign Latvia cannot not be questioned, they were inclined to construct the defence forces according to Soviet practices, for example with a disproportionately top-heavy rank structure. They also tolerated some long-standing Soviet military practices, such as the bullying of recruits; habits that were greatly disliked by society. As a consequence, 'public support for the professional military was low; [and the perception was] that training and experience ... had been gained in a very different Soviet system'. There was inertia of old thinking, planning and organisation. Paradoxically, despite widespread contempt of the Soviet Army, during the early 1990s, Latvia's armed forces began to resemble a small-scale version of the old Soviet forces.

Views among the minorities sometimes differed from Latvian ones. They had no historical image of a former Latvian Army or of a Latvia as a sovereign independent state. Neither did they necessarily view the Soviet Army with intense dislike and contempt. Nor were their views towards Soviet armed forces uniformly positive. The former Soviet military (a handful of them remained in Latvia) longed for past prestige and privileges. As to the others, their attitudes were similar to those in the rest of the Soviet Union, which, after the invasion of Afghanistan in 1979, tended to be critical.

### The influence of the present

After a decade of development, Latvia's defence community has addressed many of these issues: it has organised coherent armed forces, determined their priorities, put together viable defence plans, and developed a mission statement. On the one hand, the sense of history has not been discarded. The armed forces again wear the uniform of the old army, at parades, on sentry duties – and in pictures in White Books submitted to parliament. The gap between the unpleasant Soviet nature of the armed forces in 1991 and the armed forces of an independent nation has been largely removed. On the other hand, new criteria have emerged by which society judges the armed forces.

Latvia's security strategy states that the missions of the armed forces are to protect the nation's sovereignty and territorial integrity, a democratic form of government and the market economy, national identity and human rights. Latvia is committed to joining NATO and the EU and has activated a tri-national Baltic Battalion. This has participated in NATO peacekeeping missions, and is a practical demonstration that a threat to one Baltic State is considered a threat to all three. The strategy also recognises that there are new security risks that cannot be met solely with military means.[5] There is considerable evidence that Latvians are judging the legitimacy of the armed forces largely in terms of their capability in performing their contemporary missions. Over the last decade, a similar attitude has also emerged among the non-Latvian ethnic groups, with a consensus that a decade after independence the Latvian armed forces must be judged according to their new missions and functions.

## Domestic, regional and international influences

### Threats and risks

Over the past decade, Latvia's political and military establishment has developed a national security concept based on threat assessment, and promoted this through debates in the Latvian parliament and through the media and public commentary. A policy declaration approved by parliament provided an assessment of the key elements of the new security environment. Mindful of the need for public support, they also appealed to the electorate to provide sufficient resources in order to provide for Latvian security needs. In 1999, the International Defence Advisory Board to the Baltic States (a group of senior western soldiers and statesmen) concluded that Latvia's security policy had been developed and promulgated in a democratic process.[6] However, judging the impact of these statements on military–society relations is complex and in part depends on the specific issue at hand.

The major issue is national defence. Latvia's defence planning assumes that Russia does not pose an immediate threat to the Baltic States, but cannot be disregarded as hostile. On this issue, the views of Latvian and Russian ethnic groups diverge, with most Latvians endorsing the consensus of the political elite, while most ethnic Russians do not consider the Russian Federation a threat now or in the medium or long term. What does preoccupy most of the electorate are so-called 'new risks', like organised cross-border crime and corruption. In a recent public survey on the benefits of Latvia's membership of NATO, giving the responses of Latvians and non-Latvians alike, less than 9 per cent said that NATO 'will defend Latvia against Russia' whereas 36 per cent responded in more general terms that NATO 'extends security' or 'precludes conflict'. To Latvia's society as a whole, Article V is a desirable guarantee of Latvian territorial integrity, but is not immediately necessary.[7] From the vantage point of 2003, to many Latvians the value of NATO appears principally to reside in its value as a security community rather than a military organisation.

## Domestic conditions

Two domestic factors shape the strength of Latvia's armed forces: demography and the economy. Latvia is a small country with no strategic depth and a small population. Moreover, it has a great power to the east and a sea to the west. Under these geostrategic circumstances, Latvia does not have enough young people available for its armed forces in order to provide for its own security. It has to do the best that it can with what is available and has to design its defence posture and force structure accordingly.

The second domestic condition is the economy, where, likewise, Latvia has difficulty in providing sufficient resources for defence. However, unlike the size of a country's population, which changes very slowly, the economy is more responsive to change. After 1991 Latvia's economy underwent quite rapid change to a market economy. As with other transition states, social demands claimed a large part of the state budget. As a consequence, the Defence Ministry lived with 'survival budgets' that sufficed only to keep the defence establishment on an even keel. 'Whilst accepting that there are always competing demands for scarce resources and that the decisions on how these resources are allocated is a political one, to be decided on the cabinet level,' wrote the International Defence Advisory Board, 'we nevertheless judge that the low proportion of GNP allocated to defence in all the Baltic States has been historically such as to ... frustrate internal military development.'[8]

The late 1990s saw a change in the resources allocated to defence, in part through improved economic performance, but in part too because the government was willing to give greater priority to the armed forces. A key driver of this change took place following the Washington Summit in 1999, when Latvia was not invited to NATO accession talks but anticipated an invitation at the next summit, and the government responded by providing the necessary resources to make membership a realistic prospect in 2002.

## Baltic defence cooperation

Latvia's security policy is based on the principle that defence cooperation between the Baltic States is an essential condition for the security of the region. This is premised on the belief that joint defence measures would not only be more effective, but would also create a better opportunity for the three Baltic States to gain admittance to NATO. Stability and security in the eastern Baltic benefits every state in the region and Latvia's defence development has thus been helped by western self-interest as well as by more selfless motivations.

The Baltic States have cooperated in defence affairs since they regained independence. Their first major project was the Baltic Peacekeeping Battalion, since renamed the Baltic Battalion. It was the first link in a network of regional security arrangements. In 1995 the Baltic Defence Ministers signed an agreement identifying further areas of cooperation, which in addition to the Baltic Battalion (BALTBAT), now include the unified air control system (BALTNET), the Baltic naval squadron (BALTRON), the Baltic Defence College (BALTDEFCOL), the unified Baltic C2 information system (BALTCCIS), the joint Baltic States registration and management system for persons subject to military service (BALTPERS), and the Baltic medical unit (BALTMED).[9]

These regional initiatives have an extremely high approval rating in Latvia's society, with almost 90 per cent of the public surveyed in 2000 supporting Baltic defence cooperation and 69 per cent believing that regional cooperation between Latvia, Lithuania and Estonia would advance the admittance of the Baltic States to NATO. The opinion of the respondents on this question was practically identical across all the socio-demographic groups in the survey. A negative opinion was held by less than 7 per cent.[10]

## Military Diplomacy: international peacekeeping missions

Latvia's National Security Concept states that the armed forces should participate in international peacekeeping missions. Latvia has a special peacekeeping unit, the Baltic Battalion, activated in 1995. The idea for the Battalion was first proposed at a meeting of Baltic defence chiefs in 1993. With it, the hope was that Baltic nations could contribute to international peace and visibly re-enter the international community.

Thus there was a political motive for the Battalion. Once Latvia's government decided to opt for NATO membership, this political aspect of the Battalion became more pronounced. In particular it fits well with the demands of the Alliance's new Security Strategy, it has participated in multinational NATO missions, and it has been willing to embrace interoperability.[11]

Moreover, the public at large favours deployment to international peace operations. There was considerable public support for the participation of units of Latvian armed forces in the operations in Bosnia, Albania and Kosovo. A public opinion poll shows that 61 per cent of those questioned approved such deployments on the grounds that on such missions the armed forces gain experience and 'become more professional'. Other reasons given are that Latvia must help other states, and 'if we help others, we too will be offered help in case of necessity'.[12]

General Wesley Clark, visiting the Baltic in July 1999, recognised Baltic contributions to IFOR, SFOR and KFOR. He also advised the defence ministries to weigh their priorities carefully and recommended more attention to national military reform and training. In Latvia's circumstances, participating in NATO peacekeeping missions means directing scarce defence resources to a special unit for political reasons, in order to be accepted by NATO.[13]

### International pressure and expectations

From the mid-1990s, the Latvian political elite has been keen to advance the case for Latvian membership of NATO – a policy which culminated in an invitation to join issued at the November 2002 Prague Summit. The NATO Study on Enlargement, the Membership Action Plan, the NATO Strategic Concept and other documents all set out the type of military reforms required for applicant states. In response, Latvia has implemented wide-ranging civil–military reforms, with the limited NATO enlargement in 1999 adding further momentum to the speed and direction of this reform process.

One of the key requirements for NATO membership is that candidate countries should provide approximately 2 per cent of their GDP for defence. (Although, specifically, this requirement is not stated in any official NATO document, there is much reason to assume that this is what NATO wants.) The Latvian government has taken steps to ensure that allocating 2 per cent of GDP was sustainable from 2002 when decisions on expansion were next to be made. Indeed, from the late 1990s, spokespeople for Latvia's Defence Ministry have been quite explicit that

'2 per cent is the price of NATO admission', and have been successful in getting parliament, in 1999, to pass a law determining that from 2003 defence expenditure would remain fixed at 2 per cent of GDP for at least five years. Undoubtedly, developing national defence capabilities with an eye to NATO requirements is an expensive proposition. However, the decision in Prague confirms that this is a strategy that at least for Latvia has made an important contribution to securing NATO membership. The challenge that both government and society now face is ensuring that budgets are sustained and that they deliver enhanced military capabilities.

## Society and defence

Latvia's Defence Ministry has a large programme designed to establish ties between the armed forces and society. In this regard, the White Book of 2001 states, in a chapter entitled 'Links with Society', that:

> The basis of the close ties between the [national armed forces] and Latvian society in general go back to the days of World War I when Latvia began its first period of independence. Pride in its own armed forces, which have deep roots in society, formed a bond that exists to this day, in spite of the fierce dislike that the Latvian people had for the Soviet occupation army.[14]

Public relations are a top priority in the work of the ministry, and each year increasing resources are devoted to them. To coordinate activities within the ministry and the armed forces, a Public Relations Council has been established. The ministry has also created an internet homepage and has personnel responsible for providing timely information. It solicits suggestions and has a 'Discussions and Comments' sections on the web page. A recent survey of Baltic defence affairs, Assessing the Aspirants for NATO Membership, carried out by the Centre for European Security Studies in the Netherlands on behalf of the Dutch Defence Ministry, states that Latvia's Ministry of Defence provides more than sufficient information to parliament, and that a 'huge amount of [official] documents' are available on the website which is assessed as the most transparent and complete one of all Baltic defence and foreign ministries.[15]

In addition, representatives of society and the media and parliamentarians are invited to 'Open House' days held in all military units. Parents of recruits are invited to observe the oath-taking ceremony, and to meet the officers and non-commissioned officers responsible for their children's service. The press has been invited to spend a day with the troops. 'This proved extremely interesting,' notes the White Book and 'was viewed very positively by the public. Such activities help the public to understand the everyday Latvian armed forces' everyday life and their mission.' In a similar fashion members of the parliamentary committee and their staff were invited to spend a day at the major training base. A picture in the White Book shows them, smiling but somewhat bemused, wearing military uniform and helmets and carrying packs and rifles.[16]

This energetic public relations programme does indeed appear to have shaped public attitudes, and opinion polls have indicated growing support for the armed forces and defence expenditure. A comprehensive public survey showed that 51 per cent of the country's inhabitants believed that the defence budget needed to be increased, that 26 per cent thought that it was adequate, and that only 9 per cent thought it could be reduced. Of those surveyed, among the non-ethnic Latvian nationalities, 43 per cent said that the budget should be increased. The majority of the younger generation, of minority groups, and people under 24, were also in favour of increasing the defence budget. Asked which areas of defence needed funds, 43 per cent of the respondents wanted to ensure the quality of military education, 34 per cent the acquisition of weapons and technical equipment, and 20 per cent thought the improvement of living conditions for service personnel should have priority.[17]

## The armed forces and ethnic minorities

As already noted, in Latvia's multinational society, there are inevitably different opinions and responses to questions concerning the armed forces. Russian views differ noticeably from the Latvian ones. However, ethnic identity does not seem to be the sole or perhaps the most important determinant of views and age and citizenship are also influential factors. In particular, public opinion polls indicate important differences in responses from those Russians who are citizens and those who are not. Assessing the Aspirants for NATO Membership found that the younger Russian generation has virtually identical views to Latvians in the same age group.[18]

Evidence of a broad and inclusive 'society' is emerging in Latvia. Writing in the journal *NATO's Nations*, former Major General of the *Bundeswehr* Dietrich Genschel described the situation in 2002 as one where Latvia has embarked on 'a social integration process, adopted appropriate naturalisation legislation and improved respective procedures. As a result naturalisation is increasing, [Russian] loyalty to the Latvian state is improving, eagerness of the younger generation to participate in a modern, free and civil society is pervasive.' As the opinion poll data indicated, there are differences of opinion among Latvians and Russians, but a key fact is that Russian views are beginning to converge with Latvian opinion. In particular, Latvian society as a whole seems to be increasingly concerned with the 'new risks' rather than the traditional threat of territorial attack.

Membership of NATO is the issue that highlights the most differences however. Surveys conducted in 2000 and 2001 show that 68 per cent of Latvians favour joining NATO compared with 44 per cent of other nationalities who are decidedly or moderately in favour. Assessing the Aspirants for NATO Membership concluded that Russian support is 'a high figure considering the enormous anti-NATO propaganda in the local Russian press and from Russia itself', which paints NATO in the darkest colours as an aggressive military alliance meant for waging war. Efforts by the Latvian government to rebut the propaganda have been successful. As a result support amongst the Russians is advancing some-what faster than among the Latvians.[19] After Moscow ended opposition to Baltic NATO membership, Russian acceptance of the Alliance has grown and continues to increase.

## Current and future challenges

### International politics

The first and most important challenge to Latvia's armed forces comes from the transition from being an active 'associate' member of the Alliance through the Partnership for Peace (PfP), to a full member of NATO with all the obligations this brings. The November 2002 decision therefore marks a watershed in Latvian military–society relations, introducing new challenges for the government, society and armed forces.

### Budget and defence resources

In terms of defence expenditure, the majority of the public believes that the defence budget should be increased, as do most Latvian political parties. Experts in economic development – both within and outside Latvia – estimate that Latvia's GDP will continue to increase at a rate of between 5 to 7 per cent. Throughout the next decade, the law on defence budgets, coupled to a sustained strong economic performance, should therefore provide sufficient financial resources to continue the military reform process.[20] Paradoxically, some analysts have argued that the major challenge is that there is too much money for the armed forces, with a glut following very lean years.[21] This view argues that the Defence Ministry might not be able efficiently and effectively to manage its budget and that money might be wasted or frittered away. Eventually this may have a negative effect on public opinion on the matter of defence funding.

At the same time, according to the American Kievenaar Study, 'The speed at which Latvia can build its armed forces depends in large part upon the level of spending it provides for support as well as the economic rate of growth.' The study also observed that national defence plans are basically sound and can be implemented over the next 10 years, provided that funding is made available. Latvia's Defence Ministry has developed and implemented a Planning, Programming and Budgeting System (PPBS), with one-year, four-year and twelve-year defence planning, and the possibility of a surplus of funds being misspent is not an immediate problem.[22]

### Volunteer or conscript armed forces?

Latvia's armed forces have a core of regular forces backed by reserve components. The regular land, naval and air forces largely comprise conscripts; the reserve forces, the *Zemessardze*, are volunteers. In the next decade, the difference between the two could be reduced, with an increasing proportion of volunteer, non-commissioned officers serving with the regulars and in the reserve forces. Nonetheless, the overall balance between conscripts and volunteers is not going to change radically, not least because conscript soldiers cost relatively little, and at least for the foreseeable future Latvia's defence budget cannot sustain a volunteer force.

What is clear is that the present conscript armed forces do not appeal to Latvian society. Public opinion polls show that two-thirds of the population think that the best army would be one recruited on a voluntary basis. The argument most frequently advanced is that it would be more efficient, better prepared and more effective. The next most frequently stated opinion is that there would be a greater sense of responsibility, dedication and discipline in a professional army. At the same time, however, there is also some support for a continuation of conscription among a strong minority of 33 per cent of the population. The major argument for conscription is that it is a citizen's obligation to serve in the armed forces of a state, that young men are morally improved by military service and that, as a result, they are better citizens. This is the fundamental notion of the armed forces as a Nation Builder.[23]

In analysing the conscript system, the evidence is that in general the system is working well, but with some areas of concern. A study conducted for the Dutch Ministry of Defence concluded that conscripts for the Latvian armed forces are recruited from lower income groups and the countryside where the economy is more depressed. However, the welfare of junior servicemen is being taken seriously, and the eradication of the harassment of recruits has been a sustained concern of the Latvian military authorities. The Defence Ministry has also introduced a system of enlisted representatives, chosen at platoon level, who represent the soldiers' views to their commanders. A recent feature of conscription is that many of those eligible actually volunteer before they are called up and in general avoidance of military service has declined. Although students still use their deferment, the voluntary military training programme (reserve officers' training) is very popular. So too is the voluntary military training in secondary schools and the Ministry of Defence has had difficulty keeping up with the volunteer service demand.[24]

A further encouraging sign in this area is the high number of university graduates who want to become career officers. Here too the situation has altered and a new generation of officers is making for changes. The National Defence Academy now accepts only university graduates who have passed a competitive entrance examination. The officer cadets receive a short, intensive one-year basic military education, with subsequent assignments at other schools as a part of an officer's career path. The academy's objective is to develop military professionalism in terms of technical soldierly skills combined with high moral standards, intellectual qualities and an ability to lead by example, and good communication skills with soldiers in the unit.[25] The success of the system can at least in part be measured by the fact that the National Defence Academy currently has three well-qualified candidates for every place.

## Conclusion

After a decade of development, several patterns in Latvia's military–society relations are clear. The armed forces emerged in chaotic circumstances out of the remnants of a collapsed Soviet economy and wrecked military equipment and installations left behind by a withdrawing Soviet army. Ten years later, there is a relatively small armed force, which, however, is growing both in confidence and in its ability to perform its missions.

As the introduction to this volume argues, the military in contemporary society can have various roles: that of defending a sovereign state, the historical and fundamental purpose of all armies; the relatively new role of international assistance or peacekeeping missions; that of domestic assistance, or helping in domestic emergencies, such as natural disasters; that of Nation Builder, where the army is a school for patriotic and civic virtues; and, occasionally, that of a defender of a political regime, party, or individual. Latvia's armed forces definitely fulfil the first three roles. They do not function as a Nation Builder because they are numerically small (although a considerable number of Latvians would want them to resume this function), and they have no regime defence functions whatsoever.

Latvia's military–society relations stem from the National Security role and the defence of Latvian territorial integrity. In part, they also stem from the use of the armed forces as an instrument of military diplomacy and Baltic regional cooperation. Overlapping purposes of all the roles and the shared goal of NATO membership have given the Latvian armed forces a clear purpose based on the development of sound military capabilities, but targeted at a political goal. NATO's November 2002 invitation to the Latvian government to join is a culmination of this strategy but it is also a new point of departure for the future development of Latvian military–society relations.

Political consensus on the security orientation of a country, backed by general public support, is a prerequisite for successful internal development in security and defence matters. This chapter has argued that ethnic Latvian and ethnic Russian views on the purpose and role of the Latvian armed forces can differ. However, at times, they are similar. There seems to be a consensus on the need for Baltic defence cooperation and certainly little difference in attitudes towards international missions or using the armed forces for military diplomacy. It is the issue of NATO membership that divides opinions the most, because a strong reason why the Baltic States want to get into the Alliance is an acquisitive great power at their eastern borders. However, the gap between the Latvians and the Russians does appear to be narrowing, and in the case of the younger generation, for some issues, has virtually disappeared. In this sense, then, military–society relations in Latvia continue to strengthen and consolidate, in a process which mirrors the strengthening and consolidation of the Latvian state itself.

# Notes

1. Latvia, Defence Ministry, *Aizsardzibas ministra zinojums Saeimai par valsts aizsardzibas politiku un Nacionalo brunoto speku attistibu 2000. gada* (Riga, Defence Ministry, 2001) and http://www.mod.lv/english/09inform/ 03balta.php. Hereafter cited as *White Book 2000* or *2001*. Page references are to the electronic English-language version.
2. *White Book 2001*.
3. NATO Parliamentary Assembly, Committee Reports, 'European Security: the Baltic Contribution' (November 1998), 12.
4. The International Defence Advisory Board for the Baltic States (IDAB), *Final Report* (February 1999). The Board was established in 1995 at the request of the Baltic Defence Ministers to advise and assist with Baltic defence and security reform.
5. *The National Security Concept of the Republic of Latvia*, www.mod.lv/ english/02.politika/index.php.
6. IDAB, *Final Report*, 4.
7. *Public Opinion Survey 2000. Attitude toward Military Defence issues*, www.mod.lv/english/02.darbs/04.sab.php.
8. IDAB, *Final Report*, 6.
9. *Military cooperation of Baltic States*, www.mod.lv/english/politika/ 05starptautiska_sadarbiba.php.
10. *Evaluation of the capacity for cooperation and defence of the Baltic States*, www.mod.lv/english/06darbs/04sb.php.
11. *Attitude toward Military Defence issues*, www.mod.lv/english/06darbs/ 04sb.php.
12. Eitvydas Bajarunas, 'Baltic Security Cooperation: a Way Ahead', *Baltic Defence Review* (2000: III), 43–62
13. *Central European Review*, 9 August 1999, 23.
14. *White Book 2001*, 48.
15. Centre for European Security Studies, *Assessing the Aspirants for NATO Membership. Final Report of a Study on the Membership Action Plan (MAP) States and 'Second Wave' NATO Enlargement* (Groningen, The Netherlands: Centre for European Security Studies, July 2001), 37.
16. *White Book 2001*, 33.
17. *Attitude toward Military Defence Issues*, www.mod.lv/english/06darbs/ 04sb.php.
18. *Assessing the Aspirants*, 40.
19. *Assessing the Aspirants*, 40.
20. *Attitude toward Military Defence Issues*, www.mod.lv/english/06darbs/ 04sb.php.
21. C. Donnelly, 'Military Matters: Reform Realities', *NATO Review*, 49:3 (Autumn 2001), 32.
22. Findings of an expert group, headed by Maj. Gen. H.A. Kievenaar, US Army, in the Baltic States, *Latvian Assessment Document (NATO Unclassified)* or the 'Kievenaar Study', 1997.
23. *Attitude toward the National Armed Forces and Conscript Service*, www.mod.lv/ english/06darbs/04sb.php.
24. *Assessing the Aspirants*, 40.
25. A. Viksne, 'The Formation of the NDA', *Baltic Defence Review* (2000/3), 16–18.

# 7
# Armed Forces and Society in Lithuania

*Andrius Krivas*

In Lithuania, military–society relations have never been treated as an isolated issue. Instead, they have been focused around the demands of other, more central challenges facing an independent Lithuanian state. These include NATO accession, the development of the armed forces as the main instrument for ensuring national security, and more widely the role of the armed forces in Lithuania's democratisation process. From the vantage point of 2003, Lithuania is completing its transition from a postcommunist stage of development to a modern democracy based around the principles of a free market economy, individual freedom, and respect for human and minority rights. This transition is nearing completion and Lithuania's accession to NATO and the EU will finalise the process. This will have implications for military–society relations in Lithuania with new issues, priorities and challenges likely to appear in this changed environment.

The Lithuanian armed forces were created from scratch in 1990 to 1991. At this time, their role was inherently bound up with national sovereignty. At a functional level, their mission was to organise armed resistance should the newly independent country face external military aggression (though the Soviet/Russian military presence in Lithuania lasted until August 1993). They also played an important symbolic role, helping to illustrate the reality of Lithuanian independence and sovereignty. However, since the time of their formation, the roles of the Lithuanian armed forces have expanded considerably. This expansion has resulted particularly from the evolving European security environment and consequent changes in political and popular threat perceptions in Lithuania. This has led to a significant diversification of the armed forces' functions over the past ten years and in turn altered the nature of military–society relations.

Today, the Lithuanian armed forces play a continuing symbolic role as representatives of the nation's international and domestic image and prestige. In this Nation Builder role, they function as a symbol of national unity, a visible attribute of sovereignty, and an embodiment of Lithuanian national traditions. The Lithuanian armed forces also fulfil the Domestic Military Assistance role, and are tasked with aiding the civilian authorities if government assets prove insufficient to cope with a domestic emergency. In addition, because of the importance placed on NATO accession as a representation of Lithuania's return to the European mainstream, the Lithuanian armed forces have found themselves fulfilling an important Military Diplomacy role as a vanguard of the country's political and cultural process of westernisation and democratisation. Largely as a consequence of this role, since 1994 the Lithuanian military have participated in a number of international peace support operations (PSOs) under NATO or UN auspices. The armed forces' role in the NATO integration process is recognised and supported by the Lithuanian public, and reinforces the Lithuanian military's bases for legitimacy in society. It also adds significantly to society's willingness to pay for the development and strengthening of the country's national defence capabilities.

## Domestic and international pressures in relation to legitimacy, recruitment and funding

The legitimacy of the Lithuanian armed forces in society has been influenced by a number of factors. The first is the public recognition by the NATO secretariat and politicians from NATO countries as to the progress made by Lithuania and its military in relation to defence reform. This has contributed to growing public trust in the competence of the Ministry of Defence and the leadership of the armed forces. Second, democratic civilian control of the military was established early in Lithuania and in general this has functioned well. Indeed, this has been a central influence in the development of Lithuanian military culture and for many in society ties the armed forces closely to Lithuania's wider democratisation process. Third, international aid, defence advice and military training for the Lithuanian armed forces has been crucial in the development of their capabilities and professionalism. This professionalism has contributed directly to the military's standing in Lithuanian society. Fourth, the legitimacy of the armed forces, their public prestige, and the justification for their share of public resource allocations have been strengthened by the frequent instances when the military has offered its material and organisational assets to the civilian authorities at times of domestic emergency such as flooding.[1] For the Lithuanian public, this Domestic Military Assistance role is increasingly important, and represents a visible justification for the armed forces' existence and resource allocations.

Fifth, economic constraints have at times had a negative influence on the public debate on defence issues and especially on questions of defence spending. During periods of economic difficulties or during election campaigns, defence spending has often been seen as a diversion of resources away from more important areas of state spending, such as health-care or the welfare budget. Sixth, public debate reappears periodically on whether Lithuania's system of universal military conscription continues to be relevant. This tends to occur during election campaigns when some parties find significant political capital in opposing conscription. However, in 2003, a shift to an all-volunteer force for Lithuania does not appear to be imminent.

Finally, the Ministry of Defence in Lithuania has developed an active and quite sophisticated public relations strategy that has helped to keep the public informed about their armed forces. The Lithuanian armed forces learned to their cost in the mid-1990s that if they did not publicise their achievements in areas such as developing national defence capabilities, preparations for NATO membership, or their support to the civilian authorities, then public perceptions of them would be dominated by largely negative and scandal-driven reporting in the media. In the past, this tended to focus on breaches in discipline, abuses of authority, accidents or instances of crime or suicide in the military. Even if these instances occur only rarely in Lithuania, if they are the only information the public receives about its armed forces through the media, they will contribute to a distorted image of the military. As a result, in 1998, the Ministry of Defence launched a comprehensive public information drive on the situation in the armed forces. This was strengthened in 2000 by the establishment of a public relations department in the Ministry of Defence, and the allocation of a portion of the defence budget for public information campaigns. This work has proceeded in parallel with public information initiatives on NATO issues, and much of it is conducted through cooperation between the Ministry of Defence and the Ministry of Foreign Affairs.

## Context

### General history, prestige through previous achievements

Lithuania has a deeply-rooted, many-layered national military tradition within which the medieval, twentieth-century interwar and post-Second World War periods are of particular significance. The first layer dates back to the days of the Grand Duchy of Lithuania, which expanded in the thirteenth and fourteenth centuries to stretch from the Baltic to the Black Sea. This expansion resulted only partly from military power, and there was no Lithuanian tradition of glorifying military prowess or celebrating great battles. In practice, the main force that held the Duchy together was a common need for defence against stricter, crueller or more demanding rulers such as the Teutonic Order, the Golden Horde or the Russian principalities. The Grand Duchy of Lithuania was fragile, vulnerable, strongly decentralised and often internally unstable. Nonetheless, for the time it was characterised by a genuine linguistic, cultural and religious tolerance, and gave shelter to many foreigners escaping persecution in their home countries. The Grand Duchy's independent political tradition lasted until its union with Poland, first concluded in 1385 and frequently challenged by Lithuanian rulers until its final design in 1569. The Union entailed the linguistic, cultural and ultimately political Polonisation of the Lithuanian nobility, a secondary role for Lithuania in political affairs, and the virtual abandonment of the Grand Duchy's military tradition.

The second historical layer relates to the armed forces of independent Lithuania between 1918 and 1940, when the military was widely respected and favoured by the government and society. In part this stemmed from their central role in the country's struggle for independence against the Red Army between 1918 and 1920, and their actions against Polish and German troops during the same period. Government policy at this time focused on the strengthening of the armed forces, with the objective of regaining those Lithuanian-populated territories – including the capital Vilnius – that remained under foreign rule. The region of Klaipeda in the west was incorporated into Lithuania in 1923 and Vilnius was regained in 1939. While their reincorporation did not take place as a result of military action, the Lithuanian armed forces did play an important and visible role. In 1940, Lithuania was forcibly incorporated into the Soviet Union. As a result of the politicians' indecisiveness, the armed forces were not deployed in defence of the country's sovereignty. Upon annexation, the Lithuanian units were soon disbanded, and most military officers were either imprisoned, exiled to Siberia or executed.

During the Second World War, no part of the Lithuanian military tradition developed within the German Wehrmacht. Despite tenacious efforts, the Nazi occupation authorities were not able to recruit a Lithuanian SS battalion on either a voluntary or compulsory basis between 1941 and 1944 and Lithuanian men massively avoided the Nazi draft. Offering them a way to escape severe punishment for draft evasion, the Lithuanian general Povilas Plechavicius did form a so-called 'Local Force' (LF) that took orders from the occupying regime and was tasked with the defence of the country from any Soviet reinvasion. However, when the Germans ordered the LF's deployment on the eastern front beyond Lithuanian territory, the force fell apart. Most of its leaders and members who fell into Nazi hands after this – including Plechavicius himself – were executed.

After the end of the Second World War, it was the remnants of Lithuania's interwar armed forces that provided the backbone cadre for the country's guerrilla resistance against the Soviet reoccupation. This began in 1944, and its participants – many of whom wore interwar military uniforms – were known as 'partisans' or 'forest brothers'. Their struggle constitutes the third historical layer of Lithuania's military tradition, and comprised almost a decade of ferocious guerrilla warfare against the Soviet regime. The last battles of the partisans against Soviet NKVD troops occurred as late as 1953, and the last active partisan leader was trapped by the security forces and shot himself in 1956.

The role of the Soviet period in the development of Lithuanian military tradition was limited, though it did have an impact in the early days of Lithuanian independence. At this time the Soviet legacy was twofold. First – and with the exception of those few Lithuanians from diaspora communities with a western military background – Soviet military doctrine was the only source of expertise known to and accessible to Lithuanians with a previous (generally Soviet) military background. Second, military issues were closely associated in the popular mind with the widely despised Soviet regime and its occupying forces. As a consequence, in the early 1990s, Lithuanian attitudes towards military issues were characterised by anti-militarism and pacifism. This led to a considerable lack of public respect towards the newly-formed Lithuanian armed forces, and an opposition among young people to both conscript and volunteer service. However, this public mood did not last long. Indeed, in the mid to late 1990s occasional public dissatisfaction with the military had more to do with the poor economic position of the armed forces and the lack of credible defence value they represented. When these more practical difficulties were resolved, the Lithuanian armed forces' popular standing improved.

For military–society relations in Lithuania today, the actual historical roles played by the military in the past matter less than what the general public believes them to have been. The image of the Lithuanian warrior is both mythologised and idealised in today's public perceptions. This idealised historic legacy is an important – though probably not determining – factor in the Lithuanian public's attitude towards its armed forces. Significantly, the military clearly associates itself with their historic traditions, and it is an important motivation for many of those who decide to join the armed forces.

## Current roles of armed forces

Since the creation of the Lithuanian armed forces in 1990 and 1991, their original purpose – to provide for the effective military defence of the country in time of war – has developed in scope and content. Initially, the military's focus lay in preparations for in-depth defence of national territory by a regular force supported in times of crisis by the mobilisation of pre-trained reserves. However, Lithuania's changing national security environment, declining popular threat perceptions, and its decision to apply for NATO membership created new imperatives for its armed forces. These include issues such as interoperability with other NATO forces, and the need to address a wider range of tasks than simply opposing a foreign military attack on national territory. As a consequence, in addition to their national defence function, the Lithuanian armed forces have developed a number of other roles.

First, the Lithuanian military have revived some traditions of significance to national identity and pride in their role as Nation Builder. They provide a mechanism for assisting the societal integration of ethnic minorities, as well as for education and skill transfer for some of the more disadvantaged parts of the Lithuanian population, such as young men from rural areas. As conscripts, these groups acquire the chance to gain qualities that will be useful for them in their future civilian careers such as leadership and teamwork or specific skills such as vehicle maintenance and first-aid. For ethnic minorities in particular, military service provides an opportunity to develop or improve their command of the Lithuanian language. The multi-ethnic nature of the military also means that it plays an important role as a symbol of national unity and cohesiveness.

Second, the Lithuanian armed forces have also developed a strong contribution to international peacekeeping efforts that has been internalised and accepted by Lithuanian society more widely. Thus, for example, Lithuania has regularly contributed forces to international PSOs under both the UN and NATO since 1994. Lithuanian contingents have served as part of UNPROFOR II in Croatia between 1994 and 1995; IFOR/SFOR in Bosnia since 1996; AFOR in Albania in 1999; and KFOR in Kosovo since 1999. In 2002, Lithuania also dispatched troops to the anti-terrorist 'Operation Enduring Freedom' in Afghanistan and to the International Security Assistance Force in Kabul. Furthermore, the military have been instrumental in the proliferation and dissemination of western norms and values to Lithuania's wider security culture. This has been possible due to their active participation in NATO cooperation programmes and to generous western defence-related assistance.

Third, the Lithuanian military has developed an important Domestic Military Assistance role. Thus, pre-identified military assets such as helicopters or naval vessels can be rapidly allocated to the civil authorities to help them in search and rescue operations.[2] In addition, the air force occasionally assists in medical emergencies by transporting patients or transplant organs, and some military assets have been employed in police operations.[3]

The Lithuanian armed forces have not played a Regime Defence role since the country's independence, despite widespread perceptions that part of the armed forces – the Voluntary National Defence Service (VNDS)[4] – was politically connected to the leadership of the right-wing Conservative Party (CP). The CP was at the vanguard of Lithuania's independence struggle in 1990, and the country's first military units, especially the VNDS, were predominantly formed from its supporters. The Conservatives were defeated in the 1992 general elections, but were returned to power for the 1996 to 2000 period. In the main, however, the VNDS and its successor the NDVF has generally served Lithuania faithfully, irrespective of political changes in the government. The one exception was the so-called 'Kaunas Woods' incident of July 1993 when a group of VNDS personnel armed with light weapons retreated to a forest in the vicinity of Kaunas and attempted to make a number of demands on government.[5] This situation was defused relatively quickly, did not require the use of force, and there has been no repetition. Since 1998, the service has been reorganised, and today the NDVF is fully integrated within the regular armed forces and responsible for the provision of reserve training, as well as some support military functions such as guarding military bases and key civilian infrastructure facilities.

## Domestic and international influences

### Threat perceptions and the geostrategic context

Military–society relations in Lithuania have been shaped by the country's evolving security environment – and correspondingly by threat perceptions at both popular and elite levels. Three general trends in this evolution are of particular note. The first trend has been the gradual integration of Lithuania into western security institutions through the NATO accession process and through direct security cooperation with NATO and EU members and candidates. Second, there has been a decrease in security concerns with regard to Russia. This has occurred through Lithuania's increased experience and self-confidence as an independent sovereign state as well as through the development of cooperation with Russia on issues of mutual interest, such as the Kaliningrad region. In addition, the slow strengthening and consolidation of democracy in Russia and its generally positive relations with the West have contributed to a decline in Lithuanian worries over the intentions of its eastern neighbour.

Finally, the appearance of so-called 'new' security challenges – such as international crisis management and terrorism – have required new approaches on the part of nations, societies, alliances and policy planners, as well as new capabilities for the armed forces to ensure their continuing relevance. In Lithuania, this has meant that national threat perceptions have gained a wider international perspective that goes beyond a purely military understanding of security. As a consequence, Lithuania's motivations for wanting to join NATO have also evolved. Alongside the traditional collective defence function of the Alliance, Lithuania has also been keen to participate in addressing its 'new functions'. These include international (that is, out of area) PSOs and the fight against terrorism. Thus, Lithuania expects NATO membership not only to provide security reassurance, but also to function as a mechanism to facilitate further cooperation with Russia in the security field. Moreover, the developing security agenda poses new questions for the armed forces in terms of their structures, capabilities and interoperability, and also in relation to their need to prove their effectiveness to society at large and to justify the substantial resources invested in them.

These developments have had two somewhat contradictory impacts on military–society relations. First, Lithuanian society has become less concerned about the armed forces' ability to defeat a conventional military attack on the country. This has allowed the military to shift its focus to those security challenges that are of a lower order but higher probability. As the process of economic integration with western Europe stimulates better economic performance and an improving standard of living, the public is also more at ease with properly financing national institutions, including the armed forces. Second, however, in the absence of a direct military threat, Lithuanian society sees much less urgency in the need to develop effective armed forces, and the popular pressure to spend money on defence should, logically, decrease. Nonetheless, the declining importance of national territorial defence as the military's primary *raison d'être* has been supplanted by its new roles and functions as a justification for defence spending in Lithuania. In particular, the prospect of NATO membership has proved a much stronger incentive for the public to spend money on defence than the sense of imminent Russian threat.

### International aid and externally generated 'expectations'

The NATO enlargement process has been the major external factor influencing military–society relations in Lithuania at both popular and political levels. NATO membership is a goal that is strongly supported by Lithuanian society, and the armed forces have been centrally important in the country's preparations for accession and its ultimate success. Because of a popular perception of their competence in fulfilling this task, their public prestige has been boosted considerably. NATO integration requirements have shaped the armed forces' development priorities, focused international military aid, led to the establishment of mechanisms to provide feedback on the progress of military reform, and created a willingness amongst Lithuania's politicians and public to contribute to international PSOs.

Not all international assistance to the Lithuanian armed forces has been directly related to NATO accession. Some foreign governments chose to assist Lithuania in the development of its armed forces as part of their efforts to promote democratisation in the region. Thus, for example, defence assistance has also occurred at a bilateral level through individual defence attaché offices, or multilaterally through groups such as the Baltic Security Assistance Group (BALTSEA). Lithuanian military personnel have also undergone large-scale, high-quality training programmes in western countries. This has helped develop both their professional skills and their mental attitudes. The officer corps has become an integral part of the Lithuanian social elite, and is regarded by many in the country as a catalyst of modernisation more widely. International training opportunities also contribute to the attractiveness of military service among potential volunteers or draftees.

## Domestic political factors

Perhaps the most important domestic political factor that has influenced military–society relations in Lithuania was the early establishment of a working system for democratic, civilian control over the armed forces. This system is addressed in the Lithuanian Constitution and in subsequent defence and security legislation – notably the Law on the Fundamentals of National Security (1996) and the Law on the Organisation of the National Defence System and Military Service (1998) – as well as in strategic planning documents such as the National Security Strategy (2002) and the National Military Defence Strategy (2000, currently under review). In all these documents, democratic civilian control of the armed forces is mentioned as a fundamental principle of Lithuania's defence system. Formal civilian control arrangements focus on two main issues. The first is the subordination of the military leadership to the democratic civilian authorities. Second, limitations are placed on the political activities of the armed forces and their personnel. In relation to this latter point, the political constraints placed on military personnel are quite tough. They are prohibited from making any public criticism of decisions approved by the political authorities, and political advertising is not allowed in any places of military service. In practice, almost the only way in which military personnel are legally allowed to express their political will as citizens is through voting in local or general elections or in public referenda.

Many of these restrictions were inspired by popular suspicion of the military engendered by the totalitarian system of Soviet civil–military relations, where the armed forces were often used as a tool of political intimidation and functioned as a pillar of the communist regime. The principle of the political isolation of the armed forces was instituted in the early days of Lithuanian independence as the safest means of preventing their political manipulation for partisan interest. However, in Lithuania today, many of these restrictions appear somewhat obsolete or superfluous. They are partly justifiable in relation to the professional elements of the armed forces as long as they are clearly part of the 'deal' when a free individual accepts the conditions of military service. However, in relation to conscripts, any infringement of their freedom to express and argue personal political views raises concern.

In practice, however, these laws are interpreted flexibly in Lithuania today. This is illustrated by the 2002 debate caused by the participation of the Commander of the Armed Forces Major General Jonas Kronkaitis in a conference organised by the US Lithuanian community while he was on leave. During the conference, he criticised – at a fairly philosophical level – practices of social and economic management in Lithuania, attributing many of the country's problems to post-Soviet attitudinal legacies among the political elite. The left-wing ruling coalition attacked the Commander of the Armed Forces. He was called for account before the President and the Speaker of Parliament. The right-wing opposition on the other hand argued that as he was expressing his views as a citizen (rather than as a military officer), Kronkaitis had neither abused his authority nor exceeded his legal powers.[6] The debate was somewhat artificially heated by the political context in which it took place. At the time of Kronkaitis's appointment the current opposition had been in government, and he was widely considered to be sympathetic to their political cause. Nonetheless, however politicised, the debate touched upon serious issues that may need to be addressed in the future. Over time, Lithuania may find it more relevant to its circumstances to move away from the present 'isolationist' model of democratic civilian control to one based around the idea of the 'citizen in uniform'. This would rely not on the isolation of the military from the political life of the society, but on a more profound understanding by the military of the political circumstances of the country, as well as the nature and purpose of various democratic institutions and practices including the role of the political parties. This might provide a stronger link between the military and society, and would ensure that the armed forces functioned as one of the key institutions of the democratic society. Any new legal arrangements should, of course, retain the strict prohibition of the use of military power in pursuit of internal political objectives.

### Economic constraints

Economic factors have had an important influence on Lithuanian military–society relations. This has especially been the case at times of economic difficulty – such as in the aftermath of the 1998 Russian financial crisis – or during election campaigns. Traditionally, the political opposition has been quick to suggest that resource allocations to the defence sector have the potential to act as a reserve for remedying funding insufficiencies in other – by implication more important – areas of state funding. In practice, once they come to power, these forces have tended to reconsider their approach and have yielded to internal and international pressure towards ensuring adequate defence funding. Perhaps the most visible example of this was the campaign of the Social Liberal Union (SLU) during the 2000 elections, which included a reduction in defence spending as one of its core demands. However, on joining the ruling coalition after the elections, the SLU took a more balanced approach, entering willingly into the Defence Policy Agreement with other parliamentary parties in May 2001. This contained a political commitment to keep annual defence expenditure at a level of at least 2 per cent of GDP until the next parliamentary elections in 2004.

## Actions of the armed forces towards 'society'

Since the middle of the 1990s, both the government and the armed forces have made deliberate and sustained efforts to inform society about the life and activities of the military. This consistent information campaign – strengthened over the past four years – contributes significantly towards the transparency of the armed forces and has helped to strengthen their public image. In late 2000, the Ministry of Defence's public relations policy was institutionalised by the establishment of a public relations department. The PR department's functions include the promotion of the public image of the armed forces and the stimulation of public support for NATO membership by educating the population on NATO policy and broader security issues. Its activities include producing publications, regular television and radio broadcasts, the appearance of military personnel in the media and other public activities. These include initiatives like 'armed forces days' that allow civilians to see the life of the military close up, as well as educational activities with groups such as politicians, teachers, journalists and children. In this context, the military's provision of assistance to the civilian authorities in the areas of disaster relief, search and rescue, medical emergencies or support to police operations is very important; and providing timely and accurate public information about instances when this occurs has helped to add to the popular prestige of the armed forces.

## Societal factors

One of the most important factors in military–society relations in Lithuania is the country's use of universal conscription as a basis for military organisation. From the point of view of military–society relations, conscripts embody a real, physical link between civilian society and the military, and conscription in Lithuania has been significant in helping to keep public attention on the situation within the armed forces. Nonetheless, conscription has been the subject of often fierce argument in Lithuania, though to date the decision has always been made to retain it. In the early 1990s, conscription appeared attractive because it was the cheapest way to recruit the armed forces. Subsequently, other arguments have become more relevant to support conscript service. In particular, compulsory military service creates a considerable pool of individuals with a minimum standard of military skill, thus ensuring a credible defence of national territory by a large, reasonably well-trained force in times of war. In peacetime, only a small proportion of this force is maintained and trained from public funds.

In addition, many argue that conscription plays an important social-ising role – allowing young men the chance to gain shared experiences, to acquire skills such as teamwork and personal leadership, and provid-ing the opportunity for non-Lithuanian ethnic communities to better integrate into Lithuanian society. However, in practice, these impacts have actually been relatively limited because of the insufficiently uni-versal character of conscription. The Lithuanian armed forces do not have either the requirement or the ability to absorb the bulk of conscript age youngsters. In addition, the law contains a variety of bases on which military duty can be postponed or waived, such as being in further edu-cation or being the main provider for a family. As a consequence the annual intake of conscripts in Lithuania is about 6000 – only 24 per cent of potential draftees. Nonetheless, conscription is generally accepted by those areas of society to which it most applies (and paradoxically is opposed most by those who deal with it at a hypothetical level).[7] This is partly a result of a sustained drive since 1997 to improve the quality of life for both professional soldiers and conscripts in the armed forces that has increased the attractiveness of the armed forces in the labour market. This is further illustrated by the fierce competition for places at the National Defence Academy and remarkably high cadet and young officer retention rates.[8]

The Lithuanian armed forces are in theory open to women, though in practice the bulk of military personnel – almost 90 per cent – are men. Normally women serve in support functions as medics, typists or accountants. There are only a very few female junior officers and NCOs who serve as army squad or platoon leaders. Despite this, the trend of employing women as professional soldiers has grown since the opening of the National Defence Academy to female cadets in 2000 at the insis-tence of the parliamentary Equal Opportunities Controller.[9] Indeed, in 2002, a woman was promoted to the rank of Lieutenant Colonel for the first time in Lithuanian history.[10]

## Major challenges of linking armed forces to society

### An end to conscription?

Given the lack of an immediate large-scale military threat to Lithuania, it is increasingly difficult politically for the government to justify the retention of conscription. The importance of being able to dramatically augment the military in the event of crisis or war through the mobilisation of conscript-trained reserves is likely to decrease significantly in future. However, as well as the argument that military service provides an important link between the military and society, there are also external influences in favour of retaining conscription. Indeed, conscription is militarily and societally central to the Nordic defence culture from which Lithuania has taken many of its basic approaches to defence. Unless Denmark, Norway, Sweden and Finland reconsider this fundamental principle of their defence policy, Lithuania is unlikely to do so on its own, whatever the current European trends towards all-volunteer forces, and despite official encouragement from NATO Secretary General George Robertson to do so.[11] Nonetheless, it is likely that the issue of an all-volunteer force will return to the public debate in the near future. However, because such a change would require an alteration in the Constitution, it will require a very broad public and political consensus on the issue which at the moment is simply not in place. But urgent challenges remain in relation to the improvement of Lithuania's alternative national service system for those who cannot join the military for ideological or religious reasons.

### Legitimising the armed forces

When Lithuania joins NATO in 2004 it will be a clear validation of the nationwide effort that has been devoted towards the accession process. Because the armed forces have been central players in this process, the success of this effort will give the armed forces much additional prestige, and increase their bases for legitimacy in society. However, in the absence of an immediate military threat to national territory, the importance of developing meaningful peacetime roles for the armed forces continues to be central to their societal legitimacy. Such roles include enhanced contributions to international – and particularly NATO-led operations – and the provision of domestic military assistance at times of crisis. In the short to medium term, these new roles may need to be further emphasised in governmental, Ministry of Defence and military public relations efforts. Finally, Lithuania's existing system of democratic, civilian control of the military may require a revision in the future to move away from the 'isolationist' model of military neutrality to a more 'integrationist' one. The requirement for this to occur will be all the more pressing if the country decides to continue with universal military service.

### Securing appropriate public expenditure

Upon acceding to NATO, Lithuania will face the challenge of maintaining momentum in the development and funding of adequate capabilities for its armed forces. At the moment, popular and political enthusiasm for defence reform has largely been sustained by the 'carrot' of accession to an alliance of like-minded democratic nations. For this commitment to continue, the government will have to work hard in relation to public education, the military's professionalism and Lithuania's sense of internal and international responsibility. It will also have to ensure that the economy continues to grow and that defence spending remains transparent. Past experience in Lithuania shows that the public generally recognises the need to allocate a decent share of public resources to national defence, as long as the economy is in a stable condition.

## Conclusions

From the vantage point of 2003, Lithuania can be seen to have emerged from a decade of postcommunist transition to become a modern, democratic European state. Throughout this decade military–society relations in Lithuania have been shaped by seven key factors. The first factor is the evolution of the European security environment and the consequent decline in national threat perceptions. This has led to a shift in the roles of the armed forces away from an emphasis on the defence of national territory to one that is also concerned with participation in international PSOs and the provision of military assistance to the civil authorities at times of crisis. The second factor has been the early establishment of working mechanisms for democratic, civilian control of the armed forces. Third, universal conscript service has been adopted as a basis for military organisation. The fourth factor has been the decision to seek NATO accession on the basis of a broad political consensus and wide popular support. Fifth, the government and the military have made good progress in the preparations for NATO membership and there has been public acknowledgement of this by the decision to invite Lithuania to join NATO. Sixth, there has been a deliberate and sustained focus on the part of the political and defence authorities on ensuring an improved quality of life for armed forces personnel. Finally, there has been generous western defence assistance.

Under the influence of all these factors, Lithuanian society has developed a better knowledge of its armed forces and a greater trust in them. Military service has gained greater social prestige and the military career has become competitive on the employment market. Indeed, the popularity of the armed forces has steadily increased and opinion polling shows a steady growth in the number of people who trust the military, up from 35 per cent in 1996 to 50 per cent in 2002. The number of those who do not trust the military has declined from 55 per cent to 35 per cent over the same period.[12]

The Lithuanian armed forces have also acquired additional roles over this period, most notably the Military Diplomacy and Domestic Military Assistance roles outlined in Chapter 1. These have included the use of the military as an instrument of diplomacy to support Lithuania's NATO membership bid; the Lithuanian armed forces' participation in international PSOs and crisis management; and their provision of domestic assistance to the civilian authorities in the areas of disaster relief and search and rescue tasks. The armed forces have also played an important role in the proliferation of western societal and cultural values in Lithuania more widely.

Lithuania's accession to NATO and the EU in 2004 will mark the ultimate success of its transition to freedom and democracy, and this is also likely to modify the agenda of military–society relations in the country. NATO membership in particular has validated the nation-wide effort towards accession and gives the military additional prestige. However, it will also create future challenges. This will entail maintaining the linkage between the Lithuanian armed forces and society over the next decade. Particular challenges are likely to include sustaining public willingness to pay for national military capabilities; enhancing meaningful peacetime roles for the armed forces; providing political justifications for the continuation of conscription; and the possible need to revise the present system of democratic control over the military from the current 'isolationist' model to one with a more 'integrationist' character. If these challenges can be met successfully, then military–society relations in Lithuania will continue to develop along the lines of those in a modern European democracy.

# Notes

1. 'Jegeriu batalionas istiese pagalbos ranka Kano miestui' (Ranger Battalion Extends Help to the City of Kaunas), http://www.kam.lt/archive.php?=525 (9 January 2002); 'Kariuomenes sarvuociai pades potvynio metu' (Military APCs to Help in Flood), http://www.kam.lt/archive.php?=589 (31 January 2002); 'Lietuvos kariai isijungia i pagalba zmonems potvynio teritorijoje' (Lithuanian Military Provide Assistance to People in Flooded Areas), http://www.kam.lt/archive.php?=595 (1 February 2002).
2. 'Karines oro pajegos isgelbejo i audra patekusius zvejus' (Air Force Saves Fishermen in Storm), http://www.kam.lt/archive.php?=164 (10 September 2001).
3. 'Karines oro pajegos perskraidino organa transplantacijai' (Air Force Transported Human Organ for Transplantation), http://www.kam.lt/archive.php?=405 (15 November 2001); 'Karines oro pajegos skubiai perskraidino suzeistaji' (Air Force Transported Swiftly an Injured Person), http://www.kam.lt/archive.php?=618 (10 February 2002); 'Karines oro pajegos kartu su policija iesko nusikalteliu' (Alongside Police, Air Force Chases Criminals), http://www.kam.lt/archive.php?=262 (10 October 2001); 'Kariniu juru pajegu narai padejo tirti sunkius nusikaltimus' (Navy Divers Helped Investigate Atrocious Crimes), http://www.kam.lt/archive.php?=578 (28 January 2002).
4. This was today's National Defence Volunteer Force (NDVF) before its reorganisation in 1998 and subsequent integration into the regular armed forces.
5. For further details of the Kaunas Woods incident, see V. Urbelis and T. Urbonas, 'The Challenges of Civil–Military Relations and Democratic Control of Armed Forces: the Case of Lithuania', in Andrew Cottey, Timothy Edmunds and Anthony Forster (eds), *Democratic Control of the Military in Postcommunist Europe: Guarding the Guards* (Basingstoke: Palgrave Macmillan, 2002), 110–12.
6. 'Kariuomenes vadas aiskinasi Seimo vadovui' (Armed Forces Commander Gives Account to Leader of Parliament), *Lietuvos rytas* (14 February 2002); 'Parlamentarai bande paaukleti generola' (MPs Tried to Teach General a Lesson), *Lietuvos rytas* (28 March 2002).
7. I. Verbiene, 'Vietoje karines tarnybos – darbas uzsienyje' (Jobs Abroad Instead of Military Service), *Lietuvos zinios* (19 June 2002).
8. See, for example, 'Norinciu studijuoti Lietuvos karo akademijoje vis daugiau' (Increasingly Many Wish to Study at Lithuanian Defence Academy), http://www.kam.lt/archive.php?=163 (10 September 2001).
9. See, for example, 'Prisieke 107 Lietuvos karo akademijos kariunai' (107 Cadets Sworn in at Lithuanian Defence Academy), http://www.kam.lt/archive.php?=280 (15 October 2001).
10. 'Pulkininko leitenanto laipsnis suteiktas pirmajai moteriai' (First Woman Promoted Lieutenant Colonel), http://www.kam.lt/archive.php?=566 (23 January 2002).
11. ' "No Future" for Conscript Armies, says Robertson', *DPA* (13 June 2002).
12. 'Organizacju reitingai. Kitimas laiko intervale' (Ratings of Organisations. Evolution over Given Period), http://www.5ci.lt/ratings/lit/cgi-bin/ikli.asp (14 June 2002).

# Part III
# Southeastern Europe

# 8
# Ahead of the Curve: the Military–Society Relationship in Romania

*Larry L. Watts*

The Romanian military is popularly associated with every significant advance in state-building and national consolidation since the formation of the Romanian people. Its status as an institution under full national control since the 1960s, coupled with the hostility shown it by Romania's communist leadership, maintained the popular prestige of the military before 1989. This popularity was reinforced when the army joined with the population in the December 1989 revolution. The Romanian Armed Forces (RAF) thus emerged from the communist period as a popular and fully field-capable army, and its relationship with society free of the civil–military antagonism common among other former Warsaw Pact countries.

These unusual circumstances have enabled the RAF to engage in new Military Diplomacy roles of peacekeeping and regional security provider more rapidly, reinforcing Romania's national security and advancing NATO and EU integrationist goals. Since 1990, over 10,000 military personnel have been sent to various peace support and military operations, from the Persian Gulf and Somalia to Kosovo and Afghanistan. Continued regional instabilities and the new threats that arose after 11 September 2001 have invested both traditional and new roles with greater currency.

Freed from basic institution-building tasks, and enjoying popular support, the RAF has been able to address 'next generation' problems associated with personnel reconversion, professionalisation, diversity training, minority recruitment and anti-corruption relatively early, further increasing its social standing as the state's most effective institutional reformer. Key to these efforts has been a media outreach programme in existence since 1991, based on the RAF's understanding that public support is an inherent component of its combat capacity and its ability to fulfil strategic missions. The principal vulnerability facing the military–society relationship over the long term is economic, although current performance and medium-term forecasts give cause for cautious optimism.

## Context

### Nation Building and National Security

As an important avenue of social mobility and critical factor in national unification and independence during the nineteenth century, in the integration of the nation-state during the First World War, and in the defence and recovery of territory during the Second World War, the RAF is firmly established in the Nation Builder and National Security roles in popular perception. Initially allied with the Axis in the Second World War, the RAF joined the Allies after German forces attempted to prevent Romania from leaving the war in 1944, contributing over 538,000 troops and suffering over 167,000 casualties in the Allied cause – the fourth largest military contribution made during the entire war.[1]

### Regime Defence and Domestic Military Assistance

The army acted as regime defender on several occasions during the nineteenth and twentieth centuries, most notably in two domestic crises: the Peasant's Rebellion of 1907, and against a coup attempt by the fascist Iron Guard in 1940. The very substantial (5000–10,000) casualties of 1907 created an aversion for internal security tasks within the officer corps despite legislation stipulating a greater police role for the army in 1907, 1917 and 1920.[2] In response, the General Staff issued special instructions in 1932 stipulating that: 'It is strictly prohibited to use operational troops for the maintenance of order (endangered or not); this task devolves upon the police organs and rural gendarmes.'[3]

Under communism, the RAF was considered the least reliable military within the Warsaw Pact for purposes of defending the regime against an internal threat.[4] In January 1999, President Emil Constantinescu and the Democratic Convention government mobilised troops against a miner's protest they alleged to be a 'grave danger' to 'national security and constitutional democracy'.[5] The mobilisation was widely resented among the officer corps as an illegitimate attempt to employ the military against the population.[6]

At the same time, the RAF has traditionally filled domestic assistance roles. It regularly assisted in harvests and provided disaster relief before 1989, and it continues to provide relief during seasonal flooding, severe storms and forest fires. Until 2001, municipal firefighting was also a military task. However, it has resisted even limited policing tasks. In March 1990, for example, it reluctantly sent a small unit into Tirgu Mures to quell a local ethnic disturbance while restating its opposition in principle to internal security roles.[7]

## National control of the RAF under communism

During the late 1950s and early 1960s, Romania's autonomous policy freed the RAF from Soviet subordination and reinstated full national control over defence strategy and operational forces.[8] As of 1961 Romanian officers were no longer sent to the USSR for training, and Soviet authorities were not permitted to vet officers before appointment to senior posts. In 1963, Romania ended its participation in Warsaw Pact troop exercises.[9] By the mid-1960s, intelligence cooperation with the KGB and GRU (the Soviet Main Intelligence Administration) was terminated.[10] This ended the RAF's role as an agent of foreign control and removed a major source of popular antagonism.

In addition, the adoption of a national territorial defence strategy reduced military compatibility with the Warsaw Pact by charging the RAF with the exclusive mission of defending the country within national borders and excluding any supranational authority over it.[11] Romania then distinguished itself as the only Warsaw Pact member to refuse participation in and to condemn the Soviet-led invasion of Czechoslovakia in 1968.[12]

Introducing the weaponry, training, deployments and logistical infrastructure necessary for the redefined mission transformed the RAF into the 'least systemically integrated of any member of the Warsaw Pact'.[13] Romania also developed a large domestic defence industry, diffused its foreign sources of equipment, and drastically reduced its dependence on Soviet production and supply.[14] These provisions and measures created fundamental incompatibilities with Warsaw Pact military doctrine, rendering the RAF of limited utility for coalitional offensive warfare and recasting it as a national defence force.

In order to deter Soviet aggression, Romania created huge reserves of quasi-guerrilla *Patriotic Guards* under the 'War of the Entire People' doctrine, anticipated a Soviet attack as the primary threat in its strategy, and redeployed forces for effective territorial defence.[15] By the late 1970s, the RAF was regarded as a probable adversary of the USSR in a potential

East–West confrontation, reassuming its historic role as defender against a traditional threat from the east.[16]

Compelled to rely upon its army for support of its independent policies, the communist leadership was also forced to grant the RAF the professional autonomy necessary for creating a fully field-capable military.[17] Ceausescu resented this dependence and viewed the RAF with increasing hostility, even while he exploited it as a source of cheap labour. This was reflected in defence allocations, proportionally the lowest in the Warsaw Pact.[18]

As popular antagonism towards the regime increased, military dissatisfaction provided a natural bridge to the long-suffering population – a bond reinforced by the military's regular participation in disaster-relief actions and seasonal harvesting. The role of the RAF in the 1989 Revolution, where it sided with the demonstrators and suffered over 20 per cent of the casualties, cemented this linkage, redefining the institution as a defender of the people rather than the regime.[19]

The early reinstitution of uniquely national control and traditional roles made the RAF better able to pursue reform while maintaining combat effectiveness at the start of the postcommunist transition, earning it prestige as Romania's leading institutional reformer.[20] After 1989, the other former Warsaw Pact armies were compelled to purge officer corps largely trained in the USSR;[21] to rebuild their civil–military relationships and decision-making processes;[22] to acquire the capability to create and implement national strategy;[23] and to undertake major redeployments.[24] Romania had already accomplished these tasks decades earlier. Consequently, as Figure 8.1 illustrates the RAF began the transition with

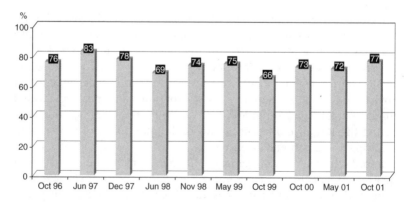

*Figure 8.1*   Public trust in the military 1996–2001

Sources: Metro Media Transylvania, Center for Urban and Regional Sociology (CURS), and the Romanian Institute for Public Opinion Polls (IRSOP).

enviably high levels of trust and prestige among the population, hovering over the past decade between 70 and 85 per cent.[25]

## International, transnational and domestic influences

Although there are no direct military threats, instability has been endemic around Romania's borders since the collapse of communism. Since 1991, ethnic and sectarian conflicts have been regular phenomena along the country's south-western border. During 1992–93, military hostilities broke out in the Republic of Moldova on the north-eastern border, and periodic socio-political unrest there continues up to the present. Romania is the closest NATO candidate to Belgrade, Sarajevo and Chisinau, and second closest – after Bulgaria – to Pristina, Skopje and Tirana. General regional instability is unlikely to disappear over the near or medium term.

### The NATO alliance

NATO (and EU) pressure and assistance have complemented and reinforced domestic pressures for internal reform and integration. In part, this reflects the popular desire to reintegrate into the West after a half-century of isolation. It is also an artefact of the security and prosperity the two organisations represent for the general population. And partly, it is due to the prestige of those organisations relative to Romanian institutions. With the exception of the military, NATO and the EU are consistently more popular and credible for Romanians than their own public institutions – the mass media included. The RAF thus benefits from its leading role in the NATO integration process.

All military reforms within the RAF are considered on the basis of their compatibility with NATO standards and practices, and are overseen by a special Directorate for Military Reform and NATO Integration. The NATO Membership Action Plan (MAP) process has proved enormously beneficial for setting priorities, monitoring fulfilment and ensuring consistent practice.[26] Although not directly concerned with the military, the EU integration process, and particularly the accession advisers placed within various ministries, has also proved a boon to military reform by establishing a framework of reforming institutions and a template of European legislation and practice. Given the high priority that the Romanian population places on NATO and EU integration, and on reform generally, effective use of international aid and response to pressure for further reform contributes to a more robust military–society relationship.

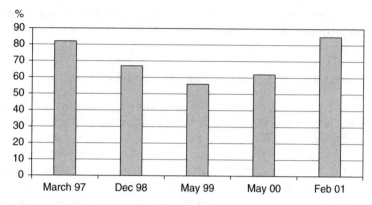

*Figure 8.2*  Public support for NATO 1997–2001

*Sources*: Metro Media Transylvania and Center for Urban and Regional Sociology.

Romanian support for NATO integration has consistently been the highest in central and eastern Europe at around 85 to 87 per cent. During the Kosovo campaign support for NATO dropped to an all-time low of 56 per cent (see Figure 8.2), partly due to Romanian scepticism regarding the utility of the operation for resolving ethnic conflict, and partly to the proximity of the bombing to the Romanian border.[27] However, even this diminished support was on a par with that of new NATO member Poland (at 60 per cent), equal to that of Germany and France, and exceeded support levels in Hungary, the Czech Republic and Greece.[28]

## Regional security and military diplomacy

During the interwar period, with French backing, Romania acted as a regional alliance sponsor and coordinator of the Little Entente and the Balkan Entente. It reassumed this regional role, this time with US support, after 1989. In 1993, Romania introduced the formula that it would be a 'regional security producer rather than consumer', terminology which quickly entered NATO's vocabulary. A major aspect of this effort was the RAF's military diplomacy during 1990, resulting in the Open Skies agreement with Hungary, at a time when the two governments were barely on speaking terms, which bolstered the RAF's reputation as a pragmatic institution advancing general national rather than partisan or particular interests. Aside from its direct linkage with stability and national security, providing regional security also boosts Romania's international reputation.

In Bucharest's appreciation, by virtue of its location, size and resources, Romania must bear significant responsibility for providing security in both the Balkan/Southeastern European region and in the Black Sea region. To this end, Romania has initiated, co-founded or participated in the Romanian–Hungarian Joint Peacekeeping Battalion; in the *Tisza* Engineer Battalion; in the UN's Stand-by High Readiness Brigade (SHIRBRIG); in the Black Sea Naval Task Group (BLACKSEAFOR); in the Central European Nations' Cooperation Initiative (CENCOOP); and is chairman of the South Eastern Europe Security Cooperation Group (SEEGROUP) which ensures connectivity between NATO's South Eastern Europe Initiative (SEEI) and regional cooperative initiatives.

The influence of the US has reinforced the regional role significantly while further anchoring Romania within NATO in terms of its goals and concerns and ultimately has been crucial in the decision to extend an invitation to the Romanian government to join NATO. A US military advisory team has been working in the RAF since 1993. Romania chairs the Political and Military Steering Committee for the Multinational Peacekeeping Force South Eastern Europe (MPFSEE) with the USA, Italy, Greece, Turkey, Bulgaria, Slovenia and Albania. In addition, it contributes an infantry battalion, reconnaissance platoon, transport platoon, engineer company and staff personnel to the South East European Brigade (SEEBRIG), which became fully operational in May 2001.

Although the strategic partnership concluded with the US in 1997 formalised cooperation on regional stability, defence reform, and in addressing transnational threats, US–Romanian security cooperation has a longer history. In 1995 Washington and Bucharest agreed to set up a regional centre for combating new non-military threats – the Southeastern Europe Cooperation Initiative for Combating Cross-Border Crime (SECI) – which has proved successful in countering illegal trafficking in the region. Romania's decision in the immediate aftermath of 11 September 2001 to act as a de facto ally of NATO was taken in full cognizance of NATO's 1999 Strategic Concept specifying that Alliance response can be triggered by 'acts of terrorism, sabotage and organised crime'.[29]

### Deployments abroad

There has been consistent political willingness across the board to put troops in harm's way in the furtherance of national security goals, including those of the NATO alliance. Again, this reflects a well-established precedent. In the mid-nineteenth century the RAF fought alongside French forces in Morocco, Italy and Mexico. During the war against the

Ottoman Empire, Romanian forces fought in Serbia and Bulgaria along-side Russian, Serb and Bulgarian forces. The RAF acted as an occupation force in Budapest at the close of the First World War, and during the Second World War it sent troops with Allied forces through Hungary and Czechoslovakia to Vienna. In fact, the duration of the Warsaw Pact represented the longest period over the last two centuries when RAF forces were not deployed abroad.

Since 1989 Romania has contributed over 10,000 personnel to various peace support and humanitarian operations in Africa, the Middle East, Asia and Europe, sending 400 personnel to the Persian Gulf during Operation Desert Storm, 700 to Somalia, and cycling over 3000 through Angola between 1995 and 1998. It is present in Rwanda, Congo, Ethiopia/Eritrea, Iraq and Kuwait. Regionally, over 1500 troops have participated in IFOR/SFOR in Bosnia (not including the 400 reserves standing by in Romania), 400 troops have participated in Operation Alba in Albania, and psyops and military police contingents have been maintained in KFOR in Kosovo. Romania also offered peace support forces for Cyprus and Macedonia and maintains liaison and observer teams in Georgia and the Republic of Moldova.

Following its decision to act as a de facto ally of NATO in September 2001, Romania offered to replace US troops in the Balkans to permit their redeployment elsewhere, and to provide peace support and military forces for operations in Afghanistan. This decision had the unanimous support of the Romanian parliament. Romania doubled its military personnel in the Balkans to ease the redeployment of US personnel and US KFOR forces rotated out of Kosovo through Romanian port and air facilities on the Black Sea.

In January 2002, Romania became the first NATO candidate to deploy forces (military police and air transport contingents) in Afghanistan under the British-led International Security Assistance Force (ISAF). In March, this presence was upgraded with a contingent of staff officers. In July, the RAF deployed an infantry battalion (the *Red Scorpions*) as part of 'Operation Enduring Freedom', where it took part in combat operations beginning in September. A new Romanian infantry battalion (the *Carpathian Hawks*) was cycled in during December.

According to a 2001 poll, illustrated in Figure 8.3, more than three-quarters of the population favour the active participation of the RAF in new normative roles of peace-support and peace enforcement.

This support rests on societal, institutional and individual motivations. First, everyone accepts the desirability of the norms and values that underpin these new roles. Second, contribution to the NATO

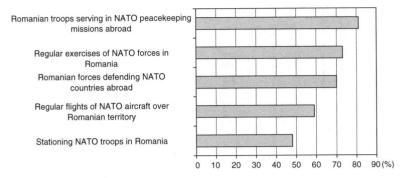

*Figure 8.3* Public support for military roles in NATO
*Source*: Metro Media Transylvania, 11–13 February 2001.

alliance – and to the US partnership – is directly linked with the defence of Romania's own national security. Third, regional peacekeeping in the Balkans and Black Sea region also contributes directly to Romanian security, while the role of regional security provider demands active involvement in order to be credible. Fourth, participation in these roles provides an efficient method of achieving full interoperability and compatibility with NATO faster, as well as providing the experience necessary for constituting a fully professional force. Finally, service in these missions is attractive to military personnel because field experience is a component of the advancement process and since pay rates are some 20 times higher than pay rates within Romania.

Post-NATO enlargement in 2004, the status of the transatlantic relationship remains a conditioning factor in support for deployments. A breakdown in US–European relations, for example, could undermine public support for deployment in NATO missions beyond the region. At the same time, the area of Romanian interest in terms of stability and security (and economic opportunity) is defined broadly in Bucharest, including not only the Balkans and Southeastern Europe – where there is likely to be continued instability over the next decade – but the Black Sea, Caucasus and Central Asia as well.

### Downsizing and conscription

The RAF has been engaged in a massive restructuring and downsizing effort since 1989 (Figure 8.4). Military and civilian manpower have been reduced from 320,000 to 120,500 and the active service peacetime army has been decreased from almost 290,000 to 93,000 as of December 2002.

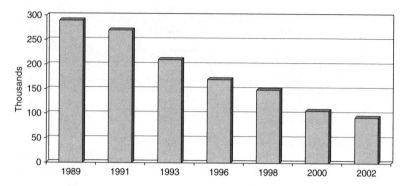

*Figure 8.4*    Military downsizing 1989–2002
Source: J-5, General Staff, Romanian Ministry of National Defence.

The final peacetime force target of 75,000 is scheduled to be reached in 2007. Since the military itself 'carried the water' for this restructuring, it did not create tension in military–society relations. The RAF's transparent personnel management system, implemented during 2001 with British assistance, established promotion boards for all ranks and clear evaluation criteria for advancement and redundancy, and has managed to avoid much of the political backlash associated with officer downsizing.

Potential social issues arising from the need to reabsorb these personnel into civilian life are being addressed through a complex reconversion process undertaken with the assistance of the World Bank. The programme provides for job placement, small business start-up counselling, and professional cross-over training. The Higher Military Academy and Staff College also provides officers within three years of retirement with reconversion training and the MOD has signed post-retirement employment agreements with several government ministries.

Conscription has been cut back periodically over the last ten years and is now less than 20,000 annually in a population of 22 million. According to the Romanian Constitution and law regarding the preparation of the population for defence, military service is obligatory for all males of 20 years of age. Conscientious objectors have been able to choose alternative service to the community since 1997. The MOD has discussed whether the elimination of conscription would not be preferable to its radical reduction.[30] In February 2002, an incident in which two recruits stole arms, shot their commanding officer, and killed two civilians provoked a thorough reorganisation of the recruitment and evaluation processes. In March 2002, the MOD proposed an amendment to the Romanian Constitution phasing out conscription in stages beginning in 2003.

Romanians are supportive of the RAF's restructuring programme, which is set to achieve a 68 per cent professional force during 2003 (reaching 71 per cent in 2004). This support is high across the board for all income levels (see Figure 8.5).

Support for a smaller professional force is also high among those eligible for service (18 to 55 years), while those of 55 and over are almost evenly split on the issue (Figure 8.6).[31]

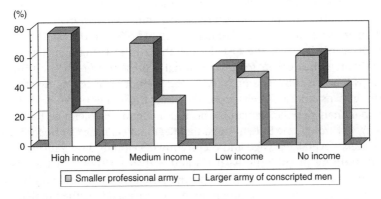

*Figure 8.5*  Public support for smaller professional army (by income level)
*Source*: Metro Media Transylvania, 11–13 February 2001.

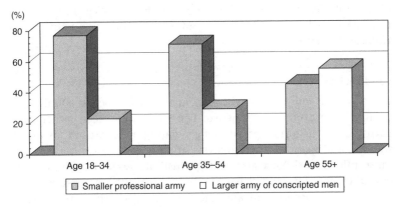

*Figure 8.6*  Public support for smaller professional army (by age group)
*Source*: Metro Media Transylvania, 11–13 February 2001.

## Minorities

Women currently make up 3 per cent of the RAF's officer and NCO corps. Their recruitment was frozen after the fall of communism and only re-introduced in 2001. Since this represents a return to previous practice, it has not raised any special problems and women continue to serve in both administrative and operational roles including, for example, as helicopter pilots. Selection criteria are similar to those for male personnel and regulations provide equal educational, training and career opportunities. However, women are not permitted to join as conscripts or contract enlisted personnel.[32] Currently, there are 1332 female officers and NCOs, with 172 women in the Higher Military College, 88 in NCO schools and 55 in the various service academies. Women make up more than 50 per cent of the civilian personnel – 18,574 – in the MOD.

Occasionally over the last decade the ethnic Hungarian party in parliament has called for proportional representation in the officer corps.[33] Since 1989, the military career has not attracted many ethnic Hungarians, and such calls probably reflect the wishes of political elites rather than popular demand. The RAF introduced tolerance training (largely through the British-Romanian Regional Training Centre for Staff Officers) several years ago and is currently developing a tolerance/diversity training programme with US and British assistance at the basic training and NCO levels. Although the Roma/Gypsy population is the main target group of such programmes, they also address the problem of minority recruitment and retention generally. A Roma commission has been set up and is operating within the RAF to work on recruitment issues and to address specific problems of military personnel from this community. In March 2002, the National Defence College introduced a Holocaust teaching unit in its programme in cooperation with the US Holocaust Museum.[34]

## Civil society

The 'strategic community' within Romanian civil society is only now beginning to exert real influence. The process has been rather slow, partly due to the former practice of generating these institutions within the RAF and granting their analysts military rank prior to 1989. The most influential defence and strategic institutes so far have been those embedded in international associations, such as the Mannfred Woerner Euro-Atlantic Association and the George C. Marshall Association. These institutes also have the greatest degree of civilian–military cross-fertilisation. In 2001 they joined forces with several other associations to form the NATO House (*Casa* NATO). Other institutions specialising in this domain, such as the European Institute for Risk, Security and Communication Management (EURISC) for example, have also begun to establish their own influence.

One explanation for the delay in the development of this community is that prior to 1996 most Romanian NGOs representing civic society were 'captured' by opposition parties and became extremely partisan. For example, the overt partisanship of the Civic Alliance culminated with its entrance into the Democratic Convention government in 1997, while the Group for Social Dialogue campaigned openly for President Constantinescu. There has been a general maturing of defence and security NGOs over the last five years, and the fact that a large number of analysts have passed through the training programme for civilian defence managers at Romania's National Defence College (established in 1991) has laid the groundwork for common approaches to these issues.

## Media

Postcommunist civilian and military elites were quick to grasp the fact that the public image of the armed forces is an inherent component of its combat capability, and that any decrease in public support and funding could diminish the military's ability to fulfil basic missions at home and abroad. In order to build and maintain public support for reform at home and operations abroad, Romania instituted a media outreach programme under the Directorate of Public Relations (DPR) within the MOD in 1991.

The DPR regularly informs the public on how public funds are spent, on the progress of reform efforts in downsizing and restructuring, and on military training, combat readiness and military living standards. It also reports on the status of NATO integration efforts and on participation in UN, Partnership for Peace, and NATO-led peace support and counter-terrorism operations. During 2001, 79 civilian-media organisations and 102 journalists were accredited to the MOD. Likewise, the MOD issued 409 press communiqués (over four times more than any other ministry), and brought journalists along on 40 working visits at home and abroad (see Figure 8.7).

The DPR produces a weekly newspaper, a weekly radio broadcast and a weekly TV programme. As part of its mandate the DPR also organises international conferences and public debates on topics such as 'The Armed Forces and Society', 'Military Careers and Youth in the Armed

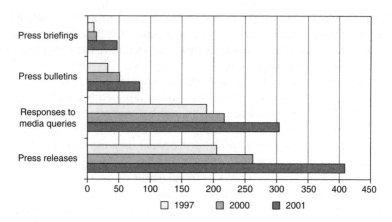

*Figure 8.7*   MOD media activities 1997–2001

*Sources*: Directorate of Public Relations, Department of Parliamentary Relations, Legislative Harmonisation and Public Relations, Romanian Ministry of National Defence.

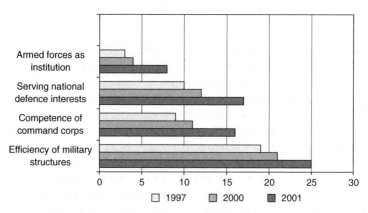

*Figure 8.8*   Positive references in the media 1997–2001

*Sources*: Media Monitoring Section, Directorate of Public Relations, Department of Parliamentary Relations, Legislative Harmonisation and Public Relations, Romanian Ministry of National Defence.

Forces', 'Transparency of Security – Security of Transparency' and 'Defence of Transparency – Transparency of Defence'. Since 2001, press briefing transcripts and recordings, backgrounders and the Romanian Military Newsletter have also been made available to the media and the public via the ministry's internet website, more than doubling the public information activities of the RAF. The MOD worked with civilian universities to introduce a syllabus on NATO studies in 2001.

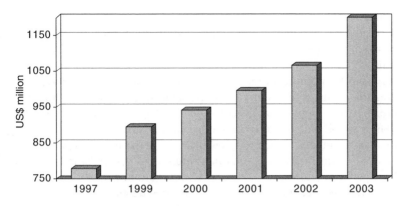

*Figure 8.9* Defence expenditures 1997–2003
*Source*: Department of Defence Policy, Romanian Ministry of National Defence.

The DPR monitors media coverage of the military (nine TV stations, three wire services and 32 publications), responding to inaccuracies and criticism. The stable frequency of negative references in the media and increase in positive references may be partly attributed to the media outreach programme (see Figure 8.8).

### Economic constraints

The most serious challenge to maintaining the linkage between the armed forces and society is economic. In 1999, under pressure from the International Monetary Fund, the government reduced the defence budget below 2 per cent of GDP for the first time since 1991. In 2000 the defence budget again reached 2 per cent, increasing to 2.4 per cent of the GDP in 2001 and 2.6 per cent in 2002 (see Figure 8.9). The present government has committed itself to defence budgets of at least 2.4 per cent of GDP through 2004.

To some degree, significant economic growth during 2001 (5.3 per cent) and 2002 (4.5 per cent) permitted the renewed financial effort. If, however, the global recession has a greater than anticipated impact on Romania, or if some other blockage should reverse current trends, then there may be greater societal pressure to reduce defence budgets that could undermine public support for financially demanding deployments abroad. Of course, this would depend upon the degree to which those deployments were perceived as directly impacting on Romanian security. The generalised understanding within the RAF that economic growth conditions Romania's military modernisation accounts for the correspondingly high levels of support within the military for continued economic reform.

In spite of the economic exigencies, and contrary to what might be surmised by popular support for a smaller professional military, the Romanian armed forces are in the enviable situation of also enjoying broad public support for larger defence budgets. According to a 2001 poll, a significant majority of the population (63 per cent) favoured increased defence allocations even at the expense of other public sectors, indicating that Romanians neither equated 'smaller' with 'cheaper', nor (currently) balked at further economic trade-offs in order to ensure their security in a relatively unstable region.[35]

### Corruption

The corruption evident between 1997 and 2000 in the administration of Emil Constantinescu and the Democratic Convention government undermined their credibility and cost them public support to such an extent that the Convention was not able to muster the minimum required to enter parliament in the 2000 elections. Likewise, the PSD government under Prime Minister Adrian Nastase has been plagued by corruption allegations. These allegations also undermine public support at the institutional level. The MOD is well aware that if corruption is not addressed in a timely and effective manner then the military could lose the public support necessary to fulfil its strategic mission.

The RAF made measurable progress in combating this phenomenon in 2001 and 2002. For the first time since 1989, it conducted a complete inventory of its military equipment and real property, and opened official investigations into property transfers and a number of high-profile procurements. The government has transferred the defence industry from military control, ended the bulk of subsidies to defence industries, and significantly downsized defence industry personnel. Since 2001, the RAF has had a programme-based budget and a functioning Planning, Programming, Budgeting and Evaluation System (PPBES). It is now possible to trace allocations to specific military units, their breakdown, and how they are actually expended.

In March 2002, within a general governmental programme of electronic public acquisitions designed partly to stem corruption problems in this sphere, a system of e-procurement was implemented. Currently, this system is obligatory for all acquisitions in the RAF under US$200,000, and the MOD is undertaking inspections to ensure that the new methodology is applied universally throughout the RAF.

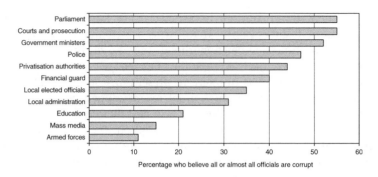

*Figure 8.10*  Public perception of levels of corruption
*Source*: World Bank.

The RAF's openness in dealing with corruption has won over public opinion, which continues to view the military as the least tainted of all state agencies and public institutions.[36] In the public estimation, the military is consistently ranked as less corrupt than even those institutions closest to the everyday life of the average citizen, including the mass media, locally elected institutions and individuals, and education authorities (Figure 8.10).

## Future challenges for the relationship

Although there are a number of issues that will remain on the radar over the next decade – such as recruitment of women and minorities, downsizing and conscription and corruption – they are all currently being addressed in a manner that suggests that they are unlikely to present a serious challenge to the military–society relationship. Some hypothetical challenges, such as serious casualties incurred in one of the deployments that might affect current willingness to place troops in harm's way, can only be tested by a worst-case scenario. However, this problem exists for all combatants and there is no sign that it would constitute a special challenge for Romania. As of the end of 2002, the RAF had suffered seven casualties in peacekeeping operations (four in Angola, two in Bosnia and one in Kosovo) with no apparent negative impact on public support.

Given the power of traditional mythos, ongoing regional instability, the new terrorist threat, and the regularity of seasonal environmental disasters requiring the assistance of the RAF, problems or difficulties in legitimising the armed forces are unlikely to appear over the next decade. The RAF will continue to be perceived by Romanian society as the last line of defence against external threat, as attempting to establish order in their immediate neighbourhood, and as directly and regularly assisting Romanian citizens in their time of need.

General recruitment is unlikely to present any special challenges during the same period, although problems may appear beyond it. The military profession is held in high esteem and there is currently more popular desire than military need for conscription. The high standing of military education institutions, which has increased with postcommunist reforms and is likely to do so for the next five years as the result of NATO-standardising improvements, will continue to draw students.

Retention issues may be more problematic over the medium term since pay differentials between the military and civilian professions are great. However, the RAF is well aware of this problem and it is expected that the achievement of restructuring and downsizing targets, coupled with improvements in housing, medical benefits and NATO-standard living conditions will help to ameliorate this problem before it begins to affect military–society relations. In any case, the situation within the military seems to be improving. Morale and expectations experienced a significant decline between 1997 and 2000 as the standard of living for military professionals and their families suffered under a shrinking economy. This trend continued into January 2001. However, for the first time in four years, in February 2001, hopes and expectations of improvement increased along three axes: in standard of living, in a more coherent military reform and in the intention of political leaders to satisfy the equipment and training needs of the military.[37]

Barring a sudden downturn in the world economy or a sudden reversal in Romanian economic reform processes and growth, securing appropriate public expenditures for defence should not arise as a problem in the next five years. This stability rests on the strong standing of the military because of its national defence and normative roles, and on predictions of fairly constant growth during this period. The Romanian population is accustomed to paying a significant proportion of its GDP for defence and it continues to feel that this expense is justified due to regional instability and the international prestige associated with peace support and anti-terrorism deployments. There also appears to be a general understanding that the standard of living of the nation's soldiers is extremely low. However, at the edge of this period and beyond, economic constraints may constitute the greatest challenge to military–society relations, all other factors being equal.

## Conclusions

The independence of the Romanian Armed Forces from Soviet control within the Warsaw Pact, coupled with the hostility shown by Romania's increasingly unpopular communist dictator towards the military, provided Romanian military–society relations with a solid foundation at the start of the postcommunist period and permitted it to develop a reputation as the most effective institutional reformer. Perennial regional instabilities, annual natural disaster relief requirements within the country, and the central importance of military performance for Euro–Atlantic integration, have maintained the salience of traditional national defender and state builder roles. Since 1990, new normative roles in regional and out-of-area peace support and humanitarian operations have reinforced national security and generated pride among average Romanians, international recognition for Romania, and social prestige for the armed forces. The salience of old military roles and the popularity of new normative roles have combined to make Romania's military–society relationship one of the more robust in the postcommunist era.

Its unusual status as a fully field-capable military at the start of the democratic transition, and the lack of inherited civil–military antagonisms, enabled the RAF to undertake a number of measures in restructuring and addressing social issues that led developments within society at large. Most important was the early recognition that public support was an inherent component of combat capacity, and of the RAF's ability to fulfil its strategic mission. The subsequent extensive media and public outreach programmes have served both the military and the public discussion of defence-related issues extremely well.

Corruption and economic constraints could still prove spoilers. The Ministry of Defence and the government have undertaken a series of measures indicating their understanding of the problem of corruption and appear determined to redress it. So far, public approval indicates that they are on the right track. While the Romanian economy grew significantly in 2001–2002, and is projected to grow similarly in 2003, it did experience severe difficulties between 1997 and 2000, and economically generated pressures did compel a reduction in defence expenditures. Substantial internationally or internally generated shocks to the economy could bring about similar consequences, which may in turn have quite important effects on Romania's military–society relations.

# Notes

1. Mark Axworthy, *Third Axis, Fourth Ally: the Romanian Army in World War II* (London: Arms and Armour, 1996), 185–218. Romania was not granted co-belligerent status at the end of the war due to Soviet veto.
2. See, for example, *Instructiuni ministeriale asupra intrebuintarii armatei in caz de tulburari* (Bucharest, n.p., 1907), 7–10, 20–3; and article 10 in *Regulamentul asupra serviciului interior pentru toate trupele* (Bucharest: n.p., 1918).
3. Arhiva Ministerului Apararii National (MApN), file no. 1476/1933, p. 1, and *Instructiune relative la tulburari interne*, file no. 333/1932, 1–3.
4. Ivan Volgyes, *The Political Reliability of the Warsaw Pact Armies: the Southern Tier* (Durham, NC: Duke University Press, 1982), 47–8; and Walter M. Bacon, Jr, 'Romania', in Daniel N. Nelson (ed.), *The Soviet Allies: the Warsaw Pact and the Issue of Reliability* (Boulder: Westview, 1984), 254.
5. *Ordonanta de urgenta privind regimul starii de asediu si regimul starii de urgenta, nr. 1/1999*, and *Cronica Romana, Romania Libera*, and *Curierul National* for 20–27 January 1999.
6. Robert D. Kaplan, 'Europe's Fulcrum State', *Atlantic Monthly*, 292:3 (September 1998), 34–6.
7. Larry L. Watts, 'Reform and Crisis in Romanian Civil–Military Relations: 1989–1999', *Armed Forces and Society*, 27:4 (Summer 2001), 610.
8. In contrast: 'At no point in the communist period was the Polish General Staff in a position to plan for an all-out defence of the country's territory', and the Polish Defence Ministry 'had no control over the Polish operational army', Andrew A. Michta, *The Soldier-Citizen: the Politics of the Polish Army after Communism* (New York: St Martin's Press, 1998), 84.
9. Christopher D. Jones, *Soviet Influence in Eastern Europe: Political Autonomy and the Warsaw Pact* (New York: Praeger, 1981), 117–18.
10. Alex Alexiev, *Romania and the Warsaw Pact: the Defence Policy of a Reluctant Ally* P6270 (Santa Monica: RAND Corporation, 1979), 17.
11. *Apararea nationala a Romaniei socialiste: Documente, 1965–1977* (Bucharest: Editura Militara, 1982), 527–54.
12. *Scinteia* (Bucharest), 15 August 1968; Radio Bucharest, 21 August 1968; and Michael Costello, 'Rumania and Her Allies: August 21 and After', Rumanian Background Report 12, *RFE Research*, 6 September 1968.
13. Bacon, 'Romania', 254.
14. *Armees D'Aujourd'hui*, 22 (July–August 1977), 60–9; Volgyes, *The Political Reliability*, 47–8; Robert W. Clawson and Lawrence S. Kaplan, eds, *The Warsaw Pact: Political Purpose and Military Means* (Wilmington, Delaware: Scholarly Resources Inc., 1982), 223–4.
15. Aurel Braun, 'The Yugoslav/Romanian Concept of People's War,' *Canadian Defence Quarterly*, 7:1 (Summer 1977), 39–43.
16. See, for example, A. Ross Johnson, *The Warsaw Pact: Soviet Military Policy in Eastern Europe* P6583 (Santa Monica: RAND Corporation, 1981), 4n, 19, 30–4; Ryszard J. Kuklinski, 'The War against the Nation as Seen from Inside', *Kultura* (Paris), 4:475 (Spring 1987), 3–57; and Victor Suvorov, *Inside the Soviet Army* (New York: Berkeley Books, 1982), 3–11.

17. Alex Alexiev, *Party-Military Relations in Eastern Europe: the Case of Romania* (Los Angeles: Center for Strategic and International Affairs, University of California at Los Angeles, 1979), 20–3.
18. Walter M. Bacon, Jr, 'Romanian Military Policy in the 1980s', in Daniel N. Nelson (ed.), *Romania in the 1980s* (Boulder: Westview, 1981), 209–10.
19. See, for example, *Armata Romana in Revolutia din Decembrie 1989* (Bucharest: Editura Militara, 1998).
20. Mark R. Shelley, 'NATO Enlargement: the Case for Romania', *Central European Issues*, 3:1 (Summer 1997), 98–9; Kaplan, 'Europe's Fulcrum', 35.
21. Thomas S. Szayna and F. Stephen Larrabee, *East European Military Reform after the Cold War: Implications for the US* (Santa Monica: RAND, 1995), 2, footnote 3.
22. Larry L. Watts, 'Reforming Civil–Military Relations in Postcommunist States: Civil Control vs. Democratic Control', *Journal of Political and Military Sociology*, 30:1 (Summer 2002).
23. According to British military analysts, 'Romania's unique military position within the Warsaw Pact ensured that the military were able to think and take decisions for themselves'. *Review of Parliamentary Oversight of the Romanian Ministry of National Defence and the Democratic Control of its Armed Forces*, DMCS Study No. 43/96 (London: Directorate of Management and Consultancy Services, 1997), 30. In contrast, US analysts concluded that 'high-ranking Polish officers never made major decisions', Michta, *The Soldier-Citizen*, 101.
24. Jeffrey Simon, *NATO Enlargement and Central Europe: a Study in Civil–Military Relations* (Washington DC: National Defense University, 1996); and Michta, *The Solider-Citizen*, 55–62.
25. See, for example, www.state.gov/www/background_notes/romania/0700_bgn.html. See also the INSOMAR poll of 24–27 April 2001, *Curentul*, 7 May 2001; and Institutul Roman pentru Sondarea Opiniei Publice (IRSOP), 8–10 October 2001; *Jurnalul National* and *Adevarul*, 12 October 2001.
26. See, for example, Larry L. Watts, 'Democratic Civil Control of the Military in Romania: an Assessment as of October 2001', in Graeme P. Herd (ed.), *Civil–Military Relations in Post-Cold War Europe* (Sandhurst: Conflict Studies Research Centre, December 2001), 14–42.
27. Metro Media Transylvania, May 1999.
28. Public opinion polls for NATO performed by Metro Media Transylvania for March 1997, May 1999, May 2000, February 2001. The December 1998 poll performed by the Centre for Urban and Rural Sociology (CURS).
29. NATO's Strategic Concept 1999.
30. *Comunicat M.Ap.N. nr.55/8 feb – Precizari SMG privind executarea serviciului militar*, www.mapn.ro.
31. Metro Media Transylvania, *Population's Attitudes Concerning the Military*, February 2001.
32. Major General Constantin Gheorghe, 'Force Restructuring', in Larry L. Watts (ed.), *Romanian Military Reform and NATO Integration* (Iasi-Oxford: Center for Romanian Studies, 2002).
33. See, for example, *Adevarul* and *Curierul National*, 4 March 2002.
34. Radio Free Europe/RL Newsline, Vol. 6, No. 52, Part II, 19 March 2002.

35. Metro Media Transylvania, *Population's Attitudes*, February 2001.
36. *Diagnostic Surveys of Corruption in Romania* (Bucharest: World Bank, March 2001), vii, 5.
37. Psycho-Social Research Section, General Staff, *Values, Norms and Mentalities in the Military Environment* (Bucharest: Romanian Ministry of National Defence, 2001).

# 9
## Still the People's Army? Armed Forces and Society in Bulgaria
*Laura Cleary*

Bulgaria's entire history has been a quest for unity and integration. Through force of arms the Balkan peoples have been unified on a number of occasions although the ultimate goal of being viewed as an integral part of European politics and culture has remained elusive. That changed on 26 May 2002, when Rafael Estrella, president of the NATO Parliamentary Assembly, announced that 'the construction of Europe and of NATO's new architecture would be incomplete if Bulgaria was not a full member'.[1] This success and indeed the November 2002 invitation to join NATO was made possible by a series of subtle changes in the way in which Bulgarian society and the military view the functional imperative. Over the last 1400 years the armies of Bulgaria have been principally concerned with state building.[2] The armed forces have also been engaged in the provision of National Security and Regime Defence, but their activities on these fronts have generally served the same purpose, the advancement of Bulgarian nationalism.

Irredentism is no longer tolerated within the European community and so the national ambitions of society and the military have had to find another outlet. The Bulgarian Armed Forces (BAF) remain concerned with issues of state building, but given that their activities on this front are increasingly socio-political in nature it is appropriate to conclude that the distinction normally drawn between state and Nation Builder roles is of diminishing significance in the case of Bulgaria. The legitimacy of the BAF is predominantly determined by the extent to which they adhere to Bulgaria's constitutional framework. Success on this front is likely in turn to enhance their National Security role, since it is widely recognised that internal political and economic instability and regional discord are the greatest threats to national security. Underpinning both roles is the BAF's involvement in Military Diplomacy. The BAF's

Military Diplomacy role is primarily concerned with demonstrating that the country adheres to the principles of the 'European project'. Bulgarian national security ultimately will be achieved through successful territorial defence *and* the nation's adherence to democratic norms. The BAF are therefore exposed to pressure from internal and external forces to adhere to this interpretation of security. However, internal political and economic constraints have made compliance far more difficult. The Bulgarian people continue to view the armed forces as necessary and legitimate, but this does not always translate into financial support. Within the foreseeable future relations between the military and civil society will be affected by two key issues, the ability of the Bulgarian political elite and the electorate to internalise the European identity, and the state of the national economy.

## Context

Bulgaria's geostrategic location has had a direct bearing on the development of Bulgarian national identity.[3] Rich in arable soil and at the intersection of several major trade routes, the lands which constitute modern Bulgaria were of interest first to a number of nomadic tribes, chief among these being the Bulgars and the Slavs, and then to existing or emerging great powers.[4] The foundations of a Bulgarian state were made possible by a gradual fusion, from the sixth century onwards, of the warlike tendencies of the Bulgars with the pastoral and mercantile interests of the Slavs. A clear delineation of responsibilities was achieved; the Bulgar nobles coordinated the defence of the state, while the Slav nobility oversaw the political and cultural development of the people.[5]

The creation of a national identity, as well as the very existence of a Bulgarian state independent of the great powers, was dependent upon the ability of the leaders to play the competing interests of the great powers off against one another and adopt opposing influences. Under the leadership of rulers such as Khan Krum (804–14), Boris I (865–93) and Tsar Simeon I (893–927), the armies of Bulgaria succeeded in repulsing challenges from the Byzantine Empire and the nascent Kingdom of Rus, unifying the indigenous peoples and extending the frontiers of the state. These military feats were accompanied by equally impressive political machinations. Boris I's successful manipulation of both Rome and Constantinople resulted in the extension of the first Bulgarian Empire, the nation's conversion to Christianity, the introduction of Slavonic and the creation of an independent patriarch. The combination of these military and political activities resulted in the creation of a state and an empire, but also of an idea, the notion of a 'Greater Bulgaria'. The concept is based on the belief that a form of peaceful coexistence has prevailed among the disparate tribes, which has not been replicated in other Balkan states. Political and cultural stability allied with military strength gave rise to the belief within society and the political elites that Bulgaria had an important role to play in stabilising the Balkans.

Although Bulgaria succumbed to the Byzantine Empire in the twelfth century and was subsequently subsumed within the Ottoman Empire in the fifteenth century, the belief in a political destiny and the memory of previous military exploits fuelled the development of Bulgarian nationalism and the desire for independence from the Turks. The *haidouk* movement, a guerrilla-based organisation that staged a series of liberation uprisings from 1408 onwards, was instrumental in sustaining the morale and preserving the honour of the Bulgarians. It was this movement that formed the basis for the armed insurrections staged by men such as Rakovski in the 1860s. Ten years later the Russians would be credited with the liberation of Bulgaria from Ottoman rule, but it was the Bulgarian militias which struck the first blow.

The link between military valour and national honour formed the bedrock of the newly independent state. Prince Alexander von Battenburg (1879–86) sought to encourage the sentiments of honour and national consciousness through the establishment of an autonomous national army.[6] His task was not easy to achieve, for in accordance with the Treaty of San Stefano (1876) and the Congress of Berlin (1878), the senior ranks of the BAF had to be filled by Russian officers, appointed by the Tsar of Russia.[7] This arrangement was not conducive to good governance, as it was unclear as to whether the senior officers were loyal and accountable to the Prince, the Bulgarian constitution, or the Tsar of Russia. By many accounts the latter was the case.[8] In 1884 Prince Alexander, motivated as much by the desire to inculcate a sense of national honour as he was by the need to assert appropriate controls over the army, induced the National Assembly to pass a resolution dismissing all junior Russian officers serving in the Bulgarian army. The move resulted in the replacement of all staff officers and four-fifths of the captains by Bulgarians. The senior staff might still serve Russia, but the junior staff would fight for Bulgaria. This proved to be a decisive move, for in 1885 these patriotic Bulgarian officers would succeed in reuniting Bulgaria with Rumelia in the south-east and achieve victory over Serbia to the west.

Through his efforts to establish an autonomous army, unify Bulgaria and repulse a Serbian invasion, Prince Alexander encouraged the renaissance of 'Greater Bulgaria' and the belief among the people that the state could exist on its own. Yet despite these achievements, or indeed because of them, elements of the military staged a coup in 1886. There are two reasons for this. First, Russia continued to influence and control the senior echelons, who in turn sought to destabilise the lower ranks if it suited Russia's purpose. Second, junior officers, having been encouraged to demonstrate their autonomy and initiative by their Commander-in-Chief, the Prince, were later rebuffed and passed over for promotion by him as he attempted to placate Russia and avoid further intrusion into Bulgarian affairs. The question which individual officers had to address was which regime to defend: a puppet state, perpetually subservient to Russia, or a truly autonomous one. Public opinion was strongly in favour of the Prince and the Constitution, and it was this opinion which eventually swayed the military.[9]

The desire for national autonomy and unity led the military to intervene in politics throughout the early twentieth century. Despite military success in the First Balkan War (1912) Bulgaria did not make any significant territorial gains in the settlement. She subsequently lost territory in the Second Balkan War (1913) and again at the conclusion of the First World War with the signing of the Treaty of Neuille (1918). Having started the century with one of the best equipped and most disciplined armies in Europe, Bulgaria found itself abolishing its military service. This, coupled with the need to pay heavy reparations, led to wide-scale public unrest. The settlements were an affront not only to the military but also to national honour. Disgruntled soldiers and officers allied themselves with a variety of political movements that advocated overturning the reparations and restoring Bulgarian national honour. The military league of the Bulgarian Communist Party (BCP), the *Zveno* (Link) movement and the pseudo-fascist government, to varying degrees, received support from the military throughout the interwar period.

Samuel Finer argued that the level of political culture is a determining factor in whether or not the military will intervene in politics.[10] 'Where public attachment to civilian institutions is strong, military intervention in politics is weak.'[11] This hypothesis is only partly applicable in the case of Bulgaria. Bulgaria has been politically immature in terms of public allegiance to political parties; however there has been very strong support for the actual institutions of government. Generally the military's decision to intervene in politics has been motivated either by a desire to protect the territorial integrity of the state, or to fulfil the nation's irredentist aspirations. Public opinion has been influential on these occasions. In the case of the 1886 coup, the public did not believe that the military's action was the best means of ensuring the sovereignty of the state. In contrast, as regards the military's intervention in the 1920s, public and military opinion coalesced on the need to lift the heavy burden of war reparations.

Given the volatile political climate of the 1920s and 1930s, it is not surprising that the BCP should have sought to assert its control over the armed forces. The Communist Party's seizure of power in 1946 was not universally accepted. Despite the introduction of a regime of terror, some 30 per cent of the population dared to vote against the BCP.[12] If the regime were to survive, it was imperative that the army should no longer be available to the nationalist cause. Ironically, during the period in which it was referred to as the 'People's Army' the BAF was far more concerned with the defence of a particular regime.

The measures adopted by the BCP to exert control over the military were comprehensive. Between 1944 and 1947 a purge was conducted to eliminate officers who had been loyal to Germany during the Second World War. The armed forces became subordinate to the Communist Party, professional military personnel were indoctrinated with Marxist–Leninist dogma, and political loyalty was made a more important criterion than professional competence in the selection of new officers.[13] In the end some 80 per cent of the officer corps were members of the BCP. Nevertheless, a nationalist commitment remained and this nationalism manifested itself in a desire for a degree of autonomy. Throughout the 1950s and 1960s, the public and the military opposed Bulgaria's ever-closer affiliation with the Soviet Union. Indeed, in 1965 General Ivan Todorov-Gorunia led a failed coup attempt against President Todor Zhivkov to replace him and establish a more nationalist, less pro-Soviet leadership in the country.

Throughout its long history the BAF's principal focus has been on Nation Building and the military's ability to act as a 'symbolic embodiment of national values'.[14] The armies of Bulgaria have certainly done that, both at the time of Ottoman rule and latterly during the communist era, but they have also been involved in the establishment of the state and in state-making. Charles Tilly suggests four major elements to this: first, *war-making*: eliminating or neutralising their own rivals outside the territories in which they have clear and continuous priority as wielders of force. Second, *state-making*: eliminating or neutralising their rivals inside those territories. Third, *protection*: eliminating or neutralising the enemies of their clients. Finally, *extraction*: acquiring the means of carrying out the first three activities – war-making, state-making and protection.[15]

The armies of Bulgaria have performed all four of the activities identified by Tilly, as well as the Nation Builder role outlined in Chapter 1.
They have been engaged in war-making, eliminating or neutralising the
Byzantine Empire, the Kingdom of Rus and the Serbs. They have been
involved in state-making when they have either adhered to the constitutional framework or, conversely, when they have chosen to support
particular regimes. They have offered protection, and they have been
engaged in extraction, particularly when attempting to establish the
state between the sixth and ninth centuries and again in the nineteenth.
Throughout the entire process the military has been instrumental in
giving rise to a national consciousness. When the Nation Builder role is
understood in this way then it becomes as central in the absolute as
either National Security or Regime Defence roles. In the case of Bulgaria
the National Security and Regime Defence roles are complements to the
armed forces' Nation Building role. Since 1989 this continues to be the
case, but with a Military Diplomacy role supplanting the role of Regime
Defence.

The Nation Builder role has evolved to the extent that success is now
determined by the military's ability to adhere to the constitutional
framework and implement the social mission. Since 1989 the armed
forces and the political elite have advanced two organisational objectives:
first, to return the BAF to its traditional role of being above politics; and
second, for officers to be viewed once again as the legal representatives of
the national security interest.[16] The first postcommunist government
acted quickly in 1990 to depoliticise the BAF and ensure their political
neutrality.[17] This process was taken a stage further with the election of
the Union of Democratic Forces in 1997. Through an extensive series of
legislation the Kostov government of 1997 to 2001 sought to integrate
the military into the broader democratic framework of the state.[18]
This was achieved by clearly defining the role of the armed forces, their
rights and obligations, their relationship vis-à-vis the executive and the
legislature, and most importantly with society.

In the communist period, the BAF contributed to the socialisation and
education of young Bulgarian citizens. Since 1989, the BAF continues to
integrate social and ethnic groups in society, but within a 'European',
rather than a Soviet/Socialist, perspective. Perhaps the most significant
aspect of the social mission is the BAF's ability to act as a bridgehead to
Europe and here the military has been instrumental in clarifying the
goals and strategy for Bulgaria's integration into NATO and the EU.

Acceptance of Bulgarians of this social mission varies. Many Bulgarians
over the age of 45 continue to value the military's socialisation role and

feel that it achieves a level of ethnic integration but that it is also the best means of instilling patriotic values.[19] The younger generations, which are generally opposed to conscription, believe that a socialisation policy is no longer necessary and that alternative forms of education are more appropriate for the conditions in which Bulgaria now finds itself. There does, however, appear to be wide-scale support for the employment of the BAF as a link to the EU and NATO.[20] This manifests itself in general approval for the protection of the rights of service personnel, the assertion of democratic civilian control over the armed forces and their participation in joint EU or NATO exercises. It is generally felt that integration into Europe will improve conditions within Bulgaria and enhance national security. In a survey conducted in 1998, 56.9 per cent of students believed that full-rights membership of NATO and the EU would be the best guarantee for Bulgarian national security.[21]

During the Cold War Bulgarians believed that capitalism and the blatant aggression of NATO threatened their security. Today, most Bulgarians understand that security can be undermined by threats of an economic, political, social, ethnic or religious nature that can arise at both the domestic and international level, and which can be compounded by the emergence of international criminal networks. Some of these threats can be mitigated by improved economic conditions within Bulgaria itself and others by modernising the resources available to the border guards and the police. Other threats can only be countered through the coordinated efforts of external and internal security forces and the establishment of a crisis management system.

The ability of the military to combat these threats is limited and while over 60 per cent of Bulgarians are willing to give the military an 'approval' rating,[22] at the same time 66.8 per cent believe that the Bulgarian army is unable to protect the territorial integrity and sovereignty of the country.[23] Indeed, the opinion of military personnel and most of the electorate is that security can only be guaranteed through full-rights membership of the Euro-Atlantic institutions.[24]

Membership, however, is dependent upon an applicant state's ability to demonstrate its democratic credentials and its willingness to pursue a 'liberal' foreign policy and contribute to international humanitarian operations. Since 1989 the provision of humanitarian aid has become a principal task for armies throughout Europe, and they have restructured accordingly. For Bulgaria the conflict in the Balkans had a greater impact than elsewhere. For example, concern that the conflict and refugees would overspill the country's borders has informed the structure of the crisis management system and policies towards ethnic minorities within society as a whole, and the military in particular.[25] The Bulgarian military has insisted on a 'sober, peaceful and good neighbourly regional policy', and military and political elites have been in agreement on the deployment and the use of force.[26] Bulgarian society has been generally supportive of the armed forces in the pursuit of the policies outlined above; out of 17 possible missions, humanitarian assistance was rated third in a survey conducted in April 1998.[27]

The significance of these roles should not be underestimated. These engagements have contributed to national security, but have also strengthened the Bulgarian state. Participation in joint missions with EU and NATO member states has led to the dissemination of liberal principles throughout the military and society. Bulgarian defence experts are in favour of increased participation in multinational PSOs for three reasons. First, because the military acquires new skills and knowledge. Second, because it advances Bulgaria's foreign policy aim of integration into the Euro-Atlantic security structures. Finally because the act of contributing to global peace and stability reaffirms the nation's self-worth.[28] In the words of Yanakiev and Domozetov, 'Bulgarians tend to support the Armed Forces' participation in socially acceptable missions, i.e. missions connected with help and support of civil society.'[29]

In 1997 Plamen Pantev argued that 'Bulgaria lacks a normal civil society, a normal state of democratic control and a normal civil–military relationship.'[30] From the vantage point of 2003 it is possible to argue that Bulgarian political culture has evolved. Political elites have overcome their residual temptations to involve the armed forces in domestic politics, and the electorate appear to be unwilling to support those who might advocate it. Indeed, senior officers in the BAF appear to have consciously chosen to be 'pragmatic and effectively useful for their people rather than become the "glorious heroes" at the turn of the Twentieth century'.[31] They want to adhere to the constitution rather than to interpret it. As this position becomes more settled the more stable Bulgarian political culture will become and the more secure the nation.

## Domestic, international and transnational influences on the armed forces and society

Since 1989 the overarching themes in Bulgarian politics have been the search for an identity, a role for the nation as a whole, and improvement in the economic and social conditions of the people. All of these issues are closely interlinked and have a direct bearing on the state of civil–military relations.

Bulgarian national identity is fashioned from three counterpoints: the Slavic, Balkan and European identities. Andrey Ivanov suggests that the 'Slavic identity, historically, has been more cultural and less political and social, than European attitudes.'[32] The concept of Balkan identity used here refers to Bulgaria's aspiration to increase stability within the Balkans, while Europe has traditionally 'been the main symbol of social modernisation in Bulgaria'.[33]

At various points in history Bulgaria has been closely allied with Russia, but with the exception of the Soviet period Russia has never provided an appropriate social and political model to follow.[34] The Bulgarian political elite closely watched the political developments in Russia after the fall of communism, but chose not to imitate the political and military structure and culture that emerged. So, although the BAF continued to exploit Russian-made military equipment and armaments, it no longer wished to preserve the social model of civil–military relations.[35]

Neither was it appropriate for Bulgaria to resume its traditional role in the Balkans. What domestically might be viewed as the reunification of the former peoples of 'Greater Bulgaria', might very well look like 'expansionism' to those outside the state. The creation of such a view would not have been conducive to securing foreign investment for domestic economic reform. Thus the only option remaining was to promote a European identity, though as Ivanov argues 'Europe', for many Bulgarians, was simply a 'collective representation of a modern welfare society, and not a clearly defined social project'.[36]

The equation of Europe with social modernisation has meant that the Bulgarian electorate has been generally supportive of the political decision to integrate more closely with European military and political structures. Over the last three years support for EU membership has remained relatively steady at 80 per cent, although it climbed to 95 per cent in February 2002.[37] Support for NATO during the same period has been less buoyant, averaging around the 50 per cent mark, although again there has been an increase in support to 76.9 per cent.[38]

Although there is a desire for the economic prosperity and political stability that closer union with Europe would provide, there is also a general attitude that Bulgaria can take from the West 'only the products that it likes and avoid or postpone the costs'.[39] This selective approach has led to the development of a specific Bulgarian model. Its principal attributes are consistent with a general understanding of 'European values and identity (economic reforms from the bottom up; economic stabilisation and a currency board)' and an emphasis on ethnic tolerance.[40]

In many respects this model is a neutral variant of the 'Greater Bulgaria' model.

This benign model is as much the result of internal social conditions as it is of external forces. Bulgarians are deeply concerned with security; their own and that of the region. Domestic security is defined principally in terms of improved economic welfare; regional security is to be achieved through the promotion of ethnic tolerance. The role of the military is no longer to expand Bulgarian territory, but to contribute to the stabilisation of the region under the auspices of NATO and the EU.

Achieving interoperability has been the main focus of defence reform since 1997. However, the approach adopted conforms with Ivanov's analysis that Bulgaria 'can take what it likes and leave the rest'. It was relatively easy for Bulgaria to establish a democratic framework for defence; it cost little and it could be promoted to the electorate as a return to a more democratic past. Thus there was little or no opposition to the establishment of a normative framework. The 1991 Constitution and subsequent legislation on defence, the armed forces and alternative forms of service clearly delineate the rights, freedoms and responsibilities of all those personnel, military or civilian, engaged in the defence of the nation.[41] A cornerstone of this legislation is the principle that all Bulgarians, no matter what their religion, race or creed, should enjoy equal opportunities for education and employment.

However, this principle has not always been applied in practice and the two groups most frequently disadvantaged have been the Turks and the Roma, who constitute 9.5 and 4.6 per cent of the population. In discussions with serving military personnel and administrators within the Ministry of Defence one gains the sense that discrimination is less of an issue within the military than it is in civil society. It is difficult to substantiate this impression, however, since the demographic profile of the BAF remains classified.

For similar reasons it is also difficult to assess how well women have been integrated into the BAF. Women are allowed to serve in many branches of the forces, but they cannot undertake combat roles. Since 1997 over 1000 women have enlisted in the BAF without incident or public outcry. The decision to enlist is viewed by the general populace as a matter of personal choice.

The restructuring of the BAF has received the greatest public attention. There is a general consensus among the military and civilians that Bulgaria does not face a military threat.[42] As a result the military's relevance began to decline and restructuring was simply equated with downsizing. However, NATO's action in Kosovo had a significant impact on public opinion, and there now appears to be better public understanding both of the complexity of defence reform and the range of missions which the BAF might undertake.

The majority of the electorate also supports the decisions to phase out conscription, restructure the military and join NATO.[43] There is also broad consensus that a range of benefits will accrue: Bulgaria's international standing will improve; national security will be enhanced; accession to the EU will be facilitated; and improvements in force discipline, training, modernisation and prestige will be achieved.[44]

The last is an important issue, for although the electorate gives the BAF a high approval rating, fewer individuals are actually willing to join it. The reasons for this are complex but certainly include inadequate funding and a low quality of life. Moreover, the BAF is undergoing a substantial force reduction, from 100,000 to 45,000, in an immature economic environment. As Pantev et al. highlight, the poverty of the state, high foreign debt – currently just under US$10 billion, or 7.3 per cent of GDP – and inefficient economic reforms have made consistent military reform impossible.[45] At present 80 per cent of the defence budget is spent on personnel costs, and only 3.3 per cent is for future investment.[46] The officer corps is starting to lose its motivation and the military profession its prestige.

Attempts have been made to improve conditions within the armed forces and to provide retraining and resettlement packages for personnel who are dismissed. There are numerous cases, however, of senior officers now working as security guards. There are stories too of men committing suicide after receiving their orders to leave the service. According to Pantev, a level of resentment is also building within society at large. Almost one-third of the working age population is unemployed or underemployed and civilians do not have access to the types of retraining and resettlement programmes available to the military.[47] This could prove to be a significant friction point if economic conditions remain poor.

To date, however, the link between the military and the society that it serves has been retained. Bulgarian political elites and society recognise that future security and stability reside in the adherence to European norms in terms of political and economic organisation, the treatment of ethnic minorities and the appropriate use of military force in the 'post-modern' era. The Bulgarian military has willingly adhered to the democratic principles of the state and has acquitted itself well in the role of military diplomacy, thereby contributing to national security and national self-worth.

## Current and future challenges

The BAF will remain legitimate in the eyes of the people so long as it continues in the Nation Builder role. In the past, success in that role has been determined by the military's ability to fulfil the nation's irredentist aspirations. However, nationalism is no longer equated with expansionism, but with integration and the BAF makes an important contribution to this by adhering to the constitutional framework, implementing the social mission and engaging in Military Diplomacy. The greatest threat to the BAF's continued legitimacy does not therefore arise from the level of political oversight, or the nature of the roles they are asked to perform, but from insufficient financial support.

The Ministry of Defence is currently overhauling the military education system in order to meet NATO standards and recruit and retain better personnel, but success will also depend on improvements in salaries and quality of life for service personnel and their dependants. If the BAF is unable to recruit competent personnel and provide them with access to modern equipment and attractive professional careers then it will be unable to defend Bulgaria, provide domestic military assistance or engage in multinational PSOs. An inability to contribute to PSOs will diminish Bulgaria's contribution to the Euro–Atlantic institutions as a full NATO member. In short, the economy is the key to both political stability and military legitimacy in Bulgaria.

Following the total collapse of the Bulgarian economy between 1991 and 1997, steps were taken to initiate major reforms. There has been a significant improvement, but Bulgarian citizens have yet to feel the benefits. In terms of positive steps, the currency board established by the IMF in 1997 has succeeded in stabilising the Lev and improving financial discipline. Both the Union of Democratic Forces (UDF, 1997–2001) and National Movement for Simeon II (NMSV, 2001 onwards) administrations prioritised privatisation, the liberalisation of prices and the reform of the banking sector. As a result, GDP has improved and within the 2002 budget a 4 per cent growth rate in GDP was envisaged. Inflation has declined from the record levels of the mid-1990s and currently rests at 5.2 per cent. Inward investment is increasing and both the IMF and World Bank have recently promised new loans. Bulgaria has also managed to reorient its trade away from former COMECON countries towards the EU and some analysts have suggested that Bulgaria may well be able to join the EU in 2007. Unemployment, however, remains high, currently resting at 17.9 per cent. The NMSV won the 2001 parliamentary elections by pledging to improve the standard of living within 800 days. The number of strikes and protests that have occurred throughout 2001 and 2002 indicate that the electorate doubt the government's ability to deliver on its pledge.

## Conclusions

Samuel Finer once remarked that Bulgaria was an 'endowment of the army'.[48] Now, at the beginning of the twenty-first century, the BAF is in a position to make another bequest, a place in European institutions. Clearly, the desire to be part of Europe is the principal motivation behind so many of the reforms occurring in Bulgaria today. Having fashioned a national identity from three opposing influences, Bulgarians have collectively decided that the European orientation should now be the dominant theme. As this study demonstrates, the desire to be part of Europe is one shared by citizens, politicians and soldiers. All are agreed that in order to join Europe one must act 'European'. Bulgarian society is increasingly democratic and market oriented and its military is assuming the roles of a twenty-first-century European army. At present, civil–military relations are stable and the BAF considered legitimate. What is remarkable is that the armed forces have met the tough conditions for NATO membership despite inadequate funding and sporadic defence reform.

If, however, NATO accession does not lead to EU membership, if the economic miracle so long promised does not occur, then the link between society and the military may destabilise. Public allegiance to political parties has never been particularly consistent in Bulgaria. In a period of economic insecurity the danger is that political instability may also increase. The BAF has a long history of intervening in politics when it perceives such action to be in the interest of the nation. At the moment, such a scenario appears unlikely. For that to remain the case, reform of the economy must continue. The legitimacy of the BAF and of the state they serve depend upon it.

## Notes

1. RFE/RL Newsline Part II 6:97 (2002) at http://www.rferl.newsline.org.
2. C. Tilly, 'War-Making and State-Making as Organized Crime', in P.B. Evans et al. (eds), *Bringing the State Back in* (Cambridge: Cambridge University Press, 1985).
3. S.E. Finer, *The Man on Horseback: the Role of the Military in Politics*, 2nd edn. (Harmondsworth, Middlesex: Penguin, 1976), 55. See also S. Runciman, *A History of the First Bulgarian Empire* (London: G. Bell & Sons Ltd, 1930).

4. Those great powers with an interest in Bulgaria have included the East Roman (Byzantine) Empire (eight–eleventh century), the Roman Papacy (ninth century), Russia (tenth, nineteenth and twentieth centuries), the Ottoman Empire (fourteenth–nineteenth centuries) and the Austro-Hungarian Empire (nineteenth century).

5. For a history of the birth of the Bulgarian nation and the first Bulgarian Empire see S. Runciman, *A History of the First Bulgarian Empire.*

6. E. Caesar C. Corti, *Alexander von Battenburg*, trans. E.M. Hodgson (London: Cassell and Company Ltd, 1954), 110.

7. The Treaty of San Stefano essentially granted permission for the establishment of a Bulgarian state. After the treaty was signed, however, concerns were expressed about the nature of Russia's involvement in the region. In order to limit Russia's foothold in the Balkans a decision was taken at the Congress of Berlin to divide Bulgaria into three parts. The first was the principality, constituting the northern lands (Moesia), the second was the autonomous province of Eastern Rumelia under the rule of a Turkish sultan, and the third part consisted of Macedonia and part of Thrace which were returned to Turkey.

8. Corti, *Alexander von Battenburg*, 110.

9. Corti, *Alexander von Battenburg*, 186.

10. Finer, *The Man on Horseback*, 18.

11. Finer, *The Man on Horseback*, 18.

12. J.F. Brown, *Bulgaria under Communist Rule* (London: Pall Mall Press Ltd., 1970), 12.

13. Z. Barany, 'Democratic Consolidation and the Military: the East European Experience', *Comparative Politics*, 30:1 (1997), 28.

14. See Chapter 1.

15. It is worth noting that Tilly's model has been criticised for being too simplistic because it concentrates only on capabilities. Karen Rasler and William Thompson argue that the relationship of states to their domestic and transnational social context should also be considered when assessing the ability to make war. I am generally in agreement with Rasler and Thompson but in this particular instance the pared down model is more appropriate to the argument. See Tilly, 'War-Making and State-Making as Organized Crime'. Also, K. Rasler and W. Thompson, *War and State-Making* (Boston: Unwin Hyman, 1989).

16. L. Cleary, 'The New Model Army? Bulgarian Experiences of Professionalisation', in A. Forster, T. Edmunds and A. Cottey *The Challenge of Military Reform in Postcommunist Europe: Building Professional Armed Forces* (Basingstoke: Palgrave Macmillan, 2002).

17. In January 1990 Article 1 of the 1971 Constitution was revoked. The article had institutionalised the exclusive political role of the Bulgarian Communist Party in the armed forces. In September 1990 an additional law was passed requiring the army to respond to the state rather than to the ruling party. Soldiers were further required to relinquish their membership of political parties. For a full discussion of the depoliticisation of the BAF see L. Cleary, 'Out With the Old, in With the New: the Challenge of Asserting Democratic Control of the Armed Forces in Bulgaria', *Defense Analysis*, 17:3 (2001). See also L. Cleary, 'The New Model Army?'.

18. The legislation included the Constitution, the National Security Concept and the Defence of the Armed Forces Act (1995, amended 1997, 2000).
19. V. Ratchev and S. Tassev, 'Civil–Military Relations in Bulgaria', in Laura Richards Cleary and the Atlantic Club of Bulgaria (eds), *Civil–Military Relations: a Guide* (Sofia: ISV, 1999), 73.
20. A. Ivanov, 'The Crystallization of European Identities: the Bulgarian Case', in P. Drulák (ed.), *National and European Identities in EU Enlargement: Views from Central and Eastern Europe* (Prague: Institute for International Relations, 2001).
21. Y. Yanakiev and C. Domozetov, *Public Perceptions of Euro-Atlantic Partnership: Issues of Security and the Military (The Case of Bulgaria)*, Final Report NATO-EAPC Institutional Research Fellowship 1988–2000 (Sofia: North Atlantic Treaty Organisation Office of Information and Press, 2000). Available on-line at http://www.nato.int/acad/fellow/98-00/yanakiev.pdf.
22. Centre for European Security Studies, *Organising National Defences for NATO Membership: the Unexamined Dimension of Aspirants' Readiness for Entry* (Groningen: CESS, 2001), 98.
23. Yanakiev and Domozetov, *Public Perceptions of Euro-Atlantic Partnership*.
24. Yanakiev and Domozetov, *Public Perceptions of Euro-Atlantic Partnership*.
25. P. Pantev, V. Ratchev and T. Tagarev, 'Civil–Military Relations in Bulgaria: Aspects, Factors, Problems', in P. Pantev (ed.), *Civil–Military Relations in South-East Europe: a Survey of the National Perspectives and of the Adaptation Process to the Partnership for Peace Standards*, 53, at http://www.isn.ethz.ch/isis/Frame/frame3index.htm.
26. Pantev et al., 'Civil–Military Relations in Bulgaria', 43.
27. Yanakiev and Domozetov, *Public Perceptions of Euro-Atlantic Partnership*.
28. Yanakiev and Domozetov, *Public Perceptions of Euro-Atlantic Partnership*.
29. Yanakiev and Domozetov, *Public Perceptions of Euro-Atlantic Partnership*.
30. P. Pantev, 'The New National Security Environment and its Impact on the Civil–Military Relations in Bulgaria', Research Study No. 5 (Sofia: Institute for Security and International Relations, 1997). Available at http://www.isn.ethz.ch/isis.
31. Pantev et al., 'Civil–Military Relations in Bulgaria', 34.
32. Ivanov, 'The Crystallization of European Identities', 174.
33. Ivanov, 'The Crystallization of European Identities', 161.
34. Ivanov, 'The Crystallization of European Identities', 174.
35. Pantev et al., 'Civil–Military Relations in Bulgaria', 47.
36. Ivanov, 'The Crystallization of European Identities', 161.
37. Yanakiev and Domozetov, *Public Perceptions of Euro-Atlantic Partnership*; RFE/RL Newsline Part II 6:23 (2002), http://www.rferl.org/newsline.search.
38. Yanakiev and Domozetov, *Public Perceptions of Euro-Atlantic Partnership*; Ivanov, 'The Crystallization of European Identities', 169; CESS, *Organising National Defences for NATO Membership*, 97; 'Bulgaria and NATO: Dynamics of the Public Opinion (1999–2001)' (Sofia: Institute of Sociology to the Bulgarian Academy of Sciences, 2001). Available online at http://www.md.government.bg.
39. Ivanov, 'The Crystallization of European Identities', 166.
40. Ivanov, 'The Crystallization of European Identities', 165.

41. See P. Pantev, 'The Changing Nature of Civil–Military Relations in Post-Totalitarian Bulgaria', in A. Cottey, T. Edmunds and A. Forster (eds), *Democratic Control of the Military in Postcommunist Europe: Guarding the Guards* (Basingstoke: Palgrave Macmillan, 2002).

42. Yanakiev and Domozetov, *Public Perceptions of Euro-Atlantic Partnership.*

43. Cleary, 'The New Model Army?'

44. 'Bulgaria and NATO: Dynamics of the Public Opinion (1999–2001)' (Sofia: Institute of Sociology to the Bulgarian Academy of Sciences, 2002); Yanakiev and Domozetov, *Public Perceptions of Euro-Atlantic Partnership.*

45. Pantev et al., 'Civil–Military Relations in Bulgaria', 51.

46. 'Ministry of Defence Annual Report on the State of the Armed Forces 1999' (Sofia, 2000).

47. Pantev, 'The New National Security Environment', 51–2.

48. Finer, *The Man on Horseback*, 63.

# 10
## 'La Petite Muette' and Suspicious Controller: Armed Forces and Society in Slovenia

*Ljubica Jelušic and Marjan Malešic*

Slovenian military units earned high prestige during the country's so-called Ten-Day War[1] of independence against the Yugoslav People's Army (*Jugoslovenska narodna armija* – JNA) in 1991. At this time, the Slovenian armed forces were comprised of the republican Territorial Defence force (*Teritorialna obrana* – TO), which eventually evolved into the Slovenian armed forces (*Slovenska Vojska* – SV) in 1994. Throughout this period, the military developed bases for its legitimacy in society around the military and political successes of the conflict, and particularly its role in providing territorial national defence and wartime guerrilla tactics against the JNA.

Twelve years on, the legitimising power of the Ten-Day War is gradually dissipating and the SV has had to look for new bases of legitimacy in society. These come from two particular sources: its involvement in peace support operations (PSOs), and its participation in multinational military structures such as NATO. Slovenian public opinion is in favour of the development of a professional, all-volunteer SV, whose main operational tasks should be focused on the defence of national territory – the National Security role – and disaster relief – the Domestic Military Assistance role. In general, however, the SV remains a relatively weak institution in Slovenia – 'la petite muette' of the Slovenian state. This situation results from the military's lack of professional autonomy, a traditional antipathy towards military matters in Slovenian society, and a series of military reforms started in the 1990s but as yet unfinished.

## Military roles and society

The dilemma of fulfilling social, political and functional expectations in the Slovenian military has its roots in the former Yugoslav military which until the death of Josip Broz Tito in 1980 successfully balanced these imperatives. During the 1980s, however, the JNA came under increasing pressure from Yugoslav society in relation to its record on human rights, and particularly on issues such as conscientious objection and the use of national languages and freedom of religion in the military. The JNA's inadequate responses to these pressures increasingly damaged its societal legitimacy.

In 1991, senior officers in the Slovenian TO were well aware of legitimacy problems that the JNA had experienced during the last decade of Yugoslavia's existence. However, although poorly equipped, manned mainly by rather elderly reservists and relatively badly trained, the TO had a higher legitimacy in society than the JNA. Indeed, the events of the Ten-Day War illustrate that a military's strong societal bases for legitimacy can help to overcome its functional weaknesses. The JNA finished the war with empty barracks because its conscript soldiers had fled from them. In contrast, the TO units, though poorly equipped, benefited from a strategy of well-targeted information warfare as well as support from the police and the non-violent obstructionist activities of the Slovenian population more widely.

During the first three years of its existence, the Slovenian armed forces continued to struggle to balance its strong socio-political imperatives with its weak functional ones. In general, its societal acceptance derived from its national character and the fact that it was socially representative. However its war-fighting capabilities remained weak as a result of its low level of military professionalism, limited equipment and poor resources. Although this improved after 1995, it remains a great obstacle in the way of the SV achieving professional autonomy. It also contributes to the rather dysfunctional character of Slovenian civil–military relations over the past 12 years, in which civilian officials exclusively control, direct and decide on defence related matters, and the military's ability to advise on and participate in these issues is very limited.[2]

According to the Slovenian Defence Act of 1994, the fundamental tasks of SV are fivefold. The SV is expected, first, to provide defence in the event of an attack on the country; second, to fulfil Slovenia's obligations to international organisations; third, to train for defence purposes; fourth, to maintain adequate levels of combat readiness; and fifth, to participate in civil emergency operations in the event of natural and other disasters. [3]

In practice, however, it is often difficult to distinguish between some of these tasks and there are also inconsistencies in the implementation of the Defence Act, which may cause the confusion in the public. For example, opinion polls carried out in 1999 show that there are three groups of public expectations with regard to the SV's roles.[4] These are the military's 'defence' role, its 'societal' role, and its 'political' role. 'Defence' expectations focus on the National Security role – the defence of Slovenian territory in the event of armed attack. 'Societal' expectations concern the military's participation in public works such as road building, the patriotic education of young people, dealing with natural disasters, training, and – perhaps surprisingly – participation in international peace and humanitarian operations. In this respect, the Slovenian public does not therefore perceive cooperation in PSOs as a defence task, but as a task that contributes directly to the societal legitimacy of the armed forces. 'Political' expectations relate to issues such as the replacement of workers in the event of major strikes and helping the police to maintain internal order and security. 'Political' tasks are regarded as far less acceptable than those associated with the military's 'defence' and 'societal' role expectations.

## National Security: from homeland defence to international peace activist?

During the first six years of its development, the SV focused its activities on its national defence role. Despite reforms which changed the territorial guerrilla character of the TO into a standing army, by and large the SV remained reluctant to become involved in post-Cold War constabulary roles until 1997. This focus on national defence occurred for two reasons. First, because of the legacy of the military's successes in the Ten-Day War, and second because the TO/SV's historical military experience was rooted firmly in the JNA – which, after all, was designed for homeland defence. This meant that the SV was trained to provide security on a national basis, and that it was not deployable anywhere except on the territory in which it was trained. In particular, the army's manoeuvre capabilities were very limited.

In 1997, the Slovenian government recognised that the country could help to guarantee its own national security by contributing to the security of the region. The first peacekeeping deployment of SV soldiers was in operation ALBA (Albania) in 1997, immediately followed by its participation in the United Nations Peacekeeping Force in Cyprus (UNFICYP) operation. Under UNFICYP, eight contingents, each of 30 soldiers, officers and NCOs gained direct experience of PSOs. In addition, the SV has contributed two officer observers per year to UNTSO (Middle East) since 1998, and one officer per year to UNMIK (Kosovo) since 1999. The SV has also been involved in SFOR (Bosnia), contributing four transport aircraft together with support staff since 1999, a military police platoon of 26 soldiers and officers since 1999 rotated on a six-monthly basis to MSU (Multinational Specialised Unit), and a medical unit of 12 people since 2000. In 2001, the Minister of Defence increased the participation of Slovenian military police in the SFOR operation by two platoons. Moreover, since 2000, the SV has contributed six officers – rotated on a six-monthly basis – to operation 'Joint Guardian' in Kosovo. The Annual National Programme for the Implementation of the NATO Membership Action Plan 2001–2002 states that Slovenia should contribute a total of 142 participants to PSOs in 2002, of whom 112 were drawn from the SV, and 30 from the Slovenian police.

Representatives from the SV often make public statements in which they underline the importance of military cooperation in peacekeeping operations. In particular, they stress the importance of PSOs in allowing Slovenian military personnel to acquire direct military experience, in addition to the more altruistic reasons for peacekeeping deployments. This approach has created an impression in the Slovenian public that one of its military's main roles is as a kind of armed peace activist in crisis areas. Participation in PSOs is an explicit tool of Slovenian foreign policy, and is justified on the grounds that it contributes to both regional and national security. In this sense, the SV's PSO activities coincide with the Military Diplomacy role identified in Chapter 1. Slovenian politicians thus explicitly offer SV and police personnel to UN, NATO, EU and OSCE operations as proof of the country's willingness to take on responsibility for international peace and security.

However, there is also an indirect impact from PSO participation on the SV's traditional National Security role. Officers and soldiers return from missions with many new experiences, especially in relation to operational and logistical procedures. Slovenian participants in NATO-led missions are also a visible illustration of the way in which SV units can be successfully integrated – and made interoperable with – NATO forces.[5] In addition, the SV has been an active recipient of defence diplomacy and many Slovenian soldiers have participated in military and PSO-oriented courses run by the US, UK, Germany, France, Belgium, Switzerland and the Czech Republic. Because of the country's long history of conscription both pre- and post-independence, these missions and courses form an important mechanism for helping to professionalise the SV and indeed lay the groundwork for the introduction of an all-volunteer force.

While it is unlikely that the SV's role in providing homeland defence is going to increase its legitimacy in the near future, by increasing its participation in international PSOs – and thereby contributing to regional stability and security in the eyes of the Slovenian public – it has begun to establish new bases for its legitimacy in society. Although this may ultimately mean an increased defence budget, it is also contributing significantly to Slovenia's international prestige, and opinion polls show that citizens perceive this as a worthwhile military role.

## Military Diplomacy

New emphasis has also been placed on the SV's deployment doctrine after Slovenia joined NATO's Partnership for Peace Programme (PfP) in March 1994. In July the same year, the government presented NATO with its plans for the implementation of reform in both the military and civilian fields. By the end of 1994, the military had formed a special all-volunteer unit called the 10th Battalion for International Cooperation. It was trained for participation in international military exercises and later for PSOs. From the very beginning, the function of the 10th Battalion was in the spirit of the Military Diplomacy role identified in Chapter 1. Its activities helped to publicise Slovenia as a country that was both interested in international military cooperation and capable of fulfilling expert military tasks beyond the country's borders – and functioned in a very real way as a symbol of Slovenia's desire to become a NATO member. However, in practice, and despite all the public and political attention it attracted, the 10th Battalion needed almost eight years to become a fully functioning military formation. When Slovenia's official doctrine of military development changed its emphasis from homeland defence to international military cooperation in 2001, the 10th Battalion lost its privileged status; being renamed the 10th Motorised Battalion. However, its legacy has been significant, and in recent years several other SV units have followed its path in relation to all-volunteer manning and international deployment.

The SV also contributes to a variety of multinational joint peace-keeping units in the Southeastern European region, in order to demonstrate interoperability and its preparedness to add to future European defence capabilities. An important example of cooperation in this area is the joint Italian–Slovenian–Hungarian Multinational Land Force (MLF), whose units and staff are trained together in order to be ready for rapid deployment in PSOs. Similar initiatives include the Central European Nations Cooperation in Peace Support (CENCOOP), and the South Eastern European Brigade (SEEBRIG), where Slovenia has observer status. Slovenia's reasons for participating in the collaborative ventures are not only connected with peacekeeping, but also with regional confidence-building, contributing to regional security, and promoting its suitability for integration into western security organisations.[6]

Military Diplomacy tasks, pursued in the framework of multinational joint peacekeeping units or in other forms of multinational military formations, increase the legitimacy of the SV in society because they contribute to its international prestige. Moreover, with Slovenia's accession to NATO, and as the capabilities of these joint forces improve, these kinds of tasks are likely to become even more important to the future activities of the SV.

### Regime Defence

The SV was created on the premise that it should never fulfil the Regime Defence role or become involved in any internal policing tasks. This was a consequence of Slovenia's experiences with the JNA, which had been trained to fight against foreign invaders, but ended up being turned against its own citizens. This nervousness about the Regime Defence role is expressed in Slovenian military education, which is scrupulous in avoiding any activities that could be construed in this way. In addition, this role is unpopular with the general public, with tasks such as the military providing civil support in the event of workers' strikes being accepted by only one in ten opinion poll respondents in 2001.[7] In practice, the more the SV stresses its neutrality and impartiality in relation to Regime Defence, the higher its popular legitimacy.

### Domestic Military Assistance: prioritising disaster relief

Military assistance at times of natural catastrophe is one of the longest standing expectations Slovenian society holds of its military, and indeed it is this role that forms a traditional basis for the SV's societal legitimacy. Indeed, for more than 20 years, the majority of the Slovenian public understood disaster relief as the military's primary operational task.[8] According to opinion polling from 1982, the proportion of the Slovenian population who believes that 'the military should help in the case of natural, environmental and other disasters' has varied between

83 and 98 per cent.[9] In 1999 and 2001, these figures were 95 per cent and 93 per cent respectively.[10] Military participation in civil emergency operations requires specific training for SV personnel, and in practice this excludes conscripts from disaster relief during their military duty. In the event of a natural disaster, it is the decision of the Rescue and Protection Agency of Slovenia and the Commander of Civil Protection to decide whether or not they require the help of the military.

According to official national security documents, the SV is not allowed to provide assistance to the police on Slovenian territory, on the grounds that the military staff lacks the necessary training and skill for such tasks. It is also likely that the improper deployment of military units in support of the police would lead to widespread public criticism. Nevertheless, in some areas – such as illegal immigration – the Slovenian public supports military assistance to the police.[11] Opinion polling in 2001, for example, illustrated that SV missions to assist the military in this area is acceptable to 72 per cent of respondents. However, this figure drops to 59 per cent in relation to a military role in helping to maintain law and order.[12]

In sum, the SV's role in providing domestic military assistance in civil emergency operations contributes to its bases for legitimacy in society. In the future this role may be put to the test and is a central element in PSOs. As a consequence, the SV may well have to train more on human-itarian activities in order to be able to provide immediate help in case of catastrophes at home. In contrast, the provision of military assistance to the police has an opposite impact, largely because of public fears that it is a short step from this task to the Regime Defence role reminiscent of the core role of the JNA.

### The SV as Nation Builder: the last musketeer of traditional patriotism

A Nation Builder role for the military has been a long tradition in Slovenia. Indeed, this was a key element of the military's activities in the Austro-Hungarian Empire, the Kingdom of Yugoslavia, in partisan units during the Second World War, and in the Socialist Federal Republic of Yugoslavia (SFRY). In all cases, conscripts were exposed to military and political socialisation. Since independence, Slovenia has continued the military socialisation of its young men through compulsory service. Women are excluded from conscription, but are allowed to enter the military as volunteer career personnel.

When the SV was established in 1994, some military decision makers were of the opinion that the military should not just be responsible for the military education of male conscripts, but also for patriotic and military history education more widely. In response, a Patriotic and Motivation Education Course was introduced into the basic military training programme for conscripts. However, the importance of this element of conscript training has reduced significantly as the SV itself has become unwilling to remain 'the last musketeer of Slovenian patriotic education'. Moreover, in practice, the SV has rather limited opportunities to socialise young people in this way because almost half of those eligible for conscript service do not serve as a result of technical ineligibility, conscientious objection or poor health.

Public opinion polls also show decreasing support for military patriotic education. In 1988, when Slovenian conscripts served in the JNA, 74 per cent of the population believed patriotic education was an important part of military service. In 1999, this figure had dropped to 69 per cent.[13] By 2001, the figure had dropped even further – to 58 per cent – broadly comparable with the European average of 54 per cent.[14] Thus, the Nation Builder role does not contribute a great deal to the legitimacy of the SV in society at present, and in future it is likely to become even less important.

## Military roles and military legitimacy

### International and transnational influences

#### Threat perceptions and the geostrategic context

The basic official national security document of Slovenia, the Resolution on the Strategy of National Security of Republic of Slovenia, describes Slovenia as being at the crossroads of Central Europe, Southern Europe and the Adriatic region.[15] As a consequence, the country is exposed to different foreign influences and interests. Military threats, which are only likely in the context of a European or world crisis, and non-military threats such as organised crime, illegal immigration, drug, people and arms smuggling, and environmental pollution. This pattern of thinking about threat perceptions is reflected at both political and popular levels in Slovenia.

Public opinion polls illustrate a gradual change in Slovenian threat perceptions over the past decade. While the military threat from the JNA was perceived as the most serious risk in the period between the war for independence in June 1991 and the retreat of the Yugoslav Army from

Slovenia in October 1991, non-military threats became more pressing after 1994. An opinion poll in 1994/95 showed that military threats from other states were not perceived as significant. Despite the fact that there was substantial military activity in Croatia and Bosnia-Hercegovina at this time, 12 per cent of respondents identified military threats as 'strong', 28 per cent as 'medium', and 33 per cent as 'weak'. The same poll showed that economic problems, crime and environmental damage were perceived as the greatest threats to Slovenian society.[16]

An opinion poll in 1999 mirrored these conclusions. Possible military threats to Slovenia from other countries were perceived as being at the lowest level of all, with the potential for 'spillover' from conflicts elsewhere in Yugoslavia seen to be a 'weak' threat.[17] However, the same poll highlighted new attitudes towards non-military threats, with crime, drugs and unemployment being seen as the most worrying. A poll in 2001 showed a similar pattern of public thinking in relation to military threats towards Slovenia. A result of this is that the public sees concentrating only on military threats as an inappropriate use of its armed forces. As a consequence, the SV has had to broaden its approach to its roles, missions and responsibilities.

### International pressure and aid: NATO and EU patronage

When the Prime Minister of Slovenia signed the Partnership for Peace Framework Document on 30 March 1994, it was seen as the first official step towards Slovenian membership of NATO, culminating in its invitation to join in November 2002. Many activities followed, including the adoption of the first individual partner programme with NATO and Slovenia's participation in the Alliance's Planning and Review Process. The Slovenian public first became attracted by the prospect of NATO accession in October 1995, when the NATO Study on Enlargement was presented to Slovenian politicians and defence experts. This helped the public to gradually become more aware of the benefits and responsibilities involved in joining the Alliance.

Slovenia's desire to join NATO has no significant opposition among the country's parliamentary parties, and related legislation has been passed by parliament without major dissent.[18] The Resolution on Strategy of National Security of the Republic of Slovenia articulated Slovenia's desire to join the European security integration process in relation to NATO, the WEU and the EU. In April 1997, parliament unanimously adopted a joint declaration supporting Slovenia's accession to NATO, stating explicitly that Slovenia fulfils all the criteria for NATO membership, and that it is ready to bear the costs and responsibilities that go along with this. The document was prepared to show Slovenia's readiness for NATO's Madrid Summit in July 1997, which in the end did not result in a formal invitation for the country to join the Alliance.

NATO's decision at Madrid had a sobering effect on Slovenian politicians and the general public, and stimulated both to think harder about the arguments for and against membership. The public became more sceptical and less supportive as far as membership was concerned, whereas Slovenian politicians began to focus their accession activities around engagement with the post-conflict reconstruction of South-eastern Europe, as well as active participation in peace and humanitarian operations outside the country. In a very real way, 1997 was a turning point in Slovenian foreign policy. As a consequence, despite not receiving an invitation to join the Alliance in 1997, Slovenia became one of the most active contributors to conflict resolution efforts in the Balkans and both its activism and its success in this area is seen as one of the key factors for the November 2002 invitation to join NATO.

Slovenia's desire to join the EU has a longer pedigree than its approach to NATO. The country's sympathies for the EC/EU stem from the significant amount of trade it had with member states even during the Yugoslav period. At that time the majority of the foreign convertible exchange of the federal state went through the Slovenian republic. The EU was also the political reference point for the population after the JNA intervention of 1991 and it was the EU's recognition of Slovenian independence in January 1992, which helped to deepen the country's trust in the institution. This culminated in June 1996 when Slovenia signed the European Agreement and applied for full EU membership.

The period after 1997 was marked by an increasing maturity in Slovenian foreign policy, characterised by its activities while a non-permanent member of the UN Security Council, the evolution of accession negotiations with the EU, and a more sober and realistic approach to NATO membership. Slovenian engagement with NATO in particular helped it to become more self-confident and more aware of the need to contribute to international security as an investment in Slovenia's own national security. The prospect of NATO and EU membership has also framed Slovenian military thinking – forcing a more targeted and effective approach to defence reform. This policy resulted in the invitations coming from EU and NATO in late 2002, to join both organisations.

*Technological developments*

Technological development in the SV has been stalled since its formation in 1991, and this has had largely negative effects on its legitimacy
in society. The SV does not have many modern weapons systems, the
equipment available for conscripts is in poor condition and there is
insufficient ammunition to train soldiers to a high standard. In addition, procurement decisions have been widely criticised as inappropriate
and misguided. Often the government has given the impression that
military equipment orders have been based on promoting support for
the Slovenian application to NATO rather than the equipment needs of
the Slovenian armed forces. This has caused a variety of problems in
relation to the interoperability and maintenance of some weapons
systems and undermined military effectiveness.

**Domestic influences**

*Historical legacies*

Historically, Slovenian society has always seen the military's role as
being to provide a territorial, guerrilla-type warfare against aggression.
In peacetime, the military is at the margins of most people's everyday
interest. This pattern altered slightly in the 1980s when a huge public
debate on the mistakes of the JNA emerged, and civil society increasingly spoke out against the conservative and totalitarian military
authorities. Slovenian citizens became used to more open discussions
on the future of military issues in Slovenia, and this expressed itself
in ideas like demilitarising the republic (and so expelling all JNA units)
or the establishment of Slovenian republican armed forces in place of
the JNA. The shape of the independent Slovenian military when it
was finally established in 1991 was created by these anti-JNA and
anti-military debates. This in part explains why the TO/SV has been able
to fulfil its socio-political roles effectively, but has struggled in relation
to its functional tasks. The TO quickly became the military symbol of
the Slovenian victory against the JNA and this at least temporarily
served to close the civil–military gap and functioned as a source of the
military's legitimacy in society for some years. Post-1991, Slovenia's
more benign threat environment diminished these benefits, and the
military increasingly came to be seen as an unproductive consumer
of state funds. In this context, the 1997 decision to deploy volunteer
soldiers in PSOs was an effective way to keep the operational units in the
public eye.

*Domestic political context*

The SV is very sensitive about the apolitical character of its staff. By law Slovenian professional soldiers are prohibited from being party members, but at the same time are exposed to different ideologies and patterns of thinking that permeate through to them from the appointment of defence ministers from different ideological orientations.[19] In practice, even in cases where decision makers discuss questions of military and defence reform, SV officers are expected to stay well outside the debate. This exclusion from public lobbying has inhibited the development of a professional autonomy and identity among Slovenian military officers. Thus, Slovenian civil–military relations exist in an environment shaped by two unequal partners. The civilian sector lacks knowledge on military matters, but is confident in making decisions on the basis of earlier JNA experience. The military does not know how to represent its interests to the public and lacks confidence in its own professional capabilities. This imbalance undermines the military's standing in society and gives the impression to the public that it is professionally unable to represent and defend its own military and defence policy interests.

While the SV was established as a secular institution, in the past decade it has been challenged by the desire of some of its members to practice their religion within the military. As freedom of religion is one of the key elements of the Slovenian constitution, and a requirement for spiritual care was evident in SV units participating in PSOs, in 2001 the military introduced a military chaplaincy. This could significantly increase its standing among religious members of Slovenian society.

Changing patterns of social representation and diversification are also visible in the SV. One key problem in this regard is the role of women in the armed forces. Slovenia has a tradition of women soldiers that stems from their active role in the partisan units during the Second World War, and women fulfilled both combatant and command roles during the Ten-Day War. They were, however, excluded from the JNA. After 1991, the Slovenian military attempted to differentiate itself from the JNA by explicitly trying to integrate women into the armed forces at all levels. Despite this, those women who have joined the SV have tended to be given 'traditional' women's roles in areas such as education, logistics, and communication, which in practice limit their promotion opportunities within the military. In 2002, 13 per cent of the SV was made up of women in both operational and non-operational roles. Many women perceive a job in the military as a form of emancipation, and the integration of women into the SV has increased the military's legitimacy in Slovenian society.

## Economic constraints

Slovenia left the Yugoslav federation as its richest and most developed region. The Balkans war affected the Slovenian economy but it recovered quickly, and in recent years Slovenia has been cited as one of the most successful transition countries in terms of economic development and growth.[20] As a consequence the country is able to pay for an adequate national security system. However, societal attitudes towards military and defence spending are largely negative. Military threats are perceived as being very low, and the Slovenian public does not support additional spending on armed forces committed to war-fighting tasks alone. An opinion poll conducted in 2001 showed that four out of ten respondents expressed satisfaction with current defence spending levels, three out of ten were in favour of decreasing defence spending, while only one in ten supported an increase in the defence budget.[21]

## Societal change

A final influence on military–society relations is the fact that Slovenian society has always been exposed to influences from the West, mainly as a side effect of its economic orientation towards the markets of western Europe. Thus Slovenia is affected by broader European trends that no longer see the armed forces as the central national or state institution.[22] Despite this, levels of public trust in the SV as an institution remain high. This is likely to increase further when the shift to an all-volunteer force occurs and the unpopular institution of conscription is abolished in June 2004.[23]

## Conclusion

The societal legitimacy of the SV is the result of international and domestic influences. A low perception of military threat diminishes the societal need to maintain a robust military defence, but Slovenian society still thinks that a modern European state needs the military as a symbol of statehood. It also believes that the Slovenian military should fulfil the Military Diplomacy role as a public illustration of how the country is prepared for integration into western institutions. The political decision to opt for NATO membership has placed strong societal expectations on the shoulders of the military. It is seen as the main actor in Slovenia's cooperation with the Alliance – and received the most criticism when an invitation for membership was not issued in 1997. The SV has to carry the burden of conforming to 'NATO standards', which in practice means 19 different national security systems. This mixture of different ideas has caused short-term confusion in military preparedness, but in the long run it will hopefully create an effective military system, based on skills that Slovenian soldiers have acquired from PSOs and foreign military courses.

The SV's main domestic sources of legitimacy in society are the historical legacies of the Ten-Day War for independence, and the format of the army as an 'anti-military', 'anti-JNA' force. The victory in the Ten-Day War has also legitimised the territorial character of the SV. Since 1991, it has evolved into a standing army that also participates in constabulary-type operations. Old images of the war have steadily been forgotten, and new military operational experiences were needed to replace them.

However, the societal desire to fashion the SV according to modern principles and trends has resulted in a rather confused institution. On the one hand it fulfils the role of peace activist and 'demilitarised' military. On the other, it retains a war-fighting tradition particularly in its all-volunteer units. In seeking support from all social strata in Slovenia, the SV is therefore developing into a dual military: a peaceful conscript army whose training is not too arduous and a highly professionalised volunteer element motivated by good career prospects, adventurism and the development of new skills. This dualism has led to an ambivalent and very expensive military force, and in 2002 led the Slovenian government to introduce an all-volunteer force. In practice conscription will end in 2004 and the obligation to serve in the reserve will cease in 2010. By rejecting conscription the new all-volunteer army will fulfil the functions of being both anti-JNA (without conscripts) and a small, flexible, modern armed force that can play a role as a full member of NATO.

## Notes

1. The Ten-Day War was an armed conflict of minor size, which began on 27 June 1991 and finished on 6 July 1991.
2. A. Bebler, 'Democratic Control of Armed Forces in Slovenia', in A. Cottey, T. Edmunds and A. Forster (eds), *Democratic Control of the Military in Postcommunist Europe: Guarding the Guards* (Basingstoke: Palgrave Macmillan, 2002), 168.

3. Zakon o obrambi, Uradni list Republike Slovenije št.82/1994, 37.člen. (The Defence Act, The Official Gazette of Republic of Slovenia, No. 82/1994, Article 37.)

4. The analysis was made in the framework of the European COST project Defence Restructuring and Conversion, co-sponsored by the European Commission, in the period 1997–2001. See P. Manigart and L. Jelušič, *European Defence Restructuring: Military and Public View* (Brussels: Official Publisher of the European Communities, 2001).

5. I. Hostnik, 'Participation in Peace Support Operations', *Slovenia and NATO, NATO'S Nations and Partners for Peace*, Special Issue 1 (2002), 34.

6. P. Latawski, 'Bilateral and Multilateral Peacekeeping Units in Central and Eastern Europe', in D.S. Gordon and F.H. Toase (eds), *Aspects of Peacekeeping* (London, Portland: Frank Cass, 2001), 74.

7. Slovenian Public Opinion Poll Data Archives.

8. The expression 'operational' is understood in terms of Martin Edmonds's categories of operational and non-operational outputs. See M. Edmonds, *Armed Services and Society* (Leicester: Leicester University Press, 1988).

9. Slovenian Public Opinion Poll Data Archives, The Centre for Mass Communication and Public Opinion Research, and The Defence Research Centre Data Archives (Ljubljana: University of Ljubljana, Institute of Social Sciences).

10. In western European countries disaster relief is one of the postmodern military operations other than war. According to the Eurobarometer 54.1 (the public opinion poll of the European Union countries, which in 2001 measured the EU citizens' attitudes towards security issues), disaster relief is important to public opinion throughout the EU; the average acceptance of it is 91 per cent in all EU countries, and in Spain and Luxembourg it is perceived as the main military task, just as it is by the Slovenian public. For details see P. Manigart, *Europeans and a Common Security and Defence Policy* (Brussels: Royal Military Academy, Chair of Sociology, 2001).

11. Haltiner reported that: 'Such internal police assistance operations were undertaken by the military in Italy, Ireland, Austria and Switzerland.' K.W. Haltiner, 'Policemen or Soldiers? Organizational Dilemmas in the Constabularization of Armed Forces', in M. Malešič (ed.), *International Security, Mass Media, and Public Opinion* (Ljubljana: ERGOMAS, University of Ljubljana, 2000), 18–19.

12. Slovenian Public Opinion Poll Data Archives, 2001.

13. Slovenian Public Opinion Poll Data Archives, 2001.

14. Manigart, *Europeans and a Common Security and Defence Policy*.

15. The Resolution was adopted by the Slovenian Parliament on 21 June 2001. Official Gazette of Republic of Slovenia, http://www.uradni-list.si/uldemo/bazeul/ured/2001 (2 May 2002).

16. Slovenian Public Opinion Poll Data Archives, 2001.

17. The public opinion survey was conducted between 21 May and 18 June 1999, that is, mainly at the time of NATO air strikes on FRY. The detailed explanation of the data is published in A. Grizold and I. Prezelj, 'Public Opinion and the National Security of Slovenia', in M. Malešič (ed.), *International Security, Mass Media and Public Opinion* (Ljubljana: ERGOMAS, University of Ljubljana, 2000).

18. M. Malešic, *Slovenian Security Policy and NATO* (Groningen: Centre for European Security Studies, 2000), 27.
19. Bebler, 'Democratic Control of Armed Forces in Slovenia', 166.
20. According to EUROSTAT (Statistics in Focus, Theme 2-28, 2002) Slovenian GDP per capita in 2001 was US$16.300 (PPS). Institute of Macroeconomic Analysis and Development at the Government of Slovenia reports that economic growth in 2002 reached 3.2 per cent, www.gov.si/zmar/.
21. Slovenian Public Opinion Poll Data Archives, 2001.
22. This process can be referred to as the 'secularisation' of the military. K.W. Haltiner, *Milizarmee: Bürgerleitbild oder angeschlagenes Ideal?* (Frauenfeld: Verlag Huber, 1985), 39.
23. The number of applicants for conscientious objection status increased from 240 in 1991, to 2504 in 1999 and 3250 in 2001. One out of five conscripts dropped out of service because of health reasons. L. Jelušič, 'Mame ne bodo več prale vojaških oblek' (Mothers are not going to wash military cloth anymore), *Ona*, 4:9 (5 March 2002), 12.

# 11
## A Crisis of Legitimacy: the Military and Society in Croatia

*Alex J. Bellamy[1]*

During a visit to the George C. Marshall Centre in Germany in May 2000, the Croatian Defence Minister, Jozo Radoš, observed that:

> modern security cannot be built on the armed forces of one's home country alone. An international system of security is the only way to ensure stability. To this end, Croatia's military forces should be a well-organised, democratically controlled institution capable of guaranteeing the security of the country and being integrated into international military alliances.[2]

In doing so, Radoš initiated a new turn in the relationship between the armed forces and society in Croatia. Whereas prior to his tenure as Defence Minister, the primary roles of the armed forces were concerned with Nation Building and Regime Defence, Radoš proposed a new Military Diplomacy role. This new role is based on a rejection of the zero-sum security discourse propagated by the HDZ (*Hrvatska Demokratska Zajednica* – Croatian Democratic Union) government that ruled Croatia between 1991 and January 2000. According to this discourse, Croatia stood alone against Muslim and Orthodox enemies. Franjo Tuđman, president of Croatia between 1991 and his death in 1999, used the discourse of perpetual threat to justify overturning Zagreb's mayoral election results in 1996.[3] He also advanced the notion that internal opponents had been 'contaminated' by those outside Croatia who opposed the existence of the new state and used it as an excuse to politicise the armed forces and to create his own praetorian guard which was used to deter the 'internal' threat to the regime as often as it was to deter the 'external' threat to the state.[4]

The first part of this chapter charts the development of three phases of military–society relations in Croatia, identified according to the

185

principal role of the armed forces in society. In the first phase (1991–95) the military was primarily concerned with Nation Building. In the second phase (1995–2000) the distinction between the state and the regime was eroded, with the military taking on the Regime Defence role identified in Chapter 1 of this volume. Among the growing number of people who opposed the HDZ, this linkage brought the legitimacy of the military into serious doubt. In the third and current phase (2000 to the present), the armed forces are beginning to take on Military Diplomacy functions particularly with respect to interoperability and international integration. The chapter goes on to consider the imperatives that brought about these shifts, arguing that they were prompted by the shifting tide of the military's popular legitimacy, the functions that the military fulfils and its relationship with other social institutions. The final part of the chapter identifies three key debates that will shape military–society relations in the future. The first is a debate about the appropriate size of the armed forces and its recruitment practices, the second is the question of Croatia's force posture and types of deployment and the third is a debate about the appropriate level of defence spending.

This chapter argues that there is a crucial paradox at the heart of civil–military relations in Croatia. In order to pursue its new Military Diplomatic role and re-legitimise itself, the armed forces require sustained investment to enable processes of professionalisation to succeed. However, the lingering popular perception that the military is linked to the HDZ militates against such investment, thus inhibiting the potential for renewing the legitimacy of Croatia's armed forces.

## Three phases of military–society relations

It is possible to trace three broad eras of military–society relations in Croatia over the past 12 years. Between 1991 and 1995 the role of the Croatian armed forces can best be described as that of Nation Builder. The Nation Building role between 1991 and 1993 focused on the physical defence of national institutions and territory. The military was in the vanguard of developing Croatian state capacity in response to an immediate threat to state survival. The Croatian armed forces were constructed in time of war to fulfil an immediate functional goal. In 1991, in response to Croatia's declared intention to seek independence from socialist Yugoslavia, Serb militia and the JNA (*Jugoslavenska Narodna Armija* – Yugoslav People's Army) launched a series of attacks throughout Croatia, culminating with the sieges of Vukovar and Dubrovnik.

Serb forces seized around one-third of Croatia's territory and at times the front line came as close as 30 kilometres to Zagreb. One of the few vestiges of the communist era that remained in Croatia was the network of Territorial Defence Units, civilians who had undergone national service in the JNA and were then organised into local groups and trained to harass invading forces. At the outset of the Serb attacks, these units arranged themselves in an ad hoc manner from the bottom up. It was not until the war was several months old that a functioning General Staff and military hierarchy were created. Nevertheless, these military structures were among the first indigenously created elements of the new Croatian state.

At this time processes of state building and army building went hand in hand and in many cases civilian and military authority were indistinguishable. Military units were often built on ad hoc local arrangements. Even once a structure resembling a regular army was built, significant paramilitary organisations remained outside state control, and in practice the police force undertook military roles. Both the military and civilians were also involved in the illicit purchase of arms, forging contacts with illegal arms dealers throughout Europe and further afield. There were also indirect links forged with the US government through the consultancy firm Military Professional Resources Incorporated (MPRI).

The sense of standing alone against the enemy, the need to build a new state, and the need to construct new armed forces created particular patterns of military–society relations. Military formations were born out of informal local civilian arrangements. In fields such as procurement and funding there was often no distinction between civilians and the military. The military was widely seen as the defender of Croatian society and the earliest physical manifestation of the state. This close relationship and the military's connection with ideas of national liberation meant that unlike in Serbia, where enforced conscription failed to persuade even half the conscripts to report on duty, the Croatian military only recruited volunteers and was never short of such people. The main problem that the Croats faced was not one of finding soldiers, but finding the means of equipping them. Volunteers would often donate their personal belongings to the cause. For instance, private cars were given steel plating and converted into strange looking tanks. The military thus enjoyed a very close relationship with Croatian society.

Towards the end of this first period, the emphasis of the Nation Building function began to move away from institution building.

Throughout the 1990s, the Tuđman government attempted to enforce its own particular view of what Croatian national identity was – Catholic, historicist, conservative, and – in the context of the war in Bosnia – extending into western Hercegovina. In 1993, the Croatian army assisted Bosnian Croats in their fratricidal war against the Bosniaks. The use of the Croatian military in this way prompted controversy in Croatia and began to alter the military's relationship with society. Stipe Mesić, a leading moderate in the HDZ – who was elected President of Croatia in 2000 – resigned in protest at Croatia's role in the Bosnian war and indeed Croatia's role in the Bosnian war brought the close relationship between military and society into question for four reasons. First, the relationship was based upon the idea of national defence against external aggression. The use of the Croatian military inside Bosnia undermined this conception of the role of the Croatian armed forces. Second, Croatian activities in Bosnia eroded Croatia's international legitimacy and prompted some of the government's opponents to begin questioning the wisdom of the war effort. The Croatian massacre of Bosniaks in the village of Ahmici was a turning point. Not only did this lead to international condemnation, it also prompted Croats seriously to question for the first time what their military was doing and how it was controlled. Third, many Croats noted that the war with the Bosniaks implied an alliance with the Belgrade-backed Bosnian Serbs. This seemed to undermine the idea that the formation of the military, its operational activities, and the burdens it placed on everyday life (volunteer service, taxation, requisition) was necessitated by the Serbian attack on Croatia. Finally, it appeared to some that the Croatian military was being used as an instrument to deny national self-determination to the Bosniaks – the very thing that it had been created to provide Croatia with.

While relations between the majority of people within Croatian society and the military remained very close throughout the war, seeds of doubt were therefore sown by Croatian military activities in Bosnia and the subtle shift in the nature of the military's Nation Building function. However, the military retained a very large degree of support, because the defence of national territory continued to remain at the heart of both roles.

The second phase of military–society relations in Croatia can be traced from 1995 to the beginning of 2000, though many of the seeds for the most recent changes were laid in the final months of this period. Here, the military's role was primarily one of Regime Defence. With the end of the war, it became apparent not only that there was a close interrelationship between civilians and the military (evidenced by the strong personal control wielded by Tuđman and his controversial Defence Minister, Gojko Šušak) but also that there was a conflation of state and regime. Once the perception of national emergency had receded, it became evident that the military had been heavily politicised.[5] The problem was not one of civilian control of the military per se, but of how democratic that control was.[6] For example, there was no danger of a military coup because the military and the ruling party were closely interrelated, but there was a fear that this might inhibit democratic change and the military was used in a variety of ways to support the ruling party. The president was given his own praetorian guard, and the intelligence services were often used to monitor the activities of political opponents or to undermine the work of reformists within the ruling party. The role of the Ministry of Defence was often more to do with delivering patronage to political allies than managing the defence of the state. Budgeting was inaccurate, and corruption, profligate spending and wastage were endemic.

The tendency towards illiberal and undemocratic patterns of military–society relations prompted increasing international isolation and Croatia was excluded from Partnership for Peace, the Council of Europe, and the EU's PHARE programmes. Indeed, the EU retained its arms embargo – covering all forms of defence cooperation – until the very end of the 1990s, and while the US maintained contact and networks were developed, these remained arm's length relationships. Defence assistance in areas such as education, planning and budgeting were only offered through psuedo-independent organisations such as the defence consultancy Military Professional Resources Incorporated (MPRI).

This international isolation reinforced the regime's claim that it was standing alone against the threats to the Croatian nation. It repeatedly argued that it was the regime alone (rather than a conception of the Croatian state or people) that protected the nation. Thus, an attack on the regime constituted an attack on the state or the nation itself. The so-called 'Zagreb crisis' in 1995–96 stands as testament that not only were the regime and state viewed as the same thing but that both the rhetoric of 'national security' and the constitutional mechanisms put in place to defend it were used to protect the regime. In the 1995 local assembly elections, opposition parties secured 31 of the 50 seats on the Zagreb municipal council. Tuđman was faced with the possibility of an opposition mayor in the economically vital capital and feared that an opposition council could investigate the illegal activities of the HDZ.[7] Tuđman therefore invoked a national security clause in the constitution that allowed him to veto the appointment of top officials. In doing so, he rejected four opposition candidates, justifying his actions on the basis that an opposition mayor would threaten Croatian stability:

> It is important that our public understands that the situation in which Croatia finds itself regarding the problems of the liberation of the remaining occupied territories and the crisis in Bosnia-Hercegovina is such that we cannot allow that sort of opposition which would rock Croatia's stability to take root in the city of Zagreb, capital of Croatia where a quarter of the Croatian population live.[8]

The link between the military and society in Croatia began steadily to weaken and be replaced by a close HDZ–military axis. After the war the armed forces continued to receive very high levels of funding (15–20 per cent of the state budget). This funding did not, however, go towards the creation of professional armed forces. Indeed, until 1998 Ministry of Defence spending was not even audited by the State Auditing Office, nor did it provide yearly reports to parliament.[9] The Defence Ministry alone employed over 9000 people, almost one-sixth of the peacetime size of the entire armed forces. Military–society relations became bifurcated. On the one hand, conservatives, nationalists and other HDZ loyalists continued to hold the military in high regard. War veterans in particular were granted a special place in society. However, opposition to the HDZ government grew throughout the latter half of the 1990s and as it did so the military's relations with substantial sectors of society deteriorated. The opposition wanted proper investigation of alleged war crimes but the military continued to oppose this. The opposition wanted accountability of the military and intelligence services but again this was rejected. Relations deteriorated to such a level that there were genuine fears that if Tuđman died and the HDZ lost the 2000 elections, it might lead to a military coup led by hardliners.[10] In the event, no coup materialised, but military personnel were put under considerable pressure to cast their vote for the HDZ and the secret ballot was not always strenuously observed in military barracks.

The third, and current, phase of military–society relations in Croatia can be traced from the beginning of 2000 to the present. Although reform has been slower and less coherent than had initially been hoped for, there have been dramatic changes in patterns of civil–military relations. In this period the Croatian armed forces have taken on the Military Diplomacy role while also trying to establish a functioning system of democratic civilian control. This has included a reorientation of the roles of the armed forces towards preparation for peacekeeping, implementation of reforms according to the Membership Action Plan and compliance with NATO's interoperability criteria. It has also included a rapid reconsideration of the relationship between the military, parliament and the ruling party. Although the current confusion about institutional responsibility is problematic and has delayed effective defence reform, one positive aspect is that it has wrenched the military away from both a ruling party and a particular institution. The development of a national security concept, a defence law, a white paper and military doctrine all contribute towards the democratisation of military–society relations. These changes have had a palpable impact on Croatia's international relations. At governmental level, Croatia has now joined a whole host of organisations and acceded to NATO's Membership Action Plan (MAP) in May 2002. This has also spawned a wealth of transnational relationships between the defence community in Croatia and similar communities overseas. Defence intellectuals and defence ministry officials regularly attend conferences and courses overseas, and numerous international projects, such as the Regional Arms Control Verification and Implementation Assistance Centre at Rakitje, have also been inititated.[11] Elements of the Croatian military collaborate internationally, with examples of activities including joint Partnership for Peace (PfP) exercises, bilateral work with Hungary and Italy, and the attendance of officers on overseas courses such as those offered by the Royal College of Defence Studies in London.

New roles for the armed forces have begun to recast relations between the military and society in several important areas, although there remains a significant cleavage between conservatives and the rest of society. The wresting away of the military from the regime has significantly improved its domestic legitimacy. This has been coupled with moves to end conscription and professionalise the armed forces. These reforms are also placing the military at the heart of the government's European agenda. A commitment to European integration was one of the few things that bound together the six parties who formed a coalition in 2000 to oust the HDZ regime. Through its work with PfP, and more recently the MAP, the military has placed itself at the heart of the integrationist agenda. This has been a rapid turnabout because the military – though fulfilling different roles – was also at the heart of the HDZ's 'standing alone' discourse. Further, both the domestic and international legitimacy of the military is being improved by its cooperation with the International Criminal Tribunal for the former Yugoslavia (ICTY). Finally, public attempts to root out corruption and waste in the defence sector, though slower than many had hoped, have succeeded in removing some of the distrust of the military felt by sections of society.

However, the split in Croatian society that emerged as the role of the military subtly shifted during its Nation Building phase remains. For conservatives, the reforms constitute an attack on the memory of the so-called 'Homeland War' of 1991–95 and the very institution of the military. According to this view, held by most of the 600,000 people or so that supported the HDZ in 2000 and many others, the current government is waging a war against the military. On the issue of war crimes, a popular mantra is that because Croatia's war was a defensive one there could not have been Croatian war crimes, an argument originally put forward by a senior Croatian judge. On the issue of defence budget restructuring, opponents argue that cuts only provide evidence of the government's anti-military stance and that attempts to weed out corruption and HDZ patronage merely constitute the re-politicisation of defence. Finally, on the issue of European integration they argue that the government is being at best naive and at worst treacherous. Because they continue to insist that Croatia stands alone, reliance on the West for territorial defence jeopardises the very existence of the state.

From the vantage point of 2003, military–society relations in Croatia are in a state of considerable flux. In many areas the military is in the vanguard of transition, leading the way towards European integration. However, nearly 12 years of being a particular kind of Nation Builder and Regime Protector has left a legacy of mistrust in society. A relatively small but vocal minority centred upon the remnants of the HDZ, far-right parties, and various veterans' associations continue to revere the military as the defender of the nation. For them the military should be large and costly, it should be able to stand alone in the Balkans and it should be immune from unhelpful parliamentary oversight and undesirable criminal investigation.

## Factors influencing military–society relations

There are three key factors that precipitated the shift between different phases of military–society relations in Croatia. These three factors are the perceived legitimacy of the armed forces, the internal and external roles that it fulfils (functional and socio-political), and the relationship of the military to other social institutions such as parliament, the Catholic Church and the media.

## Legitimacy

The popular legitimacy of the military, which lies at the heart of the military–society relationship, is shaped by a variety of factors. According to James Gow in his study on military legitimacy in socialist Yugoslavia, the military is legitimised by its functional and socio-political roles. As Edmunds et al. point out in Chapter 1, for Gow 'the functional basis of military legitimacy derives from its "military mission" … the protection of the state from external threat'. Thus, socio-political legitimacy stems from the role the military plays as a symbol of national unity, its contribution to state infrastructure, and its role as an instrument of education and socialisation.[12] The main problem with this approach is that it separates out state legitimacy and military legitimacy. It also assumes that military legitimacy only involves the military being externally legitimised. In the Croatian case, the military was also an important source of legitimacy for the state itself.

At the beginning of the 1990s, the Croatian military played a fundamental role in legitimising the Croatian state. When the military was primarily a Nation Builder its existence and activities legitimised the state in a variety of ways. First, it gave the state a physical presence. The development of the Croatian military was therefore an essential physical component of the process of transforming a Yugoslav republic into an internationally recognised state. Second, according to classic definitions in international relations, a state should be able to defend its borders, and clearly the armed forces were central to the Croatian state's ability to do this. Third, the Croatian state was only internationally recognised after the Croatian military had halted the initial Serb attacks. Moreover, the state was only properly welcomed into the society of states after the military had successfully liberated Serb-held territory in 1995. At the beginning of the 1990s therefore, the legitimacy of the Croatian state and the legitimacy of its military were synonymous.

This began to change in 1993 when the armed forces began to take on a Regime Defence role. Indeed, after 1993 the armed forces came to be associated as much with the regime and a particular idea of Croatian national identity, as with the state. While the HDZ regime retained high degrees of domestic legitimacy, the armed forces did likewise. However, the commission of war crimes and acts of ethnic cleansing in Bosnia prompted international observers to award the Croatian armed forces moral equity with the Bosnian Serbs.[13] Although the sense of supreme emergency initially shielded the military from a similar loss of legitimacy at home, once the imminent threat receded they came in for increasing criticism from public figures such as Mesić, Vlado Gotovac and Ivo Banac, with independent newspapers such as the *Federal Tribune* leading the assault.[14] Towards the end of the 1990s, the security sector as a whole was viewed with deep suspicion by large parts of society. It was widely perceived as a haven for right-wing politics, corruption and illiberal practices. As the HDZ lost support, so this scepticism increased. The issue of democratic accountability in the security sector was one of the few areas that the opposition coalition could agree upon and – along with the ailing economy – was one of the most important issues in the 2000 elections that resoundingly despatched the HDZ from office.

The new government's development of a Military Diplomacy role for the armed forces attempts to tackle this crisis of legitimacy. Although there remains considerable constitutional confusion about the relationship between the General Staff, Ministry of Defence, presidency and parliament, much has been done to weed out corruption and end politicisation. As part of this process, for example, the Ministry of Defence discovered that it owned 2000 vehicles that were unaccounted for. Ministry officials had their 'credit card privileges' removed and several corrupt sub-contracts were rescinded. Despite these reforms and the military's emerging new image as an 'international integrator' significant problems remain as a result of the legitimacy crisis. As progress towards professionalisation gathers pace the armed forces will face recruitment problems, particularly when trying to attract well-educated career officers. Within the Social Democrat-dominated parliament, the military is regarded with deep suspicion and the defence budget is viewed as a potential area for further deep cuts.[15] The continuing perception that the military is an essentially right-wing organisation is not helped by a continuing institutional reluctance to cooperate with the International Criminal Tribunal for the Former Yugoslavia (ICTY), the right-wing and overtly pro-HDZ credentials of the many veterans' associations and widespread anti-government campaigns spearheaded by people associated with the military. One such instance was an open letter to the government signed by 12 serving and retired generals that condemned the government for defacing the honour of the Homeland War by cooperating with the ICTY. Stipe Mesić promptly sacked the generals, but the episode damaged the popular legitimacy of the military.

### Functions

As the three phases outlined earlier suggest, the changing function of the military has played an important part in determining the nature of military–society relations in Croatia. Over the first decade of its existence, the military's function has shifted from one primarily concerned with territorial defence to one where priority and finance is given to the Military Diplomacy role. The changing role of the armed forces was prompted by both domestic and international factors though the notion of territorial defence remains at the heart of what the military is for. In particular, the HDZ's oft-repeated claim that Croatia was 'standing alone' in the world prompted it to adopt a particular stance on several key issues. At the end of the war in 1995, the government feared that as volunteer soldiers returned to their pre-war occupations there would be an overall diminution of the state's fighting capability. Because the 'standing alone' discourse proved to be a self-fulfilling prophecy the government believed that it could only meet the imminent threats it perceived in the south through a programme of national service. Once instigated, national service took on both functional and socialising roles but was generally unsuccessful in both.

Despite the relatively large size of the defence budget (much of which was siphoned off by corrupt officials tied to the HDZ) national service training was poorly funded. Rather than receiving a programme of military training, conscripts performed a range of non-military duties such as 'guarding' national monuments and statues and repairing roads. In some cases, conscripts were used as forced labour available for hire to the highest bidder with HDZ connections. The socialisation aspect of national service had two elements. On the one hand, national service was seen as a way of reducing 'anti-social' behaviour among young men. The collapse of the economy, dramatic decline in the standard of living and a persistently high rate of unemployment of around 20 per cent have combined to give Croatia significant problems with drugs and crime and the government hoped that national service might tackle this. However, because the conscripted element of the armed forces was so poorly funded the problems that existed in Croatian society at large were merely transplanted into the military. Conscripts have been associated with organised crime networks and smuggling. On one occasion, a drunken conscript caused a major explosion at a weapons dump near Zagreb, causing widespread public alarm.[16] The second socialising role was one of national indoctrination. What little education conscripts were given tried to reinforce the HDZ's particular perspective on Croatian national identity by teaching a particular version of history, a particular type of language and a decidedly nationalist geography. Rather than improving society's perception of the military by forging close relations, national service only reinforced the perception that the armed forces were corrupt and supported right-wing politics.

The new Military Diplomacy role for the military has involved the incorporation of new functions. These include a desire to train for and participate in peacekeeping operations, regional arms control verification activities, de-mining, cooperation with neighbours, and participation in PfP exercises. The adoption of these new roles, underpinned by a cooperative rather than confrontational view of security, is beginning to impact on military–society relations. As observed earlier, multilateral military cooperation is at the vanguard of Croatian attempts to integrate into Euro–Atlantic institutions. Financial investment in peacekeeping training, for example, produces more than merely functional returns. Through joint exercises and projects, the military provides a physical manifestation of Croatia's entry into the West. This provides both international and domestic dividends. Internationally, successful military cooperation opens the way for cooperation and integration in other fields of public life. It is an unspoken belief in Croatian government ministries that membership of NATO will lead to membership of the EU, though there is no evidence to say that this is necessarily the case. Domestically, such cooperation could alter the image of the military as a conservative and right-wing organisation, and help to attract well-educated recruits from the universities.

## Social trends and institutions

The third key aspect of military–society relations is the armed forces' relationship with key social institutions. Although the military has often been characterised as right-wing and conservative, this has generally not been framed in terms of the so-called 'right to be different' discourse that has been a characteristic of western civil–military relations in the past decade or so. According to Dandeker, Moskos and others, the major challenge to military–society relations comes from society's rejection of core military values such as hierarchy and discipline. One of the main reasons they identify for this shift is the lack of an immediate threat to national security. The same, of course, cannot be said of Croatia. Nor can it be said that there is increasing interpenetration between civilians and the military. If anything, processes of professionalisation have decreased the amount of civilian and military interpenetration and cooperation. Moreover, the networks of corruption that challenged the military's legitimacy in the second half of the 1990s comprised both civilians and the military. Finally, there have not been widespread public discussions about the role of women and homosexuals in the military.

Although the main feature that separates the Croatian experience from mainstream western civil–military relations debates is the recent experience of war, another important factor is the continuing crisis of legitimacy identified earlier. Among the educated middle class, the military is still widely seen as tarnished by its connections with the HDZ. Rather than increasing the level of criticism this perception has tended to produce disengagement. Thus there is little discussion about the role of women and homosexuals in the military because the socio-economic groups that tend to raise such issues have not moved beyond simplistic distrust of the military's functions and political outlook. There remains only a tiny number of civilian defence experts and virtually all of them are co-opted into the state in one way or another. For example, Croatia's leading military sociologist, Ozren Žunec, was briefly head of the intelligence services and is currently devising a national strategy for security on behalf of the government.

There are signs of fragmentation between different social institutions that were related to the HDZ and this might help to reduce popular suspicion of the military's activities. The Catholic Church was a cornerstone of Tuđman's vision of Croatian national identity. At the beginning of the war the Church was itself a specific target for Serb attack and so it shared much of the HDZ's rhetoric about the importance of popular sovereignty and national defence. In 1995, however, there was a major breach between the Church and the state when both the Pope and the head of the Catholic Church in Croatia – Cardinal Božanić – publicly condemned the mistreatment of Serbian civilians during operations 'Flash' and 'Storm'. Although the rural clergy tended to continue propagating HDZ nationalism, the hierarchy in Zagreb became increasingly critical of government corruption, which was nowhere more evident than in the defence sector. This was deeply problematic for the military because of the high esteem in which the Church is held in Croatia. Unlike domestic political opponents, the Church hierarchy could not be branded as treacherous or misguided Serbophiles. However, the criticism also had a positive outcome. On one hand it showed that there was no rigid uniformity of thought among the social institutions closest to the HDZ's national project, and on the other, the Church's position also showed that it was possible to be patriotic without necessarily being 'pro-HDZ'. Much of the current government's intended reform of the defence sector is aimed at bringing it under the formal control of the institutions of state as opposed to the informal control of the ruling party as in the 1990s. Nevertheless, it could be a decade before social institutions such as universities and the Church hierarchy alter their view of the military as a bastion of corruption and partisan right-wing politics.

## Future challenges

The major challenge that confronts the Croatian military is re-legitimisation. At the end of the 1990s, the military was closely associated with the outgoing HDZ government and the 'support' it received on issues such as non-cooperation with the ICTY came from these right-wing circles. The legitimacy of the military is shaped by a variety of internal and external factors including cooperation with the ICTY, PfP participation, NATO membership, active participation in UN operations, the quality and scope of national service, democratic accountability and transparency, corruption and the military's relationship with other social institutions. Three major issues can be identified as key future challenges: recruitment/force size, force posture and deployment, and defence spending. The key point to note is that if the government is to succeed in its plans to professionalise the armed forces, it will need to win support on each of these issues and it will need to persuade society to legitimise the military and allow military matters to form part of the 'normal' political discourse.[17]

### Recruitment/force size

Croatia's armed forces are overmanned. The need to reduce their size produces a number of socio-political problems. Given the scale of unemployment in Croatia, laying off thousands of soldiers merely creates more unemployment. Even the limited downsizing that has taken place so far, for example, retiring the 3000 full-time personnel who were permanently inactive due to ill health, prompted fierce opposition from within both the armed forces and the vocal veterans' associations, which believed that it was the beginning of the end of their special privileges. Another problem is that in some parts of Croatia, particularly around Knin, the military is the major economic actor, and downsizing will have a serious impact on many local economies. There is also widespread concern that with the phasing out of conscription, the retreat of the military's socialisation role could worsen the social problems associated with unemployment, in particular the drugs problem and crime. On the one hand, therefore, downsizing is a fundamental part of the professionalisation which the government hopes will re-legitimise the armed forces, although without considerable external assistance the costs in socio-economic terms may outweigh the benefits and alienate the nationalist section of society that continues to hold the military in high esteem. On the other hand, a long-term programme of professionalisation, military education and international integration may re-legitimise the military among the educated middle class, providing a new pool of career officer recruits.

## Force posture and deployment

The re-legitimisation of the military is intimately linked with the internal and external roles that it fulfils. There is currently a debate within the Croatian defence community about the type of force posture the armed forces should adopt. Conservative voices within the General Staff argue that land-based territorial defence has to remain the priority. Although the rhetoric of 'standing alone' has been toned down, there is a lingering belief that Croatia must be able to deal single-handedly with any threat that emerges from Serbia or Bosnia. This continuing perception mitigates against thorough reform of the armed forces and the redirection of resources towards more specialised activities such as peacekeeping and de-mining. However, opinion polls show that Croatian society does not share the belief that there is an imminent danger, revealing a disjuncture between military and civilian perceptions of threat.[18] For many civilians, this reinforces the belief that despite the government's reformist claims, the military remains anachronistic and conservative. For the military, it prompts concern that the 'westernisation' of society will make it more difficult to mobilise the nation in its own defence.

## Defence spending

All these issues contribute to debates over the appropriate level of defence spending. To the extent that records are available, Croatian defence spending is extraordinarily high. Over 60 per cent of the entire defence budget is spent on immediate personnel costs while another 15 per cent is spent purchasing goods to support personnel. Thus, to many politicians from the government coalition, and to the people that voted for them, the defence budget is an area where significant cuts can be made. In the past two years the government has saved money by reducing the number of personnel, particularly the thousands who drew a salary without doing any work, and by putting an end to corruption wherever it can find it. Nevertheless, within a context where the government it trying to cut the size of the state's overall budget, there are continuing calls for further reductions in defence spending. The challenge is that the professionalisation which lies at the heart of the plan to re-legitimise the military is inherently expensive. The paradox of reform is that if piecemeal professionalisation is to be avoided, the government needs to invest in military equipment and education and this cannot be done with a declining defence budget. There is therefore a tension at the heart of military–society relations. The re-legitimisation of the military depends on recasting its functions, on threat perception and international outlook. However, the continuing perception that the military is linked to the HDZ mitigates against resources being given to accomplish these goals.

## Conclusion

Military–society relations in Croatia have passed through three phases. After a period of state/nation building, the military became inextricably linked to the ruling HDZ regime. During the war and in its immediate aftermath, both the HDZ and the military were held in very high esteem as a result of their successful defence of the national territory. However, in the second half of the 1990s both were brought into question. Beginning in 1993, serious doubts were raised about the role of the military in the war in Bosnia. There were also questions about the commission of war crimes and corruption. Both the HDZ and the military lost support, though prominent military figures such as Generals Agotić and Stipetić retained their personal standing. By 1999, the military faced a crisis of legitimacy, because as an institution it was viewed as closely linked with the discredited government. The new government, elected in 2000, is trying to address this crisis by giving the armed forces a new function in Military Diplomacy and hence a crucial role in a wider integrationist policy. Placing the military at the forefront of integrationist efforts is beginning to change societal perceptions, but not to the extent that the majority of the population are willing to put aside demands for cuts in defence spending. According to Edmunds et al. in the introduction to this volume, the military– society relationship is influenced in two ways. First, there are changes to the drivers that shape the military's role. Each of the three phases of military–society relations in Croatia had different drivers shaping the military's role. In the first it was the immediate physical need to build and defend the state. In the second, it was the desire to build a particular vision of the Croatian nation and defend the regime from domestic and foreign opponents. In the third, military reforms form part of a much wider effort aimed at Euro–Atlantic integration. The second key influence identified by Edmunds et al. is, 'a societal perception that the military is not effectively fulfilling the roles which are the foundation of its legitimacy'. This is clearly the case in Croatia since the military and state were mutually reinforcing. The military was at the heart of state building, and the defence of the state provided the rationale for the establishment of the military. That began to change once the armed forces became involved in the Bosnian war in 1993.

The crisis of legitimacy came to a head at the end of the 1990s when it became clear that the military's role was not about the defence of the state but the defence of the regime. The new Military Diplomacy agenda is an attempt to recast the military's legitimacy by basing it on new roles. Territorial defence remains important, but the new foundation of its legitimacy also incorporates its role in international cooperation. In order to do this successfully, however, a crucial paradox needs to be overcome. If the military is to be re-legitimised by becoming a member of NATO it requires sustained investment to meet its MAP goals which in turn is dependent on the military's legitimacy. NATO itself can play an important role in this by clearly and publicly mapping out the criteria that Croatia needs to fulfil in order to become eligible for membership and lending its own credibility to the defence reform process. This would allow the armed forces and defence establishment to articulate clearly a strategic vision that linked the allocation of resources with tangible consequences. If this occurs, then the refashioning of the Croatian armed forces' bases for legitimacy in society will be brought one step closer.

## Notes

1. I would like to thank Tim Edmunds, Anthony Forster and Andrew Cottey for their helpful comments on an earlier draft of this chapter. I would also like to thank the Croatian Sociological Association for inviting me to present the main arguments at their annual conference in Zagreb. In particular, I owe a debt of thanks to Ozren Žunec and Vjeran Katunarić.
2. Radio Free Europe/Radio Liberty (RFE/RL) (15 May 2001).
3. See Chapter 4 of A.J. Bellamy, *The Formation of Croatian National Identity: a Centuries-old Dream?* (Manchester: Manchester University Press, forthcoming 2004).
4. For further details see A.J. Bellamy, 'Like Drunken Geese in the Fog: Developing Democratic Control of the Armed Forces in Croatia', in A. Cottey, T. Edmunds and A. Forster (eds), *Democratic Control of the Military in Postcommunist Europe: Guarding the Guards* (Basingstoke: Palgrave Macmillan, 2002).
5. O. Žunec, 'Democracy in the "Fog of War": Civil Military Relations in Croatia', in C. Danopoulos and D. Zirker (eds.), *Civil-Military Relations in the Soviet and Yugoslav Successor States* (Boulder: Westview, 1996).

6. See Bellamy, 'Like Drunken Geese'.
7. L.J. Cohen, 'Embattled Democracy: Postcommunist Croatia in Transition', in K. Dawisha and B. Parrott (eds), *Politics, Power and the Struggle for Democracy in South-East Europe* (Cambridge: Cambridge University Press, 1997), 109.
8. British Broadcasting Corporation, Summary of World Broadcasts, Part 2, Central Europe, The Balkans, EE/D2453/A.
9. R. Vukadinović and L. Cehulić, 'Development of Civil–Military Relations in Croatia' (2001), 71, www.isn.ethz.ch.
10. See A.J. Bellamy, 'Croatia after Tuđman: the 2000 Parliamentary and Presidential Elections', *Problems of Post-Communism*, 48:5 (2001).
11. The Rakitje project is discussed in greater length in A.J. Bellamy, 'A Revolution in Civil–Military Affairs: the Professionalisation of Croatia's Armed Forces', in A. Cottey, T. Edmunds and A. Forster (eds), *The Professionalisation of Armed Forces in Postcommunist Europe* (Basingstoke: Palgrave Macmillan, 2002).
12. James Gow, *Legitimacy and the Military: the Yugoslav Crisis* (London: Pinter, 1992).
13. See Brendan Simms, *Unfinest Hour: Britain and the Destruction of Bosnia* (London: Allen Lane, 2001).
14. See S.W. Malović and G. Selnow, *The People, Press and Politics of Croatia* (London and Westport: Praeger, 2001).
15. Author's interviews with Zdenko Franić, Social Democratic Party management committee member and Božo Kovačević, Liberal Party politician and former government minister.
16. I owe these points to Ozren Žunec and Lt. Col. Simon Cleveland.
17. On the government's professionalisation plans see Bellamy, 'A Revolution in Civil–Military Affairs'. On the difference between 'normal politics' and 'securitised politics' see B. Buzan, O. Wæver and J. de Wilde, *Security: a New Framework for Analysis* (Boulder: Lynne Rienner, 1997).
18. When asked to identify their main foreign and defence policy concerns, respondents prior to the 2000 elections identified 'European integration' rather than homeland defence as the chief concern. See *Globus*, 7 December 1999.

# 12
# Legitimacy and the Military Revisited: Civil–Military Relations and the Future of Yugoslavia

*James Gow and Ivan Zveržanovski*

The Federal Republic of Yugoslavia (Serbia and Montenegro – the FRY), with a complicated web of security forces and other armed groups operating on its territory, has become established as the exception to the European pattern of civil–military relations. As a result, relations between the Yugoslav Army (*Vojska Jugoslavije* – VJ) and Yugoslav society are difficult and complex. At the start of this decade, in many senses, military–society relations had fallen to low point. Indeed, similar issues of legitimacy and civil–military relations confront the FRY to those which confronted and, in the end, resulted in the demise of the Socialist Federative Republic of Yugoslavia (SFRY), to which the FRY was one of the successor states. The SFRY's fate was a function of the interaction of regime legitimacy and military legitimacy, where both required renewal in face of crisis, with the latter necessary to the former. In that case, military legitimacy was lost – and with it, so too was any chance of regime legitimacy renewal. The circumstances are different and the number of actors is smaller, but central aspects remain the same today. An uncertain federation faces potentially critical challenges. The only element that covers the federation as a whole is an armed force predominantly oriented to one of the constituent elements in the federation and with a history, both distant and recent, of direct involvement in political processes.

The VJ currently performs two of the formal roles identified in Chapter 1: National Security and Regime Defence. In addition, throughout the 1990s it performed a somewhat perverted Domestic Military Assistance role. The FRY's international isolation meant that the opportunity to undertake international UN operations was not an option for a long time. However, following the fall of Slobodan Milošević at the end of 2000, the scope for this type of engagement has widened – even if it has not immediately been cultivated. Additionally, despite being the successor to the Yugoslav People's Army (*Jugoslavenska Narodna Armija* – JNA), the absence of a defined and accepted political community has impeded the VJ in its attempt to perform a role as 'Nation' Builder.[1] Regime Defence was – and continues to be – oriented primarily towards Serbia. The VJ served at various times as an instrument of Milošević's policy, as well as an active participant in Serbian politics and, since the democratic changes of 2000, in the dispute between the two main parties of the ruling Democratic Opposition of Serbia (DOS) coalition that replaced Milošević. Similarly, National Security, although covering the whole FRY territory (except for Kosovo), has been perceived as legitimate in Serbia, but as predominantly threatening in Montenegro.

This chapter will explore the various roles performed by the VJ and analyse how they have affected its legitimacy and relations with society. It will then explore the determinants of those roles. Finally, the chapter will consider current military–society challenges that the VJ is facing and those that it is likely to face in the future.

## Armed forces and society in the FRY

As the successor of the JNA, the VJ enjoyed a good reputation and good relations with society.[2] In particular, despite its failures, the JNA's National Security role gave it some sort of legitimacy. However, today's VJ comes with a history of Regime Defence throughout the 1990s. Although it took Slobodan Milošević until early 1999 to gain full control over the VJ, he managed to steer it into taking actions that would enable his regime to survive. Milošević's success was mainly due to corruption of the VJ leadership at different levels, as well as the VJ's tradition of participation in the political life of the country.[3]

While all militaries participate in political life in some degree, this feature is particularly salient in communist cases, and especially that of the SFRY. Unlike the notional 'neutrality' of armies in liberal democratic states, communist militaries often had a designated political function. The civil–military relationship in communist systems was both direct and formal. The existence of a direct, formal channel between the military and civilian political authority made the military a legitimate actor in political processes – whether the scope was large or small. This legitimacy had considerable implications for the study of civil–military relations in communist systems. Whereas in non-communist societies, military involvement in politics presented a question of legitimacy, in communist states, the politicisation of military activity provided a base for the armed services to act with political legitimacy. The federal structure of the old Yugoslavia, in which the JNA had a formal political role, amplified this position.

The transition from the JNA to the VJ, alongside the transition from the SFRY to the FRY, posed questions for the relationship between armed forces and society. As the successor to the JNA, the VJ inherited the bulk of the equipment as well as a large portion of the officer corps and mentality of its predecessor.[4] It also inherited the JNA's history and its relationship with society. In order to understand the VJ's relations with society, it is necessary to look at the historical influence of the JNA. The JNA's three main roles were National Security in relation to both the USSR and the West; Regime Defence against internal dissent; and Nation Building (especially after the 1974 Constitution, where the JNA was the only truly Yugoslav institution). Domestic Military Assistance was always a possibility, but was marginal to the other three (although the JNA was deployed to Kosovo in 1981) and the SFRY engaged only in the most limited sense in something that might be termed Military Diplomacy within the Non-Aligned Movement.

After the formation of the VJ, it became clear that National Security was the military's primary role. The VJ's primary role is the defence of the 'sovereignty, territory, independence and constitutional order of the Federal Republic of Yugoslavia'.[5] This was partly inherited from the JNA (see below) but is also the product of the Military Doctrine inaugurated by Milošević prior to the elections that brought his downfall. The National Security role is the founding purpose of the VJ, and the only role provided by the FRY constitution other than the possibility of being committed to an operation run by an international organisation. However, although its organisational structure is geared towards the defence of the FRY, the VJ has been put to other uses, which at times have compromised it.

The VJ spent the first half of the 1990s engaged in military action in Croatia and Bosnia and in Hercegovina assisting the Army of Republika Srpska (*Vojske Republika Srpska* – VRS) in Bosnia and the Armed Forces of the Republic of Srpska Krajina (*Oružane Snage Republika Srpska Krajina* – OS-RSK) in Croatia. During that period, and despite appearances, there was, in the words of then Chief of Staff General Momčilo Perišić, one force and not three.[6] Even when Milošević severed ties with the Bosnian Serbs, the VJ saw it as its duty to continue support for the VRS. Likewise, the Dayton Agreement did not deter the VJ from keeping its connections, albeit more discretely.

The Kosovo problem raised a new dilemma for the VJ. The emergence of the Kosova Liberation Army (UÇK) and its seemingly successful campaign in the spring of 1998, showed the deficiencies of Interior Ministry police (*Ministerstvo Unutrašnjih Poslove* – MUP) forces acting in the province. The General Staff found itself under intense pressure to engage in support of the police and paramilitary units. Perišić was hesitant in demanding the proclamation of a state of emergency in the province which would allow the VJ to act. Nevertheless, the VJ became engaged in the summer of 1998 and cooperated with MUP units throughout the period of armed conflict and well beyond. Milošević strengthened his grip over the VJ by creating a parallel command structure in Kosovo, which bypassed the General Staff in favour of the then head of the Third Army and future Chief of Staff General Nebojša Pavković. Perišić himself was sacked in October 1998, a move which finally placed the VJ under Milošević's full control.

The VJ's real test came during the NATO bombing of Yugoslavia in 1999. Indeed, despite its retreat from Kosovo in early June 1999, it emerged from the conflict with its reputation enhanced. For many Serbs, the VJ was seen to have stood up to a much stronger enemy, and to have successfully defended the country. The political decision to sign the Kumanovo Agreement – the military–technical agreement between the VJ and NATO on the deployment of the latter's troops in Kosovo – did not involve the military, although the Third Army was expected to negotiate the terms. In this position, the army appeared to emerge with considerable credit – it had fought the Alliance, given a good defence and maintained its honour, while it was perceived that political expediency had prompted an end to hostilities by Belgrade. But this high point of VJ–society relations would soon turn sour, as the corruption of the new VJ leadership led it away from its main National Security role towards Regime Defence.

The VJ's co-option into the Regime Defence role finally ended the distance between Milošević as political leader and the military. Throughout a decade of federal dissolution, political chaos and war, the remnants of the JNA had sought to establish themselves in a new home. That home was now offered by Milošević. The trade-off for taking this role was involvement in war and alignment with Milošević either formally as President of Serbia or President of the FRY against his opponents. Given the formal status of the FRY as a federation of two states (Montenegro and Serbia), perhaps the most egregious example of the VJ's implication in Milošević's politics – and one of the key reasons why its legitimacy and that of the FRY were challenged – was the military leadership's preparedness to take action against the smaller partner in the federation, Montenegro.

Over the weekend of 19–20 August 2000, VJ Chief of Staff, General Nebojsa Pavković acknowledged the birthday of FRY President Slobodan Milošević in a telegram complimenting him on the 'wise state policies' with which he had led the country and the 'diplomacy' through which it had maintained its dignity. This was a reflection of the close and loyal relationship that Milošević had come to have with the leadership of the army at this point, in contrast to most of his time as Serbian and FRY leader. This was confirmed the week before by the FRY President's adoption of a new military doctrine for the VJ, which, while retaining central elements from the Belgrade military's tradition, placed key emphasis on internal and non-conventional forms of defence. The new military doctrine illustrated the FRY President's reliance on and confidence in the VJ, as the FRY headed towards divisive elections on 24 September in which it was conceivable that Milošević might actually lose.

In response to the new doctrine, former VJ Chief of Staff Perišić – now leader of a Serbian opposition movement – declared it a gimmick for the elections. However, in practice, the doctrine's significance was a warning signal of the type of response that Milošević's defeat in the elections themselves might prompt. The elections were therefore the starting pistol for an unfolding set of events involving the VJ – whether in terms of a state of emergency in the event of Milošević's defeat, or in terms of their impact on Montenegro.

The new doctrine maintained a standing commitment to the defence of the FRY through appropriate use of armed force. However, it was notable for three distinct though apparently minor augmentations of this concept: first, there was emphasis on the use of 'other forms of resistance'; second, and more significantly, there was explicit mention of Montenegro and Serbia, the two states that form the FRY, rather than of the FRY per se; and finally there was mention of working in alliance with 'friendly states and nations'. The reference to history and to possible alliance with 'friendly' states and nations was significant. For most of the communist period, the then-Yugoslav federation officially had a non-aligned position, while in the period since the end of communism in its traditional guise, the question of allies was not formally a consideration. Although historic alliance could be attributed to Britain, it seems far more likely, in the context, that Russia was the real candidate. This might be confirmed by the presentation of the military doctrine and of changes in military organisation in the Russian Federation. While the latter were presented in the Milošević controlled main daily

*Politika* under the banner headline 'Changes to Armed Forces Structure' as though the forces in question were those of the FRY, the former was presented as a small front-page item the following day under the headline 'President of the Republic adopts FRY military doctrine'. Reporting of Russian changes was treated as though it was not a foreign news story and was given major treatment, while the shorter domestic story received greatly reduced status in terms of presentation. The message Milošević and his military intended to send to the people was that of Russian solidarity with beleaguered Serbia. While there is undoubtedly a close link between parts of the Russian military and Belgrade, this is certainly not a relationship formalised at the state level. Neither did this link serve the Milošević regime in the end. References to 'other forms of resistance' probably referred to the conduct of war by non-conventional and indirect means and was a complement to the implicit concerns for internal security and relations between Serbia and Montenegro indicated by the naming of both states in the doctrine. That explicit linkage of the two member states was, however, of considerable significance.

The doctrine declared 'the determination of both the Serbian and Montenegrin people to defend and protect their sovereignty, territorial integrity, independence and constitutional order'. It was this part of the doctrine that was highlighted by VJ press releases. Whereas a commitment to protect the constitutional order was consistent with previous Yugoslav constitutions, the specific mention of the two states and their relationship was ominous. It occurred at a time when there was considerable concern about Serbian or VJ action against Montenegro and there was much discussion of Montenegro leaving the FRY. By declaring the commitment of the Montenegrin people to defend the sovereignty of the FRY where many of them were already engaged politically in trying to protect Montenegro's sovereignty, the doctrine constituted a commitment to VJ action, based on maintaining territorial integrity, in the event of a move by the government of Milo Đjukanović in Podgorica to protect itself by leaving the FRY.

The same provision regarding constitutional order was also capable of being invoked in the event of a numerical victory for the opposition in the coming FRY elections. The elections might have been a potential trigger for trouble over the succeeding weeks. If Milošević had won, the pressure on Montenegro to turn its suspension of FRY constitutional provisions into a more decisive historic split might have spelled a VJ clampdown on behalf of the FRY President. If the opposition candidate Vojislav Koštunica gained more support in the election than Milošević, the doctrine provided for a clampdown in Serbia that would enable the FRY President and his cronies to hold on to power, should the VJ choose to back him.

A further implication of the new doctrine appeared to be a stronger relationship between the VJ and the Serbian Interior Ministry Special Forces. In particular, the potential for internal action in the new doctrine implied even greater coordination and cooperation between the two organisations, based in part on experience over Kosovo. It seemed likely that something akin to a fusing of some parts of the VJ and MUP structures was being considered.

According to the VJ, military doctrine plays a 'direct role' in the activities of the state and military leaderships. It seemed certain that Milošević and his generals would have interpreted this as meaning protection of their own leading positions. Although on the same day that the new doctrine was announced General Pavković, while visiting the town of Nikšić, declared that the VJ had no plan to carry out a coup in Montenegro, the new doctrine suggested that there was good reason to prepare for conflict there, as the attention to Montenegro and Serbia in the doctrine suggested a strong possibility of VJ engagement if Milošević were to win the elections. At the same time, it held out some prospect of the VJ's playing a different role to protect Milošević and themselves in the event of an opposition win in Serbia.

Events took a different course. Despite attempted gerrymandering and disruption, the elections made it clear that Milošević did not have popular support and should leave office. Rather than standing with him, the military command chose to form an alliance with the man who had beaten Milošević, Vojislav Koštunica. However, the positive link to the new FRY president, whom the VJ helped install by obliging Milošević to leave office, was of limited benefit for the army. The majority of the Serbian opposition remained sceptical of a military leadership that had previously appeared prepared to defend the Milošević regime, and numerous calls were heard within the DOS coalition to replace Pavković. However, Koštunica refused, making the VJ a tool in the political battle between him and the Prime Minister of Serbia, Zoran Ðinđić, firmly in control of the Serbian MUP.[7]

After a few years of cat-and-mouse confrontation, there was little chance of an easy and early relationship with Montenegro, even after the fall of Milošević. Moreover, the VJ's record in Kosovo and its links to the Serbian MUP, meant that military re-legitimation was necessary. Significantly, this military re-legitimation was necessary to regime re-legitimation, given that there was a clear absence of agreement on the

FRY, which the VJ nominally served, as an appropriate form and level of political community.

## Domestic, international and transnational influences on the armed forces and society

The relationship between the VJ and society is determined by a combination of domestic pressures, economic problems, threat perceptions, international engagement and, perhaps above all else, the lack of obvious correlation between armed forces and political community. The last of these is ultimately the most important, though in itself it is likely to be shaped by other influences, and particularly international engagement and domestic pressures. There is little sense in seeking to separate discussion of domestic pressures from those of political community and the future of the FRY, as is presented below.

An unavoidable problem since the disputed dissolution of the SFRY has been the correlation of armed forces and statehood in some of the successor states, notably the FRY and Bosnia-Herzegovina (BiH). While it is reasonable, in general, to assume an equation that may be stated as one country, one military, the reality for the FRY is different, as there is one formal armed force of the FRY, but three separate territories (Serbia, Montenegro and Kosovo) that need to be considered. Connected to this is a complex of other relevant forces that cannot be ignored in considering the civil–military landscape. First, each of the constituent states in the federation has its own internal force – the MUP, each of which embraces police and paramilitary units. Second, the Serbian Security Service has been responsible for the organisation and control of quasi-autonomous paramilitary forces and special military units. Third, on the territory of the FRY, there has been an insurgent force, the UÇK in the Serbian province of Kosovo, fighting for independence for the mainly ethnic Albanian land. Fourth, the conflict on the territory of the FRY between the UÇK and Serbian and Yugoslav forces also led to the deployment of an international force in the province, with NATO organisation at its core. Fifth, the VJ and the Security Service paramilitary units have been engaged in war on the territory of two neighbouring former Yugoslav states, Croatia and BiH. The FRY is exceptional in having such a complicated web of civil–military relationships which in large part can be credited to a decade of war.

A lack of stable international relations has also been an important factor in FRY's evolving military–society relations. This resulted from engagement in a series of campaigns involving Slovenia, Croatia, BiH,

Kosovo and the West, as well as international isolation and sanctions. This situation is unlike any other case (even if Bosnia and Hercegovina has experienced its own form of uncertainty derived from war). Later, extending from that decade of war, uncertainty at the interface of national and international relations persisted, even after the triumph of democratic forces. Indeed, it grew even after the fall of Milošević because of a continuing political dynamic to dissolve the FRY. Montenegro, as a sovereign state according to its own and the FRY constitutions, is entitled to independence, should a referendum there favour such a move, while the province of Kosovo lacks that formal qualification, but is in many senses de facto separated.

The FRY does not represent an agreed political community, and until the end of 2000, there was no more than a skein of democracy in its major component state, Serbia, and no settled correlation between armed forces and statehood. In addition to these problems of politics, political community, statehood and transition, three further factors influence the relationship between armed forces and society in the FRY. These are threat perceptions, economic constraints and societal change. These three have led to the many calls for the abolition of conscription and other changes regarding the VJ. As a result, there was a reduction in the period of conscript service from twelve to nine months and the announcement of a future reduction to six months. In addition the ability of the VJ to fine draft-dodgers has been limited.

The FRY's international security environment is still unstable. The unresolved status of Kosovo and the plight of the few remaining Serbs there as well as the recent insurgency in the Preševo Valley have all influenced relations between the armed forces and society. The VJ has been seen in a positive light due to its good performance in the Preševo Valley in south-east Serbia, where a form of monitoring cum cooperation with the OSCE and NATO has permitted the return of Serbian and FRY forces to the Ground Security Zone around Kosovo. Nevertheless, popular threat perceptions are changing. The FRY is painfully and slowly emerging from its international isolation and today faces fewer threats from abroad. Improved relations with NATO and the possibility of joining NATO's Partnership for Peace (PfP) have further relaxed threat perceptions.

Economically, the FRY faces the combination of a run-down post-communist economy and the consequences of a decade of isolation. The VJ currently consumes 70 per cent of the FRY budget. Taking into consideration the size of the VJ in comparison to the other federal bodies (that is, the presidency and the government) and the size of the FRY budget, this is not an enormous sum in real terms. However, discussion on the state of VJ finances, as well as revelations of financial abuses by senior military officers, have trained a spotlight on a lack of oversight over the VJ budget. Although it is no secret that the VJ has been suffering from financial difficulties since its creation (as has the whole country), revelations about misuse of VJ funds have appalled many. Lastly, although a survey in spring 2002 showed that the VJ was still the most trusted institution among the public in Serbia, the changes discussed above and the demands for shorter conscription were prompted, at least in part, by fatigue in society with anything warlike and militaristic.

As a result of this situation, the VJ recognised the need to reform and, with it, the still awkward and unwanted need for international engagement – resulting both in opportunities and pressures. Since the fall of the Milošević regime, reform of the security sector and the establishment of democratic civilian control over the armed forces have become a crucial test of how effective reforms have been. However this imposed test has so far been only marginal to the interests of the two main power brokers in the FRY. Although mentioning democratic civilian control over the VJ has been a must in almost every speech, there was little movement to draft a well-balanced law that would provide the basis for such a control. It took a major scandal involving the shady application of domestic laws and the violation of the Vienna Convention on Diplomatic Relations to kick-start the process. The arrest in March 2002 of former Chief of Staff Perišić and US diplomat John Neighbor on suspicion of espionage brought to light the total lack of institutionalised control over the VJ. It became apparent that reform was necessary and not merely a matter of political utility. As establishing civilian democratic control over the VJ is a precondition of joining PfP, as well as the Council of Europe, it is becoming apparent that the VJ is a stumbling block for the FRY. In particular, the issues of dealing with war crimes suspects and the legacy of a strategy predicated on the commission of war crimes appeared to be some way from resolution. Yet, until Belgrade has successfully dealt with the war crimes question, other matters remain unfinished business, given the conditionality of international cooperation.

## Military legitimacy, regime legitimacy and the future of the FRY

The future of the FRY is by no means assured. Indeed, throughout 2002, the federation's demise has seemed almost as assured as that of the SFRY a decade before. Kosovo has remained under international transitional authority, with no formal Serbian or FRY presence. Montenegro continues to threaten to hold a referendum on leaving the FRY and gaining full independence. Serbia, in the meantime, has remained the core of the FRY, but is focused primarily (and inevitably) on its own fate – with or without Kosovo. However, a final blow to the Yugoslav idea has been delayed by the EU-sponsored effort to preserve a Union of Serbia and Montenegro. Although the full extent of that project continues to be a matter of debate and the drafting of the new Constitutional Charter has been slower than expected, there seems little chance that the FRY will remain unchanged.

The future of the VJ, in political, functional and organisational terms, as well as in terms of its character, will need to be adjusted in line with any constitutional changes. Indeed, it is vital that the military re-legitimise itself – making itself appropriate and acceptable to whichever political arrangements emerge. Military legitimation is a necessary component of and instrument for regime re-legitimation. There are three ways in which the VJ might do this: non-intervention in processes of change at the level of political community, as well as in politics more broadly; restructuring and democratisation; and professionalisation.

Resolution of the final status of Kosovo remains a long way off, and in all probability will depend on political developments in Serbia and the FRY. Whether the province is to remain associated with the federation on some new basis, or whether it will become completely separated, will depend on attitudes in the remainder of Serbia. For Kosovo to remain associated with Serbia would require a rearrangement of political structures and relationships so that, whatever the relationship, it would be on a new and legitimate basis. Similarly, for Kosovo to separate from Serbia and the FRY, Serbian political culture would have to be capable of absorbing this in the context of democratisation and approaches to European institutions, which, in themselves, would be key elements in a new legitimacy compound.

The same is true of Belgrade's relationship with Montenegro. Despite continuing talk of full independence, the more likely outcome is a re-negotiation of the relationship between the two republics and the establishment of a new arrangement – a Union of Serbia and Montenegro. This would be established on the bases of both clear agreement between the two countries and their developing relationships with the EU and possibly NATO. Once again, this would constitute a new compound of legitimacy.

There were three ways, as noted, in which the military can contribute to the overall legitimation of whatever political arrangements emerge. The first of these is non-intervention in politics. The crucial focus for this would be the need to adjust to potential independence for Montenegro, or even simply a reorganisation of relations between Serbia and Montenegro (and possibly Kosovo). This would present challenges to the military as one of only three federal elements in the FRY (alongside the presidency and the federal government). Any restructuring of state relations and political community would mean some commensurate change in the VJ. Given both the military's record of involvement in politics over several decades, and especially its recent service to the Milošević regime, there remains a chance that the military could cause difficulties in any transition. Indeed, during 1999, General Pavković spoke publicly of a forcible return to Kosovo, a sentiment that may not have receded, even if any prospect of challenging NATO militarily had done so. Regarding Montenegro, where the whole of the navy is based, as well as elements of the ground and air forces, there is the possibility that some in the armed forces would repeat the mistake of their JNA predecessors in 1990 and 1991 and undermine any chance of military or political renewal by using force in an attempt to try to preserve that which had, in practice, already expired.

Scandals in FRY politics seem to indicate that far from being apolitical the VJ is still very much active in FRY and Serbian politics. The arrest of Momčilo Perišić and the US diplomat showed the extent to which the different elements of the VJ were involved in the dispute between the former coalition partners Vojislav Koštunica and Zoran Djindjić. Not only did this scandal reveal the extent to which the VJ and more precisely its Security Service feel themselves outside normal institutions and processes, it also revealed the divisions within the VJ created by the political ambition of its leaders and their political collaborators. The June 2002 sacking of General Nebojša Pavković, his initial refusal to accept the decision of his Commander-in-Chief and his revelations of orders the VJ received to storm a Serbian government building have also proved to be a very low point in the VJ's legitimacy.

The best way for the VJ leaders to avoid the mistakes of the JNA command is to adjust to change through restructuring and democratisation. This is something that might well have made sense in the SFRY and still has some useful potential in the FRY (or whatever replaces it). Restructuring should include development towards a more regionally-based regimental system and greater professionalisation. Some steps in that direction have already been taken with the recent switch from a three-army system to a six-corps one.

The JNA was Serb-dominated and its successor, the VJ, clearly remains a Serbian army to a very large extent.[8] Any change in the constitutional status of Montenegro is likely to have important implications therefore – particularly in relation to the VJ's basing rights and the position of Montenegrin personnel. Indeed, the Montenegrin government has already announced that Montenegrin conscripts will not serve outside Montenegro in the future union. Additionally parts of the VJ will need to be apportioned to and aligned with the elements of whatever political structure emerge. Military reorganisation of this kind is vital to its own re-legitimation and to processes of regime legitimation, whatever the final outcome of these are.

An important corollary of restructuring is professionalisation. This is essential to meeting the first two ways in which the military can contribute both to its own re-legitimation and that of whatever regime might emerge. Professionalisation presents a path out of the shadows for an army deeply implicated in a decade of war characterised by the extensive commission of war crimes, as well as with a record of intervening in politics. The role played by a Joint Security Force – combining VJ and MUP elements – over ethnic-Albanian armed insurgency in the Preševo Valley has been indicative of the potential benefits of professionalisation. EU and OSCE military monitors deployed in cooperation with the JSF quickly reported positively on the professionalism of the Joint Force. In an operation that was a mixture of observation and cooperation, the image of professional competence and demeanour offers the chance of greater collaboration in the future. This would be likely to involve international involvement, whether through the OSCE and the EU, or NATO and its arrangements, in working with the VJ. Cooperation based on professional qualities could well provide the context in which international involvement might facilitate processes of transition, restructuring and military re-legitimation. The issue of war crimes remains a major obstacle in this context – but it is conceivable that international cooperation might actually provide a helpful framework for addressing that question, given the importance of respect for the laws and customs of war inherent in the professional notion. Overall, professionalisation, in its various aspects, would undoubtedly contribute in no small way to establishing the conditions for a renewal or legitimation at the regime level.

## Conclusion

The FRY emerged from its first decade with severe challenges as a political community. A renewal of military legitimacy is vital to regime re-legitimation. However legitimacy might be restored at the regime level, this will require adjustment and alignment at the military level. The more negative aspects of the VJ's legacy, and especially the earlier preparedness of some of its leaders to be used against constitutional elements of the FRY, renders the institution deeply compromised. Both the military's reputation and its re-legitimation depend on three factors. The first is its not intervening in any processes of political realignment and re-legitimation of the territories encompassed by the FRY. The second is the VJ's proving itself capable of readjustment and restructuring in harmony with whatever changes there might be at the level of political community. The last – and the one upon which the other two depend – is the military's capacity for professional development, including coming to terms with the war crimes issue – most probably in cooperation with international organisations.

## Notes

1. This is used here with the caution that in the South Slav context the term 'nation' is deeply problematic – indeed, different interpretations of the term (some absorbed from lazy international usage) fed the political conditions that generated war. See J. Gow, *Triumph of the Lack of Will: International Diplomacy and the Yugoslav War* (New York: Columbia University Press, 1997).
2. Unless otherwise stated, the reference to society means Serbian society.
3. See James Gow, *Legitimacy and the Military: the Yugoslav Crisis* (London: Pinter, 1992).
4. James Gow, *The Serbian Project and its Adversaries: a Strategy of War Crimes* (London: Hurst and Co., 2002).
5. VJ website at http://www.vj.yu/.
6. 'Afera Perišić – Uprava Bezbednosti Prikazuje: Noć Generala', *Vreme* No. 585. See also Gow, *The Serbian Project*, Chapter 3.
7. International Crisis Group, *Fighting to Control Yugoslavia's Military*, ICG Balkans Briefing, Belgrade/Brussels, 15 July 2002.
8. The Montenegrin component of the VJ is relatively insignificant both at the conscript level and in the officer corps, while ethnic Albanians are as good as absent and other groups so small as to make no real impact.

# Part IV
# The Former Soviet Union

# 13
## The Army and Society in Ukraine
*James Sherr*

The relationship between a country's armed forces and its society is an obvious and important aspect of the relationship between its state and its society. But it is not always a simple reflection of it. There are many countries in which the armed forces have a greater or lesser legitimacy than the state itself in the eyes of ordinary citizens. Ukraine is becoming such a country. As in many other states of the former Soviet Union, the level of trust in state institutions is low, and this is also true for most of the state's 'power structures'. In Ukraine, only 11.9 per cent of the population express trust in the *militsia* (civil police) and 11.8 per cent trust the courts.[1] Yet 55 per cent have either 'complete trust' in the country's armed forces or are 'inclined to trust' them.[2]

What is more, this relationship between state legitimacy and the legitimacy of armed forces has not been constant over time. The December 1991 referendum, in which over 90 per cent of voters endorsed Ukraine's declaration of independence (24 August 1991), did not simply ratify the loss of the Soviet state's legitimacy; it proclaimed confidence that a Ukrainian state would belong to citizens in a way that the Soviet state did not. Ten years after these events, there is no hard evidence that a majority of Ukraine's citizens wish to forfeit their independence; yet there is much evidence to suggest that they no longer trust their state authorities to govern in the interests of the country. Therefore, if we are to understand how the legitimacy, image and saliency of the armed forces has evolved in Ukraine, it is important to consider not only historical and geopolitical factors, but the political context: the evolution of relations between the *vlada* (powers) and those who are subject to them. Three stages are discernible (though other schema are possible, and one should never be theological about 'stages').

But before examining this evolution, we should take note of several factors which have endured over time. These factors put western debates about armed forces and society into perspective – a *western* perspective, which is rather distinct from that which obtains in Ukraine. First, although debates about the armed forces are both sharp and widespread in Ukraine, there is virtually no discussion among experts or in society at large about the armed forces' 'right to be different'. This is because civil society and the institutions protecting it are both weak and deficient. There is no place for a debate about 'extending' social and economic rights to the armed forces in a society in which these rights are inadequately recognised and poorly observed. Rights are a serious and bitter issue in Ukraine, but they dominate a prior and far from resolved debate about the relationship between society and *state*, as opposed to society and *army*. The armed forces are not immune from pressures about rights, but they are not the main target of this pressure, and in this respect at least, no one would consider them 'different'. As Ukraine's armed forces proceed to implement an ambitious programme of professionalisation, rights do enter the equation, but indirectly. The direct focus is far more practical: how can the army attract and retain good people?

Second, although the cost of the military establishment is also a subject of debate, no one accustomed to Ukrainian conditions could reasonably propose 'civilianisation' of military functions as a solution. In Ukraine as in most other parts of the former Soviet Union, the collapse of the 'command administrative' economic system has not ushered in free markets, but rigged markets, which in large part are distorted, uncompetitive and corrupt. Far from equating civilianisation with efficiency, most Ukrainians would equate it with crime. State policy rightly calls for reducing costs by streamlining bureaucracy, closing facilities, winding up excess command organs and eliminating 'duplicating structures', not transferring services to civilians.

Third, few would accept that security threats have become indirect and transnational. To Ukrainians, insecurity is experienced not only at a national level, but at a personal one. The framework for thinking about international security remains geopolitics; the framework for understanding internal security is *bor'ba za vlast'* (the struggle for power), and on a personal scale, most ordinary people find themselves living in a world of institutionalised Darwinism, in which power is largely unaccountable and the ultimate authority is money. Given these realities, the (1997) National Security Concept rightly identified 'strengthening civil society' as the country's greatest security priority.[3] In a country still deeply marked by the Chernobyl catastrophe, it also gave prominence to economic, industrial, 'informational' and ecological dimensions of security. But these are understood as national and acute risks, not transnational and remote ones. These three conditions have a direct bearing on the views which society holds about the roles of the armed forces.

## The roles of Ukraine's armed forces

### National Security

Among political and security elites, it is widely recognised that Ukraine is a geopolitically vulnerable country: a country with seven official neighbours (and a destabilising unofficial one – the Pridnestrovian Moldovan Republic), as well as complex border problems; a country which forms the northern littoral of the Black Sea, which lies in the strategic rear of the Balkans and Caucasus;[4] and a country which finds itself the ambivalent host (until at least 2017) of the Russian Black Sea Fleet. The Minister of Defence, Army General Volodymyr Shkidchenko has recently stated that 'transient, limited, possibly very fierce local interstate conflicts' remain possible.[5]

To what extent is this perception shared by society? Not surprisingly, this is not easy to document. In a recent poll (8–16 January 2002) conducted by the well-respected Razumkov Centre, respondents placed 'military policy' as the country's eighth national priority (2.4 per cent), well behind the first priority, 'economic policy' (32.9 per cent).[6] But does that mean that military policy is not seen as a problem, or simply that there are other more urgent ones? Asked in a separate poll (by the same institution and in the same month), 'how do you assess the present level of budget expenditures on national defence?', almost 70 per cent said that it was insufficient.[7] Moreover, 58.7 per cent stated that they did not believe that the armed forces were 'capable of effective defence of the state's sovereignty against military threats', and a roughly equal percentage rejected the view that 'the present military–political situation in the region and in the world allows radical reduction of the armed forces'. The opinions of those favouring professionalisation – 69 per cent of respondents polled in April 2002 – are equally illuminating. Asked why they favoured it, 63 per cent cited social rather than national security reasons; nevertheless, 47.2 per cent responded that they expected to see an 'increase in combat readiness, ability to safely defend the state and its national interests'.[8] Asked what attributes they associated with professional soldiers, the largest category of respondents (33 per cent) identified 'staunch defender of the native land, true patriot', and the next largest category (21.5 per cent) identified 'a warrior who is able to perform the most complex tasks'. Only 12.5 per cent described the professional soldier as 'the present-day serviceman, but better maintained', and only 11.8 per cent equated the professional with 'a mercenary fighting for money'.[9]

In the round, these data (as well as data about public trust in the armed forces) not only suggest that the military institution has an essential legitimacy, but that national security is seen as a genuine problem by ordinary people. In fact, opinion polls provide only one indication of the interest (and apprehension) that conflicts in the Caucasus and the Balkans have aroused on the part of Ukrainian citizens. The perception that Ukraine is a vulnerable country forced to manoeuvre between powerful political–military blocs is not an elite perception, but a Ukrainian perception. Although public opinion is considerably better disposed towards NATO than it was in the wake of the Kosovo conflict (and highly ill-disposed to joining the Collective Security Organisation of six CIS states), it is still the case that almost 30 per cent of the country regard NATO as an 'aggressive military bloc'.

### Nation Builder

For most Ukrainians, there is no contradiction between sentiments of national patriotism and feelings of cynicism about the political order. The equation between military professionalism and patriotism is one of many indications that, rightly or wrongly, ordinary citizens view the armed forces as a defender of the nation rather than as an instrument of the political authorities. Does 'building a Ukrainian nation' strengthen support for the state or weaken it?

The political and military leadership have tended towards the opposite conclusion and for good reason. Ukraine is a country bound together by a heritage of suffering and survival (in the words of the country's anthem, 'Ukraine is not yet dead'). But it is also a country with a contested history. The prevalence of patriotic sentiment about 'nation' and 'state' disguises sharp differences about what Ukraine is, where it is headed and who at various times has threatened it. Should the 1654 Treaty of Pereyeslav (which united Ukraine with Muscovy) be a cause for lament, or should it be turned into an official holiday (as President Leonid Kuchma decreed in spring 2002)? Was the (Soviet) 'Great Patriotic War' Ukraine's patriotic war, and was it fought against one merciless enemy or two? Who were the heroes, and who were the traitors in this war?

Ukraine is also a country relatively relaxed about language and ethnicity. In the 1989 census, 19 per cent of inhabitants defined themselves as ethnic Russians, and a far larger percentage can claim ethnic Russian relatives, in-laws and friends. Yet outside Crimea (transferred to Ukraine only in 1954), this is a well assimilated minority, and there is no discernible connection between ethnicity, political loyalty and way of life. Moreover, thanks to the biases of the Soviet educational system, some 40 to 50 per cent of the population still find it easier to speak Russian than their own official language, yet most of them would bitterly resent the suggestion that they are therefore less Ukrainian than somebody else. In contrast, many proponents of nation building in Ukraine have also been proponents of *Ukrainisation* and some have sought to draw lines that the majority of people have chosen to blur. By defining 'Ukraine', does one strengthen support for the state or weaken it?

### Regime Defence

It stands to reason that society does not view Regime Defence as a legitimate role for the armed forces, but as we note below, this was not always the case. Fortunately, the armed forces have been exempt from this role, and this undoubtedly helps to account for the relative affection in which they are held. Yet they have been spared this task only because others perform it. The Soviet Union left in its wake highly militarised formations outside the framework of the Ministry of Defence. Whereas the Ministry of Defence had no branches in Union republics such as Ukraine, this was not true of the Ministry of Internal Affairs (redesignated MVS – *Ministerstvo Vnutrennykh Sprav*) and KGB (redesignated Security Service of Ukraine: SBU – *Sluzhba Bespeki Ukrainiy*), which in 1991 maintained over 700,000 troops on Ukrainian territory. While the number of these troops (still unpublished) has greatly diminished, the variety of specialist formations within and outside these bodies has proliferated since independence, leading a respected authority, Anatoliy Grytsenko, to conclude in 1999 that 'military forces are proliferating on their own'.

### Domestic Military Assistance

The Soviet armed forces not only possessed the manpower and means to provide assistance to the civilian economy, they frequently found themselves obliged to do so, contributing men and equipment for construction projects, the harvest and civil emergencies. Against this background, it is perhaps unsurprising that the armed forces of Ukraine have supplemented troops of the Ministry of Emergency Situations (MChS)[10] in flood relief and provide a variety of more routine services to regional authorities in exchange for provisions, food and occasionally petrol. Nevertheless, with the exception of the civil emergency role, this is seen as an unsatisfactory and unsustainable state of affairs. For one thing, the Soviet armed forces were a privileged institution operating in a 'command administrative' economy which gave priority to military needs. The Ukrainian armed forces are a financially stretched institution operating in a post-totalitarian system in which state funding is meagre and in which declared priorities are rarely met. No one of consequence believes that restoration of the Soviet model is either desirable or feasible. In present conditions, the diversion of military personnel from military tasks contradicts the provisions and spirit of a State Programme of Reform and Development designed to produce a 'mobile', 'well equipped' and (by 2015) all-professional force with 'Euro-Atlantic' characteristics. The Ministry of Defence and General Staff are also adamant that as soon as possible, the armed forces should be funded entirely from the state budget and not from barter, uncollected debts and commercial activity, legalised or not. These sentiments are echoed by society.

### Military cooperation and diplomacy

Among countries of the former USSR, the intensity of Ukraine's engagement in military cooperation and diplomacy is matched only by the three Baltic states. This engagement takes place at two levels. First, as of January 2002, approximately 20,000 Ukrainians have participated in UN mandated (but often NATO-led) peacekeeping operations.[11] Second, Ukraine's engagement with NATO under Partnership for Peace (which it joined on 8 February 1994) is in absolute terms unrivalled. In 2001 approximately 250 multilateral activities, ranging from large-scale exercises to expert-level seminars and exchanges took place between Ukraine and NATO, and an additional 500 such activities occurred at bilateral level 'within the spirit of PfP'.

But the purpose of Ukraine's activity in these spheres differs from that often observed elsewhere. First, participation in international peacekeeping tasks is not one of the elements of the National Security role (although it does provide important training experience). Instead, this activity is designed to enhance the international standing of the country and provide an important source of finance. Second, and in marked contrast, Ukraine–NATO military cooperation is designed to enhance national security by transferring expertise to Ukraine's armed forces. Since serious defence reform began in 2000, the military leadership has been emphatic that the purpose of such cooperation is (in the words of former Minister of Defence, Army General Oleksandr Kuzmuk) 'to support defence reform in the country'. The leadership is equally emphatic that NATO's experience in joint training and operations, budgeting, professionalisation, civil–military collaboration and 'operations other than war' is of direct relevance to this reform. As a result, the NATO–Ukraine relationship has moved beyond exchanges and activities and has become an institutionalised process of audit and consultation.

Despite these relatively enduring features which characterise defence roles and their perceived legitimacy, the evolution of the relationship between armed forces and society has altered military roles and has also produced a number of sharp and still unresolved dilemmas.

## The post-independence period, 1991–94

From the time of its electoral success in March 1990, the Ukrainian nationalist movement perceived visibly independent armed forces to be a prerequisite of statehood. In Ukraine, this relationship was seen to be more immediate and vital than it was in Poland and Czechoslovakia, where the attributes of (and 'fitness' for) statehood were not seriously questioned by the international community.[12] So obvious was this relationship that communist opportunists, flocking to the nationalist banner throughout 1990–91, threw their support behind the effort to establish Ukrainian armed forces. Not surprisingly, therefore, the right to create independent armed forces was established in the *Verkhovna Rada's* (Supreme Soviet's) Declaration of Sovereignty of 16 July 1990, more than a year before the leadership of the *Rada* proclaimed Ukraine's independence on 24 August 1991 and eighteen months before these armed forces were formally established (December 1991).

In the immediate post-independence period, the Ukrainian armed forces were meant to serve two primary roles: Regime Defence and National Security. The problem is that, in practical terms, there were no Ukrainian armed forces in 1990–91, only formations of the Soviet armed forces on Ukrainian territory. Moreover, not since the early 1930s had units of the Soviet armed forces been organised on the national-territorial principle. At the time of the USSR's dissolution, the average regiment was composed of servicemen from 18 to 30 distinct nationalities. It was estimated that 70 per cent of officers serving in Ukraine were ethnically Russian – and also estimated that over 150,000 ethnically Ukrainian officers were serving elsewhere in the Soviet Union. Although all of these formations (including the Black Sea Fleet) were nationalised by decree on 22 October 1991, their reliability remained a pressing issue at least until the summer of 1992. To be sure, the salience of this issue was reinforced by the state policy of a Russian Federation determined to preserve the integrated Soviet military system under CIS auspices – a battle not conceded until the Russian armed forces were established in May 1992.

This compelling concern accounts for two innovations which played an influential role during this initial stage. The establishment of the first of these, the Ukrainian Union of Officers (UUO) – in defiance of Soviet law – was in itself a rite of passage to statehood. Like Soviet commissars after the Bolshevik Revolution, the UUO played a guardianship role in the armed forces. But unlike commissars, they did not stand outside the military command structure and, indeed, until late 1993, UUO membership was a prerequisite for promotion. The second innovation was the establishment of a distinct military service, the National Guard of Ukraine in October 1991. From the time of its establishment until its dissolution (December 1999), the National Guard was given the task of backing up Ministry of Internal Affairs (MVS) Internal Troops and Border Troops in a crisis. But in this initial period, its primary task was providing a politically reliable force during the period of transition.

Both the UUO and National Guard were checks and counters to a Soviet era military establishment numbering some 750,000 men at the time of independence.[13] But the actual transformation of that military establishment was the product of other measures:

- Administering an oath of loyalty to officers deployed on Ukrainian territory (spring 1992). Approximately 12,000 officers and warrant officers refused to take the oath and either left the services or joined the Russian armed forces;
- Repatriating ethnically Ukrainian officers and warrant officers from other former Union Republics (of which 33,000 had returned by 1994);
- Transforming the political deputies (*zampoliti*) of the former Chief Political Directorate of the Soviet Army and Navy (GlavPU) into a Social Psychological Service;
- Establishing an integrated system of officer education – a Herculean (and still incomplete) task, which has not only meant revising the Soviet curriculum, but filling large gaps in an all-Union system of

officer education, which did not provide for all areas of specialisation in Ukraine itself;

- Establishing, in principle, a system of universal pre-induction military-patriotic education, by transforming the Soviet DOSAAF infrastructure into a Society for Support of the Defence of Ukraine;
- Establishing a Military Counter-Intelligence Department, subordinated like its Soviet era equivalent to the security services, rather than the Ministry of Defence – but unlike its Soviet predecessor, staffed by officers recruited outside the former KGB.[14]

Yet for all these measures, a cynic would argue that the main engine of transformation was the collapse of financial support for the large, well-trained and well-equipped formations occupying the three Military Districts and the Fleet retained on Ukraine's territory (some have argued that this 'transformation' was still occurring as late as 1999). The fact remains that without turbulence or upheaval, Ukraine succeeded in establishing national armed forces and command structures within a year of independence. By 1993, armed forces subordinated to the Ministry of Defence were well on their way to becoming a Ukrainian institution. As the issue of political reliability lost its salience, and the Soviet military system's antibody, the UUO, began to atrophy, the new Minister of Defence, Vitaliy Radetzsky (who replaced Konstantyn Morozov in October 1993) saw no reason to maintain its commissar prerogatives and curbed its influence.

## The institutionalisation of statehood, 1994–99

Speaking before parliament on the fifth anniversary of Ukraine's independence, President Leonid Kuchma declared that 'the transitional period in the self-determination of the state is over'. Without too much immodesty, his predecessor, Leonid Kravchuk, might have risked making the same claim in January and February 1994, the dates, respectively, of the US–Russia–Ukraine Tripartite Agreement and Ukraine's membership of NATO's newly established Partnership for Peace. These events marked a positive turn in the geopolitical position of the state. Not only did they signify the beginning of Ukraine's unilateral nuclear disarmament (completed by June 1996) and the start of NATO–Ukraine cooperation, they were the first steps towards what became a positive and seismic turn in the policy of the United States (which elevated Ukraine to third position as a foreign aid recipient by 1995) and the first serious Russian attempts to come to terms de facto and not only de jure with

Ukraine's independence. But for three reasons, Kuchma's claim in August 1996 could be accepted without the questioning which Kravchuk's might have received. First, his own election in July 1994, secured with the support of the more Russophile eastern regions, served as the prelude not to a Russian oriented policy, but a more realistic (and warmly reciprocated) western oriented one. Second, by the spring of 1995, Kuchma's policies had stabilised the economic condition of the country. Third, on 14 June 1996, president and parliament agreed on a Ukrainian Constitution (avoiding the sanguinary preliminaries to the approval of the Russian Federation Constitution in December 1993).

These achievements greatly diminished earlier concerns about regime security, as well as national security. Conclusion of the 'Big Treaty' and Black Sea Fleet accords with the Russian Federation (May 1997) diminished the national security threat still further. Yet, two contradictory trends began to appear at the same time. First, in Ukraine as in other parts of the former Soviet Union, it was becoming clear that the 'revolution' of 1991 was a contained revolution, and that very little devolution of political and economic power had taken place. The removal of the old order's supports and certainties, coupled with the persistence of many of its more objectionable features – gross inequalities of power and opportunity, opaque and conspiratorial norms of administration, arrogant and unaccountable institutions – had greatly diminished support for the political authorities by the time an overwhelmingly left-wing parliament was elected in March 1998. No less ominous was the almost insurrectionary character of the miners' strikes of February and July 1996: a repetition of which could, in the words of the secretary of the National Security and Defence council (NSDC), create a situation where the country 'could lose independence'.[15] These trends had a subtle, but definite bearing on the debate about the internal functions of the armed forces.

According to the January 1997 National Security Concept, 'the military organisation of the state, including Ukraine's armed forces … shall counteract external and internal military threats; fight organised crime; ensure protection of the population in case of dangerous social conflicts'. But in what specific capacity? The preoccupation at the core of the Concept was the concern that internal crisis and emergency (including the type of strike mentioned above) could be provoked or exploited by internal *or external* actors with ulterior political or geopolitical ends. To more forward thinking minds in the General Staff, the question answered itself. In the words of Rear Admiral Yuriy Shalyt (now head of a department at the National Security and Defence Council), 'in local conflicts or national disasters, which can also provoke conflicts, it is precisely military units with the right training that can and should set up a zone which would make it possible to direct or influence the processes occurring outside it'.[16] In other words, the armed forces would not directly confront those engaged in disorder, but 'set up a zone' to prevent the zone of conflict expanding, underscore Ukraine's sovereignty and the commitment of the state, and deter (and if necessary prevent) actors in adjacent regions or outside Ukraine from transforming emergency into disorder, disorder into civil conflict and civil conflict into local war. By the same token, such a zone would also be set up to contain the effects of emergency situations on or in the vicinity of Ukraine's borders. Yet how would the actions of Ministry of Defence armed forces and non-Ministry of Defence military formations be coordinated? As late as 1999, some experts argued that subordination should depend 'on the conflict's character'. Yet in 1997, the General Staff was given operational authority over non-Ministry of Defence formations in all such emergencies, and this scheme of subordination has not been revised.

A second negative trend emerging in Kuchma's first term was the stagnation of military development and reform. These years were not without accomplishments in the military sphere, notably approval of the National Security Concept, already referred to, as well as the rationalisation of the command structure, delineation of functions between the Ministry of Defence and General Staff, consolidation of the educational system and the diminution of clannish networks in the forces. But it is during these years that the deficiencies of the 'state military organisation' became chronic and began to corrode the whole. These deficiencies are well documented: inadequate budgetary commitments and the failure to meet them, wholesale shortage of essential provisions and materials, uncontrolled deterioration of infrastructure, the progressive collapse of social provision, bloated service establishments, senseless duplication of facilities and, in all spheres, a fundamental lack of correspondence between policy goals and the means available.[17] Apart from their profound military consequences, these deficiencies had also transformed the armed forces into a profound social problem for the conscripts obliged to serve in it, as well as those officers who, despite depression and disillusionment, have attempted to remain in the service. By the end of 1999, 55 per cent of officers cited general conditions in the armed forces as poor and 57 per cent described their service in terms of depression.[18] To these social ills, we must add another, already discussed: the uncontrolled proliferation of what the Ukrainian Constitution terms 'other military formations' outside the Ministry of Defence.

## 'The stage of reform and development', 2000–present

By the end of 1999, a variety of factors – the Kosovo conflict, Putin's more 'pragmatic' (hard-headed) policy towards Ukraine, the deterioration of economic conditions and the widening gap between state and society – persuaded the state leadership that a thorough reform of the defence system had become unavoidable. The State Programme of Military Reform and Development 2001–2005 was the first programme to make a serious, if not altogether successful attempt to put resources and capabilities in balance; it marked a significant shift from the general war ethos, unquestioned in Soviet times, to an emphasis on preventing and managing civil emergencies and 'local conflicts'; and it launched a resolute effort to eliminate duplicate structures and surplus infrastructure. It also launched a more intense, concrete and practical programme of cooperation with NATO which, in turn, has made no secret of its desire to pursue military reform as a means of strengthening civil society (and not only civil democratic control) in Ukraine. Since this new stage officially began, the State Programme has been supplemented by the Concept of the Armed Forces 2010 and the State Programme of Armed Forces Transition towards Manning on a Contract Basis, designed to transform today's 295,000 mixed conscript and volunteer force into an all-volunteer force of 180,000 by 2015. Several deeper reductions in equipment and manning levels have been approved since the president approved the State Programme in July 2000, and more can be expected as economic realities continue to bite.

Thus far, measures taken since the programme's approval have arrested some of the processes of deterioration described above and retarded the progression of others. In the social sphere, arrears have finally been paid, salaries of officers have increased by between 37 and 46 per cent, and over the course of 2001, the number of disciplinary infringements fell by 30 per cent. But despite a salary fixed at UAH 425 (US$80) per month for newly recruited contract soldiers, the average wage of contracted servicemen, NCOs and officers in 2001 still fell below the official subsistence level of UAH 342 (US$65) per month; almost 100,000 servicemen (Ministry of Defence and non-Ministry of Defence) have no living quarters, and only 57 per cent of students attending officer training courses declared that they were actually willing to enrol as officers. In spite of some highly tangible accomplishments in other areas in the short time since implementation got underway in January 2001, it is the nearly unanimous view of specialists and practitioners that without a significant increase in state funding, the programme will not meet its objectives.

This is not an impossible task. Ukraine has experienced two years of significant economic growth. There have also been clear, even alarmist declarations by senior politicians about the need for increases in defence expenditure in the wake of the 11 September events, and public support for an increase in defence spending is substantial. Nevertheless, the 2002 defence budget of UAH 3.4 billion (US$647 million), while an improvement over last year's UAH 2.4 billion budget, will still only meet 40 to 45 per cent of 'minimal needs'. Moreover, out of this sum, the component reserved for defence reform has actually declined since 2001.[19] Until the country's political authorities take responsibility for this state of affairs, it is unlikely to change.

The authorities will also need to understand that national interests will continue to suffer until defence reform is expanded into a broader reform of the security sector. Four imperatives argue against deferring this issue further. Undoubtedly, the first of these imperatives is economic. Not only are manning levels and maintenance costs of non-Ministry of Defence formations unpublished. Remarkably enough, they have not been revealed to those who allocate budgetary resources: the Cabinet of Ministers and the *Verkhovna Rada*. In the case of some of these formations, a proportion of funding is legally 'non-budgetary'; in others (notably the civilian police – *militsia* – subordinated to the MVS) a large proportion of funding is probably illicit and illegal. The implication is clear. If the staff of the *militsia*, Tax Police and Customs Service cannot live on their state salaries, they will become entrepreneurial with the powers at their disposal and offer their services to those who can pay for them. Obviously, this is as much a national security problem as a financial one.

The second imperative is operational. If 'multi-component' (joint) operations are to be the basis for deterring and containing conflict, then there must be effective interaction between Ministry of Defence and non-Ministry of Defence formations – and hence a common ethos and working culture. The ethos and operating culture of Ministry of Defence armed forces is steadily becoming more 'Euro-Atlantic'. While this is also true for the Ministry of Emergencies, and while Border Troops are beginning to take the same path, this is manifestly not the case for troops and other personnel who form part of the Ministry of Interior and SBU. Until this changes, Ukraine will possess a defence and security 'system' which is schizophrenic in character. The third imperative is geopolitical. Even before the 23 May decision on long-term NATO membership, NATO had begun to pay progressively more attention to the linkage between defence reform and security sector reform, and so had the European Union. As Poland finally grasped in the mid-1990s, accession to NATO will not be treated as a serious proposition until this linkage is understood, established and secure. The fourth imperative comes from society. Until reform extends to those structures so deeply mistrusted today, ordinary citizens will continue to distrust the authorities of the state. Even where defence reform is concerned, society distrusts the information it is given: 40.4 per cent describing it as 'insufficient', 39.6 per cent believing that 'we are actually barred from trustworthy information'.[20] One year into implementation, only 4.4 per cent stated that they believed a 'planned process of reform' was taking place. This is a revealing symptom of the gap which exists between state and society in Ukraine. As the authors of the National Security Concept warned in 1997, this gap is the most serious security problem that the country faces.

## Conclusions

Several conclusions can be drawn, not all of them consistent with conventional wisdom. First, the armed forces are broadly trusted in Ukraine, but the state authorities are not. It is the latter whom ordinary citizens blame for deficiencies in the armed forces, not military servicemen. Second, citizens perceive the geopolitical environment as unfavourable. They are alert to the possibility that military threats could arise, and they believe that budgetary and manning policy must be adequate to these challenges. Raising defence expenditure would be a popular measure, especially if this were coupled with a serious and well publicised defence reform. Third, in the eyes of the public, no genuine defence reform is taking place. Both the political and military authorities have done a poor job in publicising the aims of the State Programme and its limited successes, not to say the practical benefits of NATO–Ukraine cooperation. Fourth, information about defence is not only inadequate, it is perceived to be inadequate, and the information which is provided tends not to be trusted. Civilian, democratic control is seen as a myth. Finally, other (non-Ministry of Defence) power structures are regarded with apprehension, contempt or downright hostility. Very few perceive that they are motivated by a sense of duty, interested in upholding the law or committed to the national interest.

Ukraine's citizens broadly support defence reform and for remarkably similar reasons to those advanced by the authors of the State Programme. Unfortunately, neither state nor society believe that the other party is committed to the task. Until this changes, the programme of reform has little chance of meeting its objectives.

# Notes

1. According to an autumn 2000 poll of the Ukrainian Centre of Economic and Political Studies (also known as the Razumkov Centre) (hereafter UCEPS), *National Security and Defence* (Kyiv), 11 (2000), 10.

2. According to a UCEPS poll of January 2002, 28.8 per cent 'completely trusted' the armed forces and 36 per cent were 'inclined to trust' them. Note that the earlier poll was taken a full month before the so-called 'presidential tape scandal' which damaged the standing of Ukraine's state institutions yet further. According to this earlier poll, 20.2 per cent trusted the Security Service of Ukraine (SBU). After the revelations surrounding the murder of journalist Grigoriy Gongadze, it would not be surprising if their standing has declined, though the author knows of no polling evidence later than September 2000.

3. On 12 June 2002, a new Concept of National Security was approved by the National Security and Defence Council, but it has not been published as of this writing.

4. During the Kosovo conflict, Russia dispatched a 'humanitarian' convoy to Yugoslavia (halted on the Hungary–Ukraine border); in April 1999, it redeployed the intelligence ship *Liman* (and prepared to redeploy other vessels) from Sevastopol to the Adriatic; and it planned to transit Ukraine with airborne troop reinforcements after the 'brilliant dash to Pristina' in June 1999. Russian Federation Naval Infantry components of the Black Sea Fleet routinely train in Crimea for combat duty in Chechnya.

5. Volodymyr Shkidchenko, 'Some Aspects of Professionalisation of the Armed Forces of Ukraine', *National Security and Defence*, 5 (2002), 4.

6. Mykola Sungurovskiy, 'Military Reform: Progress against a Background of Stagnation', *National Security and Defence*, 1 (2002), 59.

7. According to the January 2002 UCEPS poll, 43.4 per cent assessed the budget as 'low', 23.5 per cent as 'very low', 7.7 per cent as 'sufficient', and only 1.5 per cent as 'high'. As tends to be the case in Ukrainian opinion polls, a large proportion of respondents, in this case 23.1 per cent, said 'hard to assess'. Andriy Bychenko, 'Ukrainian Citizens about their Army', *National Security and Defence*, 1 (2002), 35.

8. The proportions of respondents supporting professionalisation is not as sensitive to age group as might be supposed. Whereas 77.4 per cent of respondents between 18 and 29 responded favourably, the favourable response in the 30 to 39 year category and 40 to 49 year categories was 72.9 per cent and 73.6 per cent respectively. Even a majority of those over 60 were in favour (53.6 per cent). Andriy Bychenko and Mykhailo Pashkov, 'A Professional Army in Ukraine: the Views and Assessments of the Population', *National Security and Defence*, 5 (2002), 29, 32.

9. Bychenko and Pashkov, 'A Professional Army in Ukraine: the Views and Assessments of the Population', 32.

10. The full name of this ministry is Ministry for Responding to Emergencies and the Consequences of the Chernobyl Catastrophe.

11. Since 1992 Ukraine has participated in UNPROFOR (former Yugoslavia), UNTAES (Croatia), UNPREDEP (former Yugoslav Republic of Macedonia),

UNMOP (Prevlaka), IFOR/SFOR (Bosnia), KFOR (Kosovo) and UNIFIL (Lebanon).

12. 'Without its own armed forces, Ukraine can never become a full European state' (first Congress of Ukrainian Union of Officers, 27–28 July 1991)

13. Although no exact figures were kept, the withdrawal of Soviet military units from Central Europe increased these numbers to over 1,000,000 – numbers which *do not include* servicemen from non-Ministry of Defence formations (MVS, Border Guards, SBU, Ministry of Emergency Situations, National Guard, etc.).

14. Soviet Military Counter-Intelligence officers, subordinated to the Third Chief Directorate of the KGB, should not be confused with *intelligence* officers, subordinated to the Chief Intelligence Directorate of the General Staff (GRU – GUR in Ukrainian). The same distinction applies to the Russian and Ukrainian armed forces.

15. *BBC Summary of World Broadcasts: Former Soviet Union*, 19 July 1996.

16. Ukrainian news agency, UNIAN, 28 August 1997.

17. For example, UCEPS, 'Military Reform in Ukraine: the Start, or Another False Start?', *National Security and Defence*, 1 (2000), 2–40.

18. Asked to identify the most serious factor affecting their morale, 45 per cent cited absence of housing, basic amenities and 'lack of social protection', 25 per cent cited 'loss of the moral value of military service' and 23 per cent cited the low calibre of the country's military leadership. UCEPS, 'Military Reform in Ukraine: the Start, or Another False Start?', 10.

19. Mykola Sungurovskiy, 'Military Reform: Progress against a Background of Stagnation', *National Security and Defence*, 1 (2002), 57.

20. Bychenko, 'Ukrainian Citizens about their Army', 40.

# Part V
# Conclusion

# 14
# Conclusion: Patterns and Trends in Military–Society Relations in Postcommunist Europe

*Timothy Edmunds, Anthony Forster and Andrew Cottey*

Military–society relations in postcommunist Europe have undergone profound changes in the period since 1989. These have resulted from a variety of different factors and influences, not least of which has been the collapse of communism and the elimination of the Cold War divide in Europe.

In analysing these changes, three issues are the concern of this volume. What are the various roles of armed forces in their societies? What are their bases for legitimacy? And how are these changing in the post-Cold War environment? In the framework introduced in the first chapter of this volume, we argue that the nature of states' military–society relations are intimately bound up with the military's legitimacy in fulfilling particular roles. We argue that the military's roles are often diverse and are not necessarily limited to the 'traditional' functional demands of war-fighting and the defence of national territory. We identify five broad roles for the military that we term National Security, Nation Builder, Regime Defence, Domestic Military Assistance and Military Diplomacy. The National Security role corresponds to the functional imperative identified in much of the existing military–society literature. It concerns the military's role in defending the state from military threats to its security, whether internal or external. In the Nation Builder role, the military acts as an agent of national consolidation and socialisation. In the Regime Defence role, the military supports or upholds the power of a particular domestic political regime, whether that regime is based around a political party, ideology, interest group or individual. In the Domestic Military Assistance role, the armed forces play a variety of different roles in relation to the internal governance of the state, for example in providing aid to the civil community in dealing with severe socio-economic problems such as natural disasters. In the Military Diplomacy role, the military are used as a diplomatic instrument of foreign policy to promote particular values and policies across the globe.

We suggest that the prioritisation of different roles results from a variety of domestic and international factors and influences. In turn, these shape the character of military–society relations. These influences include threat perceptions and the geostrategic context, international pressure and aid, technological change, historical legacies, the domestic political context, economic constraints and societal change. The balance between these factors explains the particular roles which develop for armed forces in different national contexts. It is to the patterns of military–society relations in postcommunist Europe and the factors influencing military and society relations that this chapter now turns.

## Patterns of military–society relations in postcommunist Europe

During the communist period, military–society relations in central and eastern Europe were characterised by both diversity and commonality. On the one hand, particular historical legacies, the nature of each country's relationship with Moscow, its place within the Warsaw Pact and its particular strategy for national defence created differences in military–society relations in the region. On the other hand, common features of communist civil–military relations – for example, the key role of the military in the relationship between the Communist Party and the state and the use of universal conscription as a means of politicisation and socialisation – created many common features in military–society relations across the region. Key roles for the communist military included National Security, Nation Builder and Regime Defence. Since the collapse of communism in the region, many of these influences on military–society relations have been transformed. While the nature of these changes sometimes differs substantially between countries, several common trends are visible across the region and identifiable patterns of military–society relations are emerging. Common and interconnected trends which have had an impact in this area include a fundamental change in the military's relationship with the state and government; a decline in popular threat perceptions; a demilitarisation of areas of society that were militarised under communism; a decline in the legitimacy and perceived utility of conscription as a method of military organisation; and, in the context of these other changes, the emergence of new roles and new bases for legitimacy among postcommunist armed forces.

With the collapse of the communist system, the military's role as defenders of that particular political regime collapsed.[1] The end of the Cold War also resulted in a decline, at least in most cases, in the importance of the national defence role and especially a lowering of popular threat perceptions. Alongside the decline of these roles, new roles and new bases for legitimacy are emerging in many central and eastern European countries. These have tended to focus around two areas: the Domestic Military Assistance role and the Military Diplomacy role. In the Domestic Military Assistance role, the legitimacy of the armed forces has been reinforced by their role in – or potential for – aid to the government and wider civilian society during times of crisis, such as during the disastrous flooding which afflicted parts of central Europe in 1998. In the Military Diplomacy role, the legitimacy of many postcommunist militaries has been strengthened by societal perceptions of their professional performance in multinational peace support operations and by their central importance to many states' integration with NATO and the West more generally. Beyond these general patterns, the case studies in this volume suggest that three distinct trends in military–society relations are emerging in central and eastern Europe. These are not necessarily mutually exclusive, but they do point to the emergence of clusters of states sharing common experiences in this area.

In the first cluster of states, which includes the Baltic republics, Poland, Slovakia, Romania, Bulgaria, and more recently Croatia, societal attitudes towards the military have either remained positive and/or improved significantly since the collapse of communism. This trend reflects the strong historical standing the armed forces have in these states and/or the success in the *re-nationalisation* and *de-politicisation* of the military since 1989. Among this group of states, the development of the Military Diplomacy role has been pronounced, and has helped to strengthen the legitimacy of the armed forces in society. Thus, as Jan Trapans and Andrius Krivas both argue, Latvia and Lithuania identified membership of NATO as a key national security priority, in particular as a security guarantee vis-à-vis Russia and as a symbol of wider political integration with the West. In this context, the armed forces have been at the forefront of the countries' wider western integration and this has formed an important new foundation of their legitimacy in society. In both cases, popular support, for NATO accession in particular, has been widespread and the armed forces' standing in society has improved as a consequence. The case of the Baltic republics additionally illustrates the connection between the National Security and Military Diplomacy roles. For these countries, integration with NATO is not simply about attempting to address geostrategic vulnerabilities through effective collective security mechanisms but also about promoting wider integration with the West and, indeed, broader liberal democratic values.

Similar dynamics are visible to varying degrees within the other countries in this group. Alex J. Bellamy points out that this process has recently developed very rapidly in Croatia, marking an important break with the pattern in that country earlier in the 1990s. Under President Franjo Tuđman, the Croatian Army (HV) was politicised, tied into the regime and viewed by many in society as a custodian of Croatian nationalism. Since Tuđman's death and the electoral defeat of his nationalist Croatian Democratic Union (HDZ) party, Croatia has actively pursued membership of Partnership for Peace (PfP) and NATO as part of its efforts to integrate itself – culturally, militarily and politically – into the European mainstream. The HV is now undergoing a process of reform and professionalisation and is changing its role from one focused on Regime Defence to one increasingly concerned with Military Diplomacy and Domestic Military Assistance. As in Latvia and Lithuania, this change of role has contributed to a shift in the HV's bases for legitimacy in society. Where previously these had rested on the military's performance in its wars with Yugoslavia and on Tuđman's particular breed of conservative Croatian nationalism, now the military's role as a 'vanguard' of reform and westernisation is increasingly prevalent. Thus, for example – and despite continuing problems in areas such as cooperation with the International Criminal Tribunal for the former Yugoslavia (ICTY) – the HV has perhaps been the most active of all of Croatia's institutions in terms of bilateral and multilateral cooperative activities with western countries and institutions, recently formalised by joining PfP and NATO's Membership Action Plan (MAP).

The *re-nationalisation* of armed forces is also an important feature of this cluster of states. In all these states, the military's legitimacy in society has been closely linked to its role as a representative of either new or newly re-emergent national values – part of the Nation Builder role identified in the framework. As Paul Latawski, Larry Watts and Laura Cleary point out in their case studies, the armed forces of Poland, Romania and Bulgaria had always had important national and patriotic associations within their societies. To varying degrees, these were suppressed during the communist period, when the armed forces came to represent a particular and unpopular regime, ideology and system of government rather than the 'nation'. While the importance of the armed forces' national legitimacy never went away in these countries – former Polish President Lech Wałęsa famously described his country's communist era armed forces as like a radish: red (communist) on the outside, but white (Polish, national) on the inside – it was overlaid by their association with the communist regimes, which diminished public support for the military.[2] With the collapse of communism, the national/patriotic importance of the armed forces has visibly come to the fore again and forms a significant source of societal legitimacy for the military.

In the Baltic republics and Slovakia, the Nation Builder role is also clear, but in a slightly different way. Here the creation of national armed forces went hand in hand with the creation of new states, adding to their value as national symbols. This is particularly striking in the Baltic republics, where, during the communist period, the Soviet military was viewed extremely negatively – as representatives of foreign occupation and an unwanted political ideology. In building their armed forces 'from scratch', the Baltic States have largely eliminated this legacy and forged new, national, bases for their military's legitimacy in society. Similarly, in Slovakia, as Marybeth Ulrich points out, the creation of independent Slovak armed forces from the remains of the Czechoslovak army has been a key element in asserting the country's independent statehood and national identity.

A second cluster of states consists of the Czech Republic, Hungary and Slovenia. Despite many similarities with the first group described above, in these states the decline in the traditional bases for the military's legitimacy in society has not been adequately matched by the emergence of new ones. As a result, military–society relations in these countries tend to be characterised by popular disinterest in and apathy towards the military and defence issues. This has resulted in societal de-prioritisation of defence issues and a reluctance to spend money on the armed forces. Significantly however, and in common with states in the first cluster, the armed forces in these countries *are* developing new roles – particularly in the areas of Domestic Military Assistance and Military Diplomacy – which are beginning to build new foundations for military legitimacy in society.

As Marie Vlachová argues, military–society relations in the Czech Republic have been shaped by a tradition of societal anti-militarism, inspired by the Czechs' negative experiences of Austro-Hungarian and Soviet domination and the inability of the Czechoslovak armed forces to defend the country in 1938 and 1968. Indeed, until quite recently, public opinion polls suggested that the Czech public consistently rated the profession of military officer poorly. For many Czechs, the military has been seen as an unnecessary and, given its history, ineffective diversion of resources away from more pressing concerns such as the health service or education. Since the mid-1990s however, new roles for the military have emerged and these in turn have begun to change societal perceptions of the military. In particular, the crucial importance of the Czech armed forces in assisting civilian society during the devastating floods of 1998 and 2002 – a Domestic Military Assistance role – helped significantly to improve Czech society's views on the utility and standing of its military, with public opinion polls showing a consistent rise in public trust in the military from the mid-1990s onwards. Similarly, a popular perception that the Czech army has performed in an effective, professional manner on peace support operations in the former Yugoslavia and elsewhere has further transformed their domestic image, by illustrating in a public manner that they *can* make a concrete contribution to the security and foreign policy interests of the Czech Republic above and beyond an increasingly de-prioritised defence of national territory mission. Indeed, in the context of our argument about new military roles creating new bases for the armed forces' legitimacy in society, it is notable that key personnel – such as members of rapid reaction forces, peacekeepers and pilots – are classed in a separate category to 'soldiers' more broadly, and are consistently rated highly in public opinion polls.[3]

Pál Dunay argues that similar trends are present in Hungary. In common with the Czech Republic, the societal legitimacy of the Hungarian military's National Security role has been diluted by its historically poor performance. Again, however, NATO membership and especially Hungarian participation in multinational PSOs has helped to create more positive views of the military in Hungarian society, and new bases for military legitimacy. As Dunay notes, for example, the Hungarian military's participation in these multinational operations publicly illustrates that it is on a par with other nations with larger and more advanced armed forces. Moreover, it visibly demonstrates that Hungary is a direct contributor to the maintenance of international peace and security – a goal that is assigned increasing importance in Hungarian society. While this process has perhaps not gone as far as in the Czech Republic, multinational collaboration and NATO accession have nevertheless brought positive benefits in terms of the Hungarian military's standing in society.

Slovenia, in common with the Baltic republics, was faced with the task of creating completely new armed forces at the beginning of the 1990s.

This, together with their successful performance in Slovenia's short war of independence in 1991, gave the Slovenian armed forces a key Nation Builder role during the early part of the decade. However, as Marjan Malešic and Ljubica Jelušic point out, since then an independent Slovenian state has been firmly established and the Slovenian public's threat perceptions have declined significantly as a result of the end of the Yugoslav wars and the country's increasingly close relations with western Europe. In this context, and combined with a legacy of societal anti-militarism, the Slovenian military has seen its legitimacy based on National Security and Nation Builder roles undermined. As in the Czech and Hungarian cases, in Slovenia new roles focused around the utility of the military in disaster relief – the Domestic Military Assistance role – and participation in multinational PSOs have emerged which are creating new bases for the military's legitimacy in society. These new roles provide clear public justifications for military and defence spending at a time when military threats to Slovenian territory appear small. However, until Slovenia was invited to join NATO in November 2002, it differed from the Czech Republic and Hungary in that its armed forces continued to be on the front line of the country's drive for NATO membership. In common with states in the first cluster, this boosted their standing in society by locating them as flag-bearers for the country's postcommunist process of reintegration with western Europe. This was particularly evident in the period after the 1997 Madrid summit when Poland, the Czech Republic and Hungary were invited into NATO, but Slovenia was not. Slovenia's failure to procure a membership invitation at this point focused popular attention on the central role the armed forces had to play in this process, and so raised their public profile and placed them firmly in the vanguard of the country's drive for western integration in the eyes of wider society.

In a third cluster of states – including, to various degrees, Ukraine, the Federal Republic of Yugoslavia (FRY, renamed the State Union of Serbia and Montenegro in February 2003) and, until 2000, Croatia – the armed forces retain a prominent role in society, but some aspects of the military are viewed negatively. While the military remains an important symbolic national institution whose popular legitimacy was reinforced – in FRY and Croatia at least – by its role in 'nation building under fire' in the 1990s, this perception is balanced by problems such as the poor socio-economic position of the military and the difficult conditions in which soldiers – and especially conscripts – are expected to serve. In some countries, these difficulties are reinforced by socio-economic problems and the negative experience of conflict, and particularly poor military performance, high casualty figures and systematic human rights abuses. In general, societal legitimacy in this cluster rests firmly in the armed forces' National Security role, though with an additional – and a diminishing Nation Builder role.

In Ukraine, James Sherr highlights the continuing importance of the armed forces in the National Security role – as guarantors of the independent Ukrainian state against potential aggression from other states. As a corollary to this, the Ukrainian military's Nation Builder role still remains relatively strong. In Ukraine, the armed forces have been a key element in the establishment of the new Ukrainian state, and as such have a very direct association with the nation building process. Additionally, the Ukrainian armed forces have been active and broadly well-respected participants in multinational PSOs. Despite these legitimating factors, the Ukrainian military continues to suffer from many debilitating socio-economic problems. These include poor living standards, severe under-funding, and – as evidenced by the accidental shooting down of a Russian civilian airliner during a Ukrainian military exercise in the Crimea on 4 October 2001 and subsequent resignation of Defence Minister Olexander Kuzmuk – questions over their professional competence. These difficulties have served to damage the Ukrainian armed forces' societal standing.

In Yugoslavia, as James Gow and Ivan Zveržanovski argue, the military continues to retain a high degree of societal legitimacy in Serbia at least, but this is being challenged from a number of different directions. The Yugoslav Army (VJ) retains a strong focus on the National Security and Nation Building roles, though this is complicated and challenged by the unclear constitutional structure and future of the Yugoslav Federation. In the National Security role, the VJ's legitimacy has been enhanced by a societal perception that it performed professionally and competently under difficult circumstances, particularly during the NATO bombing of 1999 and the subsequent crisis in South Serbia. In the Nation Builder role, the VJ continues to function as a symbol of national pride (for Serbs at least) and federal unity. In many respects, it is one of the only real federal (as opposed to republic-level) institutions remaining in FRY. In addition, the VJ is widely held to have been less responsible for war crimes activity during its involvement in the Yugoslav wars than the special paramilitary units, and the Ministry of the Interior forces (MUP). This, coupled with a perception that the VJ has been less heavily involved in corruption and criminality than the MUP, has given it the image of being 'cleaner' than other security sector organisations in the FRY.

However, as Gow and Zveržanovski point out, it is clear that the VJ cannot evade responsibility for the excesses of the wars in Croatia, Bosnia and Serbia. Several key generals have been indicted by the ICTY, and in many cases the involvement of VJ special units in war crimes runs very deep indeed. In turn this undermines those elements of the VJ's legitimacy that are based on its professionalism in the National Security and Nation Builder roles. In addition, the VJ's legitimacy in the Nation Builder role is challenged by the uncertain future of the FRY itself. Indeed, as a federal institution, the VJ's current roles and bases for legitimacy are likely to undergo a profound reassessment if the federation itself ceases to exist. Already, the Yugoslav military looks less like a federal institution and more like a Serbian one. Certainly its influence, standing and its popular legitimacy in Montenegro is very limited, where its role has been almost wholly supplanted by republican MUP forces. In Kosovo, of course, the VJ (and indeed the federal government) is viewed with hostility and its role has been largely eliminated.

In Croatia under Tuđman, as Bellamy highlights, the societal legitimacy of the Croatian Army (HV) was similarly characterised by both positive and negative influences. During Croatia's involvement in the war, the HV performed well in its National Security role, and was fundamentally linked to the new state's nation building process. However, from the early–mid-1990s onwards, the HV's societal legitimacy in these roles was increasingly undermined by its close association with the Tuđman regime, and its reputation as a source of corruption and conservative nationalism. This situation has changed significantly since the death of Tuđman and the regime change of 2000, not least because of the HV's association with PfP and the NATO accession process. This has encouraged the government to implement an important series of military and civil–military reforms and placed the army at the forefront of Croatia's bid for closer integration with western institutions.

## Factors influencing military–society relations in postcommunist Europe

In general, military–society patterns in postcommunist Europe are characterised by a questioning of traditional military roles and bases for legitimacy. These have undergone major changes in emphases, and in many cases have been supplanted by new roles and new bases for legitimacy. In each of the case studies, the causes of these changes vary according to individual country circumstances, but are often under-pinned by common regional dynamics and experiences. Broadly, these can be divided into international and transnational influences, and domestic influences. These include threat perceptions and the geostrat-egic context, international pressure and aid, technological change, historical legacies, the domestic political context, economic constraints and societal change.

Threat perceptions and the geostrategic context have clearly been of central importance in influencing military–society relations in central and eastern Europe. In the main, and for the past century and a half, the demands and threat of 'modern' warfare on the European continent meant that most European armed forces in both east and west were based primarily on mass armies and conscription. Following the Second World War, the possibility of another major European ground war dom-inated threat perceptions and military planning on both sides of the Iron Curtain, and, with a few exceptions, led to a mass, conscript-based model of armed forces. This was generally perceived as the most appro-priate force structure for the high-intensity, high-casualty conflict that a confrontation between NATO and the Warsaw Pact would have entailed. The continued threat of a European war and the dominance of mass armies had major implications for military–society relations. It meant that societal threat perceptions were both immediate and high, and that military service for most of the male population was a common occur-rence. As a result, European societies' relationships with their armed forces tended to be direct and grounded in personal experience. Moreover, the apparent depth and immediacy of military threat ensured that the demands of the armed forces – whether in financial or human terms – were in general perceived to be legitimate, although debates on the scale of defence spending were common throughout western Europe.[4]

The end of the Cold War transformed perceptions of threat in Europe. In doing so, it undermined the importance of the mass army as a system of military organisation, and introduced major changes in the nature of military–society relations. Today, the threat of a major war in Europe is arguably at its lowest for over a century. As a result, the demands on European armed forces are changing. Increasingly they are being called on to operate outside national territory, and often beyond the European continent. In addition, the kinds of missions they are required to fulfil have also changed. In today's post-Cold War, post-11 September 2001 environment, European armed forces are more likely to find themselves engaged in humanitarian interventions, peace support operations or anti-terrorist activities than they are in preparing for a high-intensity confrontation with a conventional opponent. The demands of these so-called 'new missions' are different from those of the Cold War. In particular, they require armed forces that are smaller, technically skilled, deployable and often all-volunteer. These requirements are having significant impacts on the nature of military–society relations in Europe. Moreover, and as the case studies in this volume imply, these changes go deeper than the simple war-fighting role of the armed forces. In the postcommunist region at least, they are also challenging many of the other wider functions of armed forces in society, and forcing a reconsideration of their traditional bases for societal legitimacy.

The relatively low level of direct threat to national territory in most European states means that the narrow national defence role no longer provides the primary rationale or social basis for the armed forces, and this has undermined the National Security role in its traditional sense. However, a wider conception of security – based around the promotion of stability, defence of values and collective contribution to 'the West' – amongst the countries of the region is increasingly apparent. Indeed, the importance of NATO and EU accession is a key indication of this shift in emphasis, and has been highlighted in many of the case studies in this book. This has led to an increased concentration on the Military Diplomacy role for central and eastern European armed forces, and a subsequent shift in their bases of legitimacy in society. It also illustrates elements of overlap between the National Security and Military Diplomacy roles.

The importance of NATO and EU accession highlights the increased influence of international pressure and aid on military roles – and military–society relations – in the region. Indeed, the case studies in this volume make clear that NATO accession criteria – expressed through the Partnership for Peace (PfP), individual country's Planning and Review Processes (PARPs) and Membership Action Plans (MAPs) – have been central to the postcommunist development of the armed forces in the first two clusters identified above. This has been particularly apparent in the development of cadres within central and eastern European armed forces that are able to participate in multinational military operations. In some cases, a concentration on high-cost, NATO-compatible, externally deployable units has been at the expense of countries' armed forces more widely. Thus, in many countries in the region, defence spending has concentrated on small, elite elements of the armed forces, while the bulk of the military suffers from severe under-funding and decay.[5] In these cases, military reform programmes have been dominated by the development of the Military Diplomacy role, specifically in order to meet the wider foreign policy goal of NATO accession. This in turn has had an impact on the nature of military–society relations by providing new yardsticks against which the legitimacy of the military in society is measured. In this new Military Diplomacy role, the armed forces' legitimacy in society has increasingly become dependent on a perception of their professional performance in multinational operations, the popularity of NATO membership in the country as a whole, and perceptions of the success of the multinational military operation concerned in contributing to international security.

In much of Europe and particularly the United States, technological developments have had a significant impact on the development of particular roles for the armed forces, and on the societal legitimacy of their performance in these roles. In the introduction of this book we highlighted the way in which the so-called 'Revolution in Military Affairs' (RMA) has contributed to changing expectations of acceptable casualty figures on particular sorts of military operations. In many cases it has also encouraged armed forces to take on new roles by making them easier – and less costly – to carry out. In postcommunist Europe, the influence of technological change has been evident, but in practice its influence has been marginal. Economic constraints on defence spending – and especially in the areas of procurement and research and development – have meant that extensive military modernisation programmes have been a low priority. Moreover, in much of the region, given the widespread decline in threat perceptions discussed above, societies and politicians have prioritised other areas of the national budget. In general, where technological change has had an impact in postcommunist Europe, it has tended to be indirectly, through increasing interoperability and operational cooperation with NATO armed forces.

Historical legacies have clearly had an important influence on the character of military–society relations in central and eastern Europe. In the Czech Republic and Hungary, for example, historically-informed traditions of societal anti-militarism have reinforced the de-legitimisation of many traditional military roles and hampered the development of new ones. In contrast, in countries such as Romania or Poland, the traditionally high standing of the military in society has eased their transition from communist-era roles to postcommunist ones. In many cases it has also ensured that armed forces' Nation Builder roles have remained strong. Indeed, it is remarkable that despite decades of communism and more than ten years of common postcommunist challenges, very significant national variations in military–society relations remain and these are still significantly shaped by historical legacies stretching back to the Second World War and earlier. In this sense, the legacy of the past still has an important bearing on military–society relations in contemporary central and eastern Europe.

Despite these differences, however, communist military–society relations had a number of shared features. These included, first, the role of the military as a central element in the party-state nexus. In this respect, the military played a key internal as well as external role as a mechanism for party control of the state (and, as the examples of Hungary in 1956 and Czechoslovakia in 1968 illustrate, an intra-Warsaw Pact mechanism for maintaining Soviet hegemony). Second, throughout communist Europe, there was a high level of state militarisation, with countries throughout the region having large armed forces and spending a high percentage of their GDP on defence. This militarisation was reflected in communist society. Conscription was almost universal amongst the male population, and supported by communist youth organisations with strong military elements. Reserve and civil defence systems across the region ensured that former conscripts remained on the potential call-up list long after they completed their conscript service. Third, the extensive nature of communist conscription systems allowed communist militaries to play important politicisation and socialisation roles.

These features of the communist military–society relationship had a diverse and contradictory impact on general social attitudes to the military. While these attitudes differed according to particular national circumstances, certain characteristics stand out. There were, for example, a series of factors that created a negative attitude towards the military. The fact that the military was part of the communist system, for example, made it associated with the more unpopular or repressive actions of that system. In the non-Soviet States of the Warsaw Pact (NSWP), these negative connotations were reinforced by the perception that NSWP militaries were not just defenders of an authoritarian communist regime, but collaborators in the maintenance of *foreign* communist hegemony.[6] Societal resentment of the military was reinforced by the fact that, as part of the communist elite, the (senior) officer corps often had privileged access to resources.[7] Further, negative experiences of conscription often served to undermine public confidence in the military.

As well as these negative features of communist military–society relations, however, most communist militaries also retained significant public respect. In the Soviet Union, of course, the scale of the Red Army's successes and sacrifices during the Great Patriotic War ensured that for much of the population its image was informed by its wartime role as national saviour.[8] Moreover, despite the military's integral relationship with the communist regime, across the region the military establishment *did* generally manage to maintain a degree of autonomy from the Communist Party itself. In addition, in most cases, communist militaries were *not* used for internal repression or policing purposes, which in turn served to insulate them from the more repressive domestic activities and connotations of the communist regimes proper. Indeed, in practice, these internal roles were general fulfilled by the police, interior ministry personnel, the security services, or – in the case of Czechoslovakia in 1968 and Hungary in 1956 – foreign troops.[9] Similarly, and with a few exceptions, the sheer universality of the communist conscription system meant that it was one of the few common experiences in what were arguably deeply atomised societies. In this respect, conscription played an important role as a social unifier in otherwise rather diverse societies.[10] Finally, and as the Polish case study illustrates, in many non-Soviet communist countries, the military remained to some degree a fundamentally *national* rather than *communist* institution. In this respect, the military often retained much of their national and nationalist legitimacy, despite Soviet communist hegemony throughout the region.

The case studies in this volume illustrate that the impact of these communist legacies on postcommunist military–society relations has perhaps been more limited than might have been expected at the beginning of the 1990s. In general, the overall significance of the military in society in the postcommunist context has declined. In particular, central and eastern European military–society relations have been influenced by the following three factors. First, there has been a systematic *demilitarisation* of many areas of society which were militarised under communism. Defence budgets have been reduced significantly across the region, and, in the main, there has been a reduction in the size of armed forces and in the number of military installations. In the former NSWP countries, the presence of the Soviet Army on national territories – which before had served as a constant reminder of the immediacy of the Cold War threat – has disappeared. Second, the importance of *conscription* as both a basis for military organisation and an agent of socialisation has also declined and in many postcommunist countries draft evasion is endemic. In the Baltic republics, for example, a central strategy of the national independence movements of the early 1990s was support for those evading the Soviet draft. An unforeseen consequence of this policy has been a decline in the legitimacy of conscription throughout Baltic society.[11] In countries such as the Czech Republic, a poor public image of the military has combined with improving living standards and rising popular expectations to make conscription deeply unpopular.[12] Finally, the collapse of communism engendered an abrupt break in the party–military–state nexus that had been such a feature of communist civil–military relations. This had the effect of ushering in new mechanisms for (democratic) civilian control over armed forces – and engendering a different basis for military–society relations. In particular, the central association of military with governance – and especially with a particular sort of governance – was removed. The elimination of the three-way 'Iron Triangle' of communist governance fundamentally questioned the established societal roles which the military had developed during the communist period.

As the above discussion makes clear, domestic political contexts and societal change have had an important impact on military–society relations in postcommunist Europe. In an environment of sometimes severe economic constraint, societies have de-prioritised the military in relation to other areas of state reform. In addition, the mistreatment of conscripts has been an issue across the region. Indeed, the legitimacy of conscription has undergone a rapid decline since 1989 – both as a basis of military organisation and an agent for socialisation. Young people in central and eastern Europe today have little memory or experience of the communist period and have instead spent their formative years in a rapidly demilitarising, post-Cold War, postcommunist environment. They are less deferential, and so arguably have a different – often more sceptical approach – to military service than previous generations. In practice, these factors have helped to ensure that across the region, the length of conscription periods has been or is being reduced, draft evasion is widespread, and reforming armed forces have increasingly invested in their volunteer, professional cadres at the expense of the conscript majority. This decline in the legitimacy of conscription has in some respects undermined the Nation Builder role amongst many armed forces in the region. However, our case studies highlight the way in which different bases for the military's legitimacy are emerging in new domestic political and societal contexts. Thus, in many cases the armed forces have attained a new national symbolism as representatives of newly independent states or democratic political systems. These factors are creating new opportunities and challenges for embedding and sustaining postcommunist military–society relations.

## Conclusions

We have argued that three broad patterns of military–society relations are emerging in postcommunist Europe. In the first – characterised by the Baltic republics, Poland, Slovakia, Romania, Bulgaria and, more recently, Croatia – the societal standing of the armed forces has broadly improved in the period since the collapse of communism, despite the decline of many traditional bases for military legitimacy. In this group, new bases for military legitimacy are emerging based around the Military Diplomacy and Domestic Military Assistance roles. Moreover, the 're-nationalisation' of many of the armed forces in this group has helped to support the military's Nation Builder role and provide quite robust bases for its legitimacy in society. In a second group of states – including the Czech Republic, Hungary and Slovenia – there has been a decline in the traditional bases for the military's legitimacy in society that has not been adequately matched by the emergence of new ones. While new Military Diplomacy and Domestic Military Assistance roles are emerging – particularly in the Czech Republic – these have not been supported by a strong Nation Builder role, and this has continued to undermine the armed forces' standing in society. In a third group of states – including Ukraine, FRY and, until 2000, Croatia – the armed forces retain a prominent and often positive position in the eyes of society, but some aspects of the military are viewed negatively. In this group, many of the traditional bases for military legitimacy, particularly in the National Security role, remain present. However, at the same time, many of the military's bases for legitimacy in the Nation Builder role have been undermined by processes of institutional decay in the armed forces. These include – to different degrees between each country – poor living standards for conscripts, soldiers and officers, poor performance in wartime, and in some cases continued politicisation.

In all cases, the change in the European geostrategic landscape and the reduction of threat perceptions engendered by the end of the Cold War have been fundamentally important to the change in the nature of military–society relations. In particular, the end of the Cold War in Europe has required changes in the nature of military organisation which have undermined the rationale and legitimacy of mass armies. These in turn have called into question many armed forces' traditional roles and traditional bases of legitimacy in society. However, while these geostrategic changes have necessitated change in general, the direction of this has been dependent on other factors. Of these, three stand out: first, international pressure and assistance; second, national historical legacies; and finally, domestic economic constraints.

In relation to international pressure and assistance, western institutions and particularly NATO have acted as lodestones for military reform efforts in those countries which have identified western integration as a key foreign policy goal. This has occurred in two main ways. First, the technical demands of NATO accession have encouraged armed forces to reform in a clear direction – towards greater interoperability with other members of the Alliance, and an increasing ability to deploy capabilities 'out of area' for participation in Alliance activities. Second, the broad foreign policy imperative of 'western integration' has led to a desire in many countries visibly to illustrate their commitment to the norms, values and policies of 'the West'. This has expressed itself through the active participation of elements of their armed forces in multinational – often NATO-led – military operations such as SFOR and KFOR. These influences have resulted in a prioritisation of the Military Diplomacy role for many postcommunist armed forces and this has led to the development of new bases for the military's legitimacy in society. In this context, the military's legitimacy stems both from a perception of its contribution to collective international security and from its symbolic role as a 'vanguard' of western integration more widely.

Second, national historical legacies are an important element of how postcommunist societies perceive their armed forces, particularly when they contribute to a strong national symbolism for the military. Indeed, it is noticeable that in countries where the Nation Builder role is strong – such as those in the first cluster above – societal acceptance of other new military roles has occurred relatively smoothly. This is in contrast to the countries in the second cluster, where a limited or curtailed Nation Builder role – largely as a result of negative historical associations with the armed forces – has generally been accompanied by a hesitant acceptance of new military roles. For those countries in the third cluster, societal perceptions of a positive historical legacy for the armed forces have helped to shore up a Nation Building role for the armed forces that has otherwise been damaged by persistent problems within the military as an institution.

Finally, economic constraints have been central across the postcommunist region in shaping both new roles for the armed forces and new bases for societal legitimacy. The size of communist-era defence budgets were widely seen as illegitimate by postcommunist societies. In many cases this served to damage the standing of the military in society and resulted in a subsequent de-prioritisation of defence budgets in relation to other areas of state spending. It has also meant that while old models of military organisation have been abandoned, sufficient funding has not necessarily been in place to adapt the armed forces properly to their new roles. In countries such as Hungary, this has led to a concentration of limited resources on the development of elite cadres within the armed forces who are able to participate in the Military Diplomacy role, at the expense of the (mainly conscript) armed forces as a whole. In Ukraine, economic constraints go to the heart of many of the armed forces' difficulties, with the bulk of the national defence budget being spent simply on inadequate salaries and maintenance rather than procurement and professionalisation. At the same time, the cost of a serious reform effort is such that it is unlikely to happen in the current economic climate.

Military–society relations in postcommunist Europe share many common features with those of western Europe. The end of the Cold War has introduced fundamental questions about what the armed forces are for, and how they should best be structured and financed to meet these requirements. Reduced threat perceptions, together with changing societal priorities, have led to a reduction of the significance of purely military aspects of security and a decline in the legitimacy of conscription as a means of military organisation. In the context of our framework, this has expressed itself through a reassessment of the nature of the armed forces' National Security role, with increasing importance being attached to new Military Diplomacy and Domestic Military Assistance roles. These changes in turn have altered the character of many armed forces' bases for legitimacy in their societies.

There are, however, important differences too. In much of postcommunist Europe, economic constraints have meant that societies have been faced with tough decisions as to where their spending priorities actually lie. More often than not military spending has been a casualty of these decisions, and technological change has not had anything like the impact it has had in many western countries. Moreover, many states in the region have seen the collective security offered by organisations such as NATO as a more effective way of addressing their security concerns than the wholesale reform of their armed forces. NATO integration, of which the military is of course a central component, has also become representative of a wider cultural and political 'return to Europe'. Ironically, in many cases this has placed the armed forces – often previously viewed as conservative institutions with one foot still in the communist past – at the forefront of many countries' westernisation efforts, and provided them with new bases for legitimacy in society.

Although certain patterns are observable, military–society relations in central and eastern Europe are still in transition and in many countries have probably not yet reached a 'steady state'. It is notable that in the period of just over a decade since the collapse of communism, military–society relations in a number of countries have gone through various distinct phases. In a number of the former NSWP states military–society relations have moved from an initial postcommunist phase of quite broad societal anti-militarism in the early 1990s to a new stage in which the military is viewed more positively as a consequence of its utility in promoting integration with the established democracies of the West and its adoption of new National Security, Domestic Military Assistance and Military Diplomacy roles. In contrast, in countries such as FRY/Serbia and Montenegro and Croatia the authoritarian nationalism of the early postcommunist period resulted in the military developing strong Nation Builder and Regime Defence roles, but since the collapse of the Milošević and Tuđman regimes they are beginning to develop new National Security, Domestic Military Assistance and Military Diplomacy roles akin to those in the former NSWP states. To the extent that the countries of postcommunist Europe succeed in consolidating their independent nation-statehood and democratic political systems, the Nation Builder and Regime Defence roles of armed forces are likely to further decline in significance. In this context, many of the countries of central and eastern Europe may gradually come to resemble the 'postmilitary societies' of Western Europe and North America: where the military has a relatively low domestic salience, is no more important than other state institutions and is viewed primarily as a functional instrument for the pursuit of foreign policy goals rather than an organisation having special political or social importance.[13]

With the likelihood of traditional military threats to territorial integrity declining for most central and eastern European states, the importance of the military's traditional National Security role as the defender of national territory may also be reduced further. In these circumstances, the military's role – and the bases of their legitimacy within society – may increasingly revolve around new National Security, Domestic Military Assistance and Military Diplomacy functions. In terms of military operations, Lawrence Freedman describes this as the distinction between wars of necessity (wars undertaken to defend the state against ultimately existential threats) and wars of choice (wars undertaken to pursue a range of wider foreign policy goals).[14] To the extent that most future wars are those of choice rather than necessity, debates on the role of the military – and wider military–society relations – are likely to revolve around questions of when and how to use armed forces in such operations and the extent to which such missions justify the potentially heavy resource investment required to develop and maintain power projection forces. The development of sustainable new bases of legitimacy for armed forces within society may therefore depend on the development of broad societal consensus on the circumstances in which military forces should be deployed beyond national territory. Although some central and eastern European societies and states may be more 'martial' (more willing to use force beyond their borders) than others, all are likely to face controversial debates over the use of armed forces for peacekeeping, humanitarian intervention, counter-terrorist and counter-proliferation operations. Thus, military–society relations in central and eastern Europe are likely to be shaped by wider debates about the circumstances in which the 'international community' should use force.

## Notes

1. In a number of cases this role metamorphosised into a 'new' one of defending authoritarian and/or nationalist postcommunist political regimes, elites and leaders.
2. T.S. Szayna, *The Military in a Postcommunist Poland* N-2209-USDP (Santa Monica, CA: RAND, 1991), 43.
3. See Chapter 3. See also, M. Vlachová and Š. Sarvaš, 'Democratic Control of Armed Forces in the Czech Republic: a Journey from Social Isolation', in A. Cottey, T. Edmunds and A. Forster (eds), *Democratic Control of the Military in Postcommunist Europe: Guarding the Guards* (Basingstoke: Palgrave Macmillan, 2002), 61.
4. It is worth noting that with the exception of the rather different case of the anti-Vietnam War movement, peace and disarmament debates still generally took place firmly within the context of the Cold War confrontation in Europe. The concentration of many peace movements on the nuclear stand-off and the threat of mutually assured destruction only serves to illustrate just how intense and deep-rooted perceptions of societal threat in Europe were during the Cold War.
5. See, for example the country case studies in A. Forster, T. Edmunds and A. Cottey, *The Challenge of Military Reform in Postcommunist Europe: Building Professional Armed Forces* (Basingstoke: Palgrave Macmillan, 2002). Particularly, M. Vlachová, 'Professionalisation of the Army in the Czech Republic'; M.P. Ulrich, 'Professionalisation of the Slovak Armed Forces'; P. Dunay, 'Building Professional Competence in Hungary's Armed Forces: Slow Motion'; and M. Zulean, 'Professionalisation of the Romanian Armed Forces'.
6. See, for example, Vlachová, 'Democratic Control' and Pál Dunay, 'Civil–Military Relations in Hungary: No Big Deal', in Cottey et al., *Democratic Control*.
7. B.J. Vallance, 'Corruption and Reform in the Soviet Military', *The Journal of Slavic Military Studies*, 7:4 (December 1994), 707–10.

8. C. Donnelly, *Red Banner: the Soviet Military System in Peace and War* (Coulsdon: Jane's Information Group, 1988).
9. See, for example, James Sherr, 'Professionalisation, Civilian Control and Democracy in Ukraine', in Forster et al., *The Challenge of Military Reform*.
10. Viktor Suvorov, for example, notes that the party elite often found ways of exempting its sons from the worst elements of conscription. Viktor Suvorov, *Inside the Soviet Army* (London: Hamish Hamilton, 1982), 218–21.
11. Sapronas, 'Lithuanian Armed Forces', and Janis Arveds Trapans, 'Professionalisation of the Latvian Armed Forces', in Forster et al., *The Challenge of Military Reform*.
12. Vlachová, 'Professionalisation'.
13. M. Shaw, *Post-Military Society: Militarism, Demilitarization and War at the End of the Twentieth Century* (Cambridge: Polity Press, 1991), 164–74.
14. L. Freedman, *The Revolution in Strategic Affairs*, Adelphi paper (Oxford: Oxford University Press for the IISS, 1998), 34.

# Index